CYBERCRIME AND THE LAW

>cybercrime and the law

CHALLENGES, ISSUES, AND OUTCOMES

SUSAN W. BRENNER

NORTHEASTERN UNIVERSITY PRESS | BOSTON

Northeastern University Press
An imprint of University Press of New England
www.upne.com

Manufactured in the United States of America
Designed by April Leidig
Typeset in Arno by Copperline Book Services

University Press of New England is a member of the
Green Press Initiative. The paper used in this book
meets their minimum requirement for recycled paper.

For permission to reproduce any of the material
in this book, contact Permissions, University Press
of New England, One Court Street, Suite 250,
Lebanon NH 03766; or visit www.upne.com

Library of Congress Cataloging-in-Publication Data
Brenner, Susan W., 1947–
Cybercrime and the law: challenges, issues, and
outcomes / Susan W. Brenner.
    p. cm.
Includes bibliographical references and index.
ISBN 978-1-55553-798-2 (cloth : alk. paper)
ISBN 978-1-55553-799-9 (pbk. : alk. paper)
ISBN 978-1-55553-800-2 (ebook)
1. Computer crimes—United States. 2. Computer
networks—Law and legislation—United States—
Criminal provisions. 3. Computer viruses—United
States. 4. Computer hackers—United States.
5. Criminal jurisdiction—United States. I. Title.
KF9350.B73 2012
345.73'0268—dc23   2012014928

5 4 3 2 1

CONTENTS

CYBERCRIME AND THE LAW

INTRODUCTION:
TWENTY-FIRST-CENTURY
BONNIE AND CLYDE

The legal, practical, and political issues implicated by cybercrime and other cyberthreats have received a great deal of attention in specialized publications, most of which are directed at corporate or government professionals who work in this area. I continue to be amazed at the extent to which cyberthreats—those that already exist and those that will come into existence in the very near future—are ignored or overlooked by the mainstream media.

Those of us who work in this area know all too well that the number of cyberattacks on government and civilian targets increases in frequency and severity with every passing month. If these attacks took place in the terrestrial world—in real space rather than in the virtual space of the Internet—they would receive a barrage of media attention. Since the attacks play out in cyberspace, they remain invisible unless one knows where and how to find information about them. Finding information about cyberattacks is a challenge, in part because the major players—the corporate and government entities that become the victims of attacks and the cybercriminals and state-sponsored hackers who launch the attacks—generally have no interest in "outing" the incidence and details of an accelerating pattern of cyberconflict.

This is a book for those who would like to learn about cyberconflict—about how the traditional battle between good and evil (or, perhaps more accurately, between what some perceive as good and evil) is manifesting itself in cyberspace. More precisely, this is a book for those who would like to learn about how the law applies—and in some instances does not apply—to the two dominant types of cyberconflict: cybercrime and cyberwarfare. Each represents the migration of a traditional, real-world threat (crime and war) into cyberspace.

The migration of these threats into cyberspace alters them in ways that make the application of traditional law increasingly problematic. It also erodes the effectiveness of the control mechanisms sovereign entities—nation-states—have historically used to control the incidence and severity of these threats to social order. This, in turn, produces an increasingly untenable situation that is—or should be—of concern to both governments and private citizens. If nation-states cannot respond effectively to cybercrime and cyberwarfare, there is little, if any, disincentive for those who are so inclined to engage in either, or both.

As chapter 8 explains, governments control crime by creating disincentives to break the law; in other words, the likelihood that I will be captured, convicted, and sentenced to prison creates a disincentive that deters me, and others like me, from robbing banks and committing other crimes. The downside of criminal activity outweighs its attractiveness, and a similar set of disincentives usually discourages nation-states from warring with each other. Cyberspace makes it possible for criminals or agents of a nation-state to carry out attacks remotely and anonymously, which erodes the likelihood that those responsible will be identified, captured, convicted, and punished. That, in turn, erodes, if it does not entirely erase, the disincentives for engaging in such conduct; absent such disincentives, activities such as online bank theft become attractive endeavors, at least for some. And that creates the possibility that cybercrime and cyberwarfare will increase in incidence to the point at which they threaten the stability of nation-states, in varying ways and varying degrees.

This is a state of affairs that should be of interest to students and professionals in various fields, such as computer technology, political science, and economics, because they will likely have to deal with the consequences of cyberconflict and the insecurity it generates. These consequences will also be of interest to concerned citizens, who want to understand the national security implications of our increasing use of cyberspace.

The possibility that cyberconflict will become a phenomenon that threatens the stability of nation-states is of great concern to many governments, including the United States. The United States is perhaps the primary target for cybercriminals and is likely to become a primary target of cyberwarfare.

This book analyzes both cybercrime and cyberwarfare but devotes most of its analysis to cybercrime, for two reasons. One is that governments have been dealing with cybercrime for almost thirty years and therefore know more about the challenges it creates for lawmakers and law enforcers. The other reason is that there are so far no confirmed instances in which one nation-state has launched cyberwar attacks on another; there are instances in which it appears that one state was the victim of attacks launched by a hostile state, but the circumstances involved are too ambiguous to determine the nature of the attack with any degree of confidence, given the requirements of current law.

Approaching Cybercrime and the Law

Cybercrime and the Law deals with the intersection of cyberconflict—that is, cybercrime and cyberwarfare—and the law. Since I am a U.S.-trained lawyer, I know more about U.S. law than I do about the law of other countries; this book will therefore focus primarily on how U.S. law applies, does not apply, and perhaps should apply to various types of cybercrime and to certain manifestations of cyberwarfare. Focusing on U.S. cyberconflict law also has a utilitarian aspect: since the United States has been dealing with cybercrime for well over two decades, and since the United States is a federal system composed of a single federal government and fifty independent state governments, it generates a great deal of law, at both levels. This means that U.S. cybercrime law is diverse, complex, and at least to some extent more sophisticated than the cybercrime and cyberconflict law of other countries.

Since this is a book about cyberconflict law, and since I am a lawyer, this book uses the approach law schools take in training future lawyers and the approach lawyers take when practicing law. That is, it focuses on three dimensions of cyberconflict: the applicable law itself; the policies responsible for that law; and how discrete facts impact the application of the law.

Legal analysis is, as lawyers, law students, and law professors say, "fact sensitive." To illustrate, assume that John Doe, a convicted burglar, is incarcerated in the Monroe State Prison. Doe has a disease that is inevitably fatal; it will kill him but will take some years to do so. While in prison, Doe becomes angry with William Brown, one of the guards, and, when the opportunity arises, attacks the guard, biting him viciously.[1] Doctors examine Brown and determine that the bite infected him with Doe's fatal illness; Brown will die of the illness but, like Doe, may survive for years before succumbing to it.

The state has a statute that defines murder as "purposely causing the death of another human being." By infecting Brown with the disease, Doe has "caused" him to die of that disease (unless some other factor intervenes before it can kill him). Doe infected Brown purposely; he wanted to kill Brown, so the intent element of the crime is met. The local prosecutor charges Doe with murdering Brown. Doe's lawyer argues that he cannot be charged with murdering Brown because Brown is still alive; the prosecutor argues that, by infecting Brown with the disease, Doe killed him, in effect. Doe's lawyer argues that he cannot be prosecuted for murdering Brown (if at all) until (1) Brown dies and (2) an autopsy establishes that the disease was the sole cause of his death. The prosecutor argues that he can pursue Doe now because he did everything he could to kill Brown and has killed Brown (unless and until some other factor intervenes to cause his death).

This issue has arisen in real cases.[2] It illustrates how complicated it can be to apply even a simple statute, such as a murder statute, to a real-life set of facts. In deciding whether Doe can be prosecuted for Brown's murder (while Brown is still living), the judge who has the case will have to analyze the specific facts at issue, such as the fatality of the disease, the likelihood that a cure will be developed, Brown's possible resistance to it, and so forth, plus the plain language of the law and the policies behind the law. As to the latter, the prosecutor will probably argue that Doe has done everything he can to kill Brown and will kill Brown, absent possible intervening circumstances, and so should be treated as a murderer. The judge will have to sort all of that out and decide what is to be done with Doe while trying to ensure justice for Brown.

Hence, unlike other disciplines in which white is white and black is black or 1 is 1 and 2 is 2, in the law white can be white, black, purpose, or something other than a color, and 1 can be 1, 15, 1,999,444,122, or not even a number. Lawyers analyze and argue, and the law develops and expands through that process. Because that is the methodology of the law, law schools use casebooks, books that compile relevant, illustrative cases to train future lawyers. Students read cases—like the hypothetical case outlined above—and then analyze the arguments that can be made for both sides and argue about what is the correct outcome.

This book uses statutes and cases to illustrate the various aspects of cyberconflict law, its strengths and limitations, and how it plays out in particular instances. Some of the chapters—such as chapters 1 and 2—explain why cyberconflict, and particularly cybercrime, have required the creation of new law. Many of the activities that fall into the category of cybercrime simply do not fit into traditional law; in effect, they create challenges for existing law that are far, far more complicated than the issues involved in the Doe-Brown hypothetical outlined above. To understand the law as it currently exists, it is necessary to understand why that law was needed and how it was crafted. Understanding both also helps the reader to understand how, and why, many of our cybercrime laws are works in process, that is, might need to be revised as our experience with the dark side of cyberspace increases.

A Note on Cybercrime

Readers of this book may wonder how, if at all, cybercrime differs from crime.[3]

Crime consists of engaging in conduct that has been outlawed by a human social grouping, such as a tribe, city-state, or nation-state, because it threatens the society's ability to maintain social order.[4] Social order cannot exist without rules that proscribe certain harmful types of activity and institutions that enforce these rules. These rules constitute a society's criminal law. Criminal law is designed to prevent the members of a society from preying on each other in ways that undermine social order. It does this by defining certain types of behavior as intolerable, as crimes.

Crimes take many forms because each targets a particular harm. As we all know, there are crimes that encompass harming individuals (murder, rape, and assault), property (arson, theft, and vandalism), government (obstructing justice, treason, and riot), and morality (obscenity and gambling). Since societies have dealt with crime for millennia, they have developed standardized definitions of the core real-world crimes. In addition to these core crimes, modern societies also have new crimes that target evolved harms, such as antitrust and environmental violations.

Cybercrime, like crime, consists of engaging in conduct that has been outlawed by a society because it threatens social order. Cybercrime differs from crime primarily in the way it is committed: real-world criminals use physical tools—such as guns—to commit their crimes; cybercriminals use computer technology to commit cybercrimes. As we will see in the next chapters, most of the cybercrime we see today simply represents the migration of real-world crime into cyberspace. That is, cyberspace becomes the tool criminals use to commit old crimes—like fraud, theft, and extortion—in new ways.

Their use of computer technology does not fundamentally alter the nature of the activity at issue; fraud is fraud, whether committed online or off line. But while the result—the harm—may be the same, the criminal activity is not. The use of computer technology impacts the commission and investigation of these crimes in ways of which the law has been required to take cognizance.

Criminals' use of computer technology lets them commit crime on a scale far exceeding what is possible in the real world; the magnitude of the harm cybercrime causes is therefore one factor that differentiates crime and cybercrime in ways the law must address. Another differentiating factor is that the use of computer technology makes it difficult—and often impossible—for law enforcement officers to identify and apprehend those responsible for cybercrimes. Finally, all cybercrime does not merely represent the commission of traditional, core crimes by new means: all cybercrime is not simply the online replication of old crimes; there are new, distinct cybercrimes, and more might emerge in the future.

The Cybercrime: Kentucky, 2009

In the last full week of June 2009, cybercriminals operating from outside the United States surreptitiously extracted $415,989 from an account at the First Federal Savings Bank in Shepherdsville, Kentucky.[5] The account belonged to Bullitt County; it held funds the county used to pay its employees.

On June 22, "someone started making unauthorized wire transfers of $10,000 or less from the county's payroll to accounts belonging to at least

25 individuals around the country."[6] It was not until June 29 that First Federal Savings Bank employees "realized something was wrong"; once they realized the transfers were unauthorized, First Federal employees froze the account and contacted banks that had received transfers, asking the banks to reverse them.[7] And it was on June 29 that a First Federal employee called Melanie Roberts, the Bullitt County judge-executive who was one of the two people authorized to initiate fund transfers from the county's account, to tell her about the unauthorized transfers.[8]

Since no one in Bullitt County had any idea who was responsible for the transfers, county officials contacted the FBI, which began an investigation.[9] The investigation showed that the unauthorized transfers—the thefts—originated in Ukraine, a country known to be a base of operations for cybercriminals.[10] The cybercriminals responsible for the Bullitt County thefts used a sophisticated scheme to bypass the security measures the county and the bank had put in place to prevent the kind of unauthorized transfers that occurred in this case. Since the tactics these cybercriminals used illustrate the technical sophistication typical of contemporary cybercrime, it is useful to analyze this particular scheme in some detail.[11]

Bullitt County used a dual-authorization system to protect the five accounts it maintained at the bank; wire transfers of funds had to be authorized by two county employees—the county treasurer and the county judge-executive. The treasurer initiated transfers, and the judge-executive approved them. The bank relied on several methods to protect the funds for which it was responsible, one of which was to use special programming to analyze customers' computer systems and "create a unique fingerprint" of their computers.[12] This meant that if a cybercriminal tried to log into a customer's account from a computer other than the one the customer routinely used, the bank's system would detect that because the "fingerprints" of the two computers would not match. When the bank's system detected that a log-in attempt was being made from a computer with an unknown fingerprint, it would not allow the log-in and would send the owner of the account an e-mail that contained a "one-time passphrase"; the customer would have to enter the passphrase, along with her or his username and password, to access the account.

The cybercriminals responsible for the Bullitt County thefts used a Trojan horse program known as Zeus to bypass both the county's and the bank's systems. They "somehow got the Zeus Trojan" on the treasurer's computer and "used it to steal the username and password" she needed to access e-mail and the county's accounts at the bank.[13] Zeus installs itself on a computer's hard drive and steals banking information by recording keystrokes typed on the keyboard; it uses an instant message to send the information to the cybercriminals who control it. Zeus also "creates a direct connection" between the infected computer (here, the treasurer's computer) and the system used by the cybercriminals; this lets them "log in to the victim's bank account using the victim's" own computer and Internet connection.[14]

The thieves began by stealing the treasurer's username and password and linking her computer with the one they would use in the thefts. Then they logged into the county's bank account by "tunneling through" the treasurer's Internet connection.[15] Since they were using her Internet connection, the bank's fingerprinting system did not flag this as a problematic attempt to log into the account. Once they were logged into the payroll account, the thieves changed the password the judge-executive would have to use to log into the account and changed the e-mail address associated with her access to the account. The next thing they did was to create "several fictitious" county employees and "a batch of wire transfers to those individuals" that would need to be approved by the judge-executive. We will come back to the fictitious employees in a moment.

After they initiated the wire transfers, the cyberthieves logged into the county's payroll account using a computer outside Kentucky and the new e-mail address and password they created for the judge-executive. When the bank's system did not recognize that computer's fingerprint, it sent an e-mail with the passphrase the judge-executive would have to use to log into the payroll account and approve the transfers. The e-mail went to the new e-mail address the thieves had substituted for the correct one—an address they controlled. The thieves retrieved the passphrase, logged into the account with the judge-executive's new e-mail address and password, plus the passphrase, and approved the unauthorized wire transfers. Since there was nothing ostensibly problematic about the transfers or the process used to approve them, it is not surprising that it took the bank a week to realize something was wrong.

Where did the transferred funds go? Weeks before the thieves compromised the treasurer's and judge-executive's computers, they hired twenty-five individuals to serve as "money mules," unwitting dupes who would receive transfers from the county's account and then unwittingly pass the money along to the thieves. The thieves hired at least some of the mules after finding their resumes on Careerbuilder.com. The Fairlove Delivery Service hired the mules to edit "documents for grammar" and promised them they would be paid eight dollars for "each kilobyte of data they processed."[16] One mule said that, after she edited text for a while, she asked when she would be paid. In response, she received an e-mail asking if she would be interested in becoming a "local agent" for the company; she was told it "had trouble getting money to its clients overseas as quickly as they needed it, and desperately needed help speeding up that process."[17] After she agreed, she received a wire transfer of over $9,900 and was told to wire all of the money except for her 5 percent "commission" to a bank account in Ukraine.[18] She was suspicious and so "only wired $3,000 of the money."[19] Other mules wired all money they received except for their "commissions." If their banks reversed the fraudulent transfers (as some did), these mules found themselves owing Bullitt County the money they wired to Ukraine.

What happened to the money that went to Ukraine and to the thieves that received it? Basically, nothing happened; the money presumably sits in accounts in Ukraine or in whatever country to which it was subsequently transferred. The only money the county recovered came from the U.S. banks that froze accounts or reversed the fraudulent transfers. The county sued the bank, claiming that the bank's negligence was responsible for its losses and that the bank is therefore required to reimburse the county for the $415,989 it lost.[20] The bank denies it was negligent; it claims the county was at fault for not having caught the unauthorized transfers.[21] The suit is pending. And none of the cybercriminals who siphoned nearly $416,000 out of Bullitt County's payroll account has been identified or apprehended—and as we will see in chapter 6, none are likely to be.

Implications of the Bullitt County Case

What happened in Bullitt County, Kentucky, in the summer of 2009 illustrates how and why cybercrime challenges lawmakers and law enforcers in the United States and elsewhere.

Unlike traditional crime, cybercrime tends to be a low-risk, high-reward endeavor for those who engage in it. The Bullitt County incident perfectly illustrates both characteristics of this new type of crime.

The reward is obvious: a group of cybercriminals (identities and location unknown) got away with almost half a million dollars in one criminal episode, which almost certainly was not, and will not be, their only foray into cybercrime. This is far from an isolated incident: in 2007, cybercriminals (variously described as Germans or Ukrainians) used similar tactics to "hijack $6 million from banks in the United States, United Kingdom, Spain and Italy."[22] And in the summer of 2010, unidentified perpetrators used the Zeus Trojan horse program and tactics similar to those involved in the Bullitt County theft to steal more than one million dollars from banks in the United Kingdom.[23] An unknown number of similar bank thefts have occurred since and are occurring as I write this (and, no doubt, as you read it), along with other types of financial cybercrime. In 2009, the FBI told Congress, "Revenues from cybercrime [had] reached an estimated $1 trillion per year."[24] This figure probably understates the actual amount cybercriminals reaped and victims lost that year; as we will see, businesses are very reluctant to report being victims of cybercrime for fear their customers will lose confidence in them.

The low risk of being apprehended is perhaps less obvious but no less significant: the unknown Bullitt County perpetrators have not and almost certainly will not be apprehended and brought to justice for the theft of Bullitt County's funds. Cybercriminals who operate domestically are likely to be apprehended, but those who operate transnationally run little risk of being apprehended and punished for their crimes. One reason for the difference is the difficulty of tracing the actual location from which offshore cybercriminals operate; the Bullitt County thieves were suspected to be in Ukraine, but they might have routed the signals they used to hack the treasurer's and judge-executive's computers and the county's account through Ukraine in order to hide the fact that they were actually operating from, say, Brazil. Tracing the origin of a cybercrime is a difficult and time-consuming process, one that is often beyond the capacity of local law enforcement agencies. And even if Bullitt County law enforcement officers—with, perhaps, the assistance of the FBI—were able to trace the cyberthieves to Ukraine, they would somehow have to be able to take them into custody. The United States does not have an extradition treaty with Ukraine,[25] which means Ukraine would not be obliged to turn the cyberthieves over to U.S. authorities for prosecution.

A third factor that differentiates cybercrime from traditional crime is the crime scene: The legal and practical challenges involved in investigating the Bullitt County thefts and apprehending those responsible for them are exacerbated by the fact that this cybercrime, like all cybercrimes, involved digital evidence and a virtual crime scene. As we all probably know from books, movies, and television shows like *CSI: Miami* and *Law and Order*, the investigation of a crime focuses on the place where it was committed: the crime scene. In traditional, real-world crimes—robberies or murders, say—the crime happens at one physical location; officers carefully scrutinize that location for trace evidence they can use to identity, locate, and convict those responsible for the crime. In cybercrimes, the crime scene—and any attendant trace evidence—is scattered across multiple locations, for example, the location from which the perpetrator(s) operated, the location where they inflicted harm on the victim, and the intermediate locations through which the bits and bytes involved in the commission of the crime traveled between perpetrator(s) and victim.

In the Bullitt County case, the crime scene was scattered across at least two continents: digital evidence existed in the county treasurer's and judge-executive's computer systems, in the bank's computer system, in the Ukrainian computer systems involved in the crime, in the mules' computers, and in all of the computers in the United States, Ukraine, and other countries through which the signals involved in consummating the crime traveled as it was carried out. This means the process of putting the crime together and assembling the evidence needed to convict the perpetrators will be extraordinarily complex and therefore must be carried out by those with expertise in digital evidence and digital investigations. Bullitt County may have investigators with some experience in digital evidence, but it probably does not have individuals with the type of expertise needed to unravel a transnational cybercrime of this complexity. The FBI was, as we saw earlier, called in to assist with the investigation, but the FBI can only do so much because it has other investigative priorities (e.g., terrorism) and because it is a comparatively small agency with limited resources.

Cyber Bonnies and Clydes

Cybercrime is not the first instance in which criminals have exploited new technology to their advantage. David Ronfeldt and John Arquilla found that the "bad guys" tend to be among the first adopters of innovative technologies and techniques because they are not constrained by existing rules and procedures.[26] This tendency manifested itself in the 1930s, when law enforcement officers found themselves dealing with criminals who used automobiles (still a relatively new technology) to increase their chances of committing financially rewarding crimes such as kidnapping and robbery without being apprehended and punished.

Automobiles gave criminals a distinct advantage in countries like the United States that use a federal governance system. They could "plan a crime in one state, execute it in another, and then return to the first state or hurtle into some other remote locality for the hiding-out . . . period."[27] Bank robbers, car thieves, kidnappers, pimps, and other criminals quickly realized they could frustrate law enforcement efforts to apprehend them if they used motor vehicles to flee a state after committing a crime there. They understood the importance of the technology. In 1934, Clyde Barrow, of the Bonnie and Clyde gang, wrote a letter to Henry Ford, thanking him for his "steel-bodied V-8 automobiles" because they made it so much easier for the gang to elude police after they committed a robbery.[28]

There were several reasons automobiles made it easy for Bonnie and Clyde and their various colleagues in crime to avoid capture. The most obvious is the one noted above, that is, once criminals who had, say, robbed a bank in Indiana crossed the border into Illinois, Indiana police no longer had jurisdiction to arrest them and the Illinois police had no jurisdiction because no crime had been committed in their state. If the Illinois police captured the robbers, there were procedures by which they could be extradited to Indiana for prosecution, but the procedures were complex and took time; and while extradition was pending, the criminals might disappear into yet another state or disguise themselves so the Illinois police would not be able to find them. Also, the Illinois police might not put a great deal of effort into investigating a crime that had been committed outside their jurisdiction.

Cybercriminals substitute cyberspace for the automobile: like the vehicles Bonnie and Clyde relied on, cyberspace lets cybercriminals exploit jurisdictional boundaries to avoid being apprehended and punished for their crimes. That was the only advantage automobile technology provided for the motorized criminals of the 1920s and 1930s.

Cyberspace, on the other hand, provides other advantages: perhaps the most obvious is that cybercriminals do not have to physically enter the territory of the sovereign entity where they commit their crimes; as we saw above, Ukrainian cybercriminals can rob banks in other countries without ever leaving their homes. That exacerbates the impact of the jurisdictional avoidance technique noted above, which was effective but far from foolproof. Some of Bonnie and Clyde's bank-robbing colleagues—including John Dillinger—were captured and briefly imprisoned for their crimes. Since cybercriminals do not have to physically enter the territory of the jurisdictions in which they commit crimes, their use of cyberspace dramatically reduces the likelihood they will be identified and apprehended.

Cyberspace also provides criminals with yet another advantage: anonymity. Even if the bank robbers of the Bonnie and Clyde era wore masks as they committed their crimes, they were easily identifiable as they fled the scene of the crime. Locals were likely to notice a strange vehicle speeding out of town, and the employees of gas stations and cafés were equally likely to notice strange people who stopped for food and fuel. Bonnie and Clyde and their bank-robbing colleagues era might escape the scene of the crime, but they could not escape being identified, which ultimately tended to result in their being arrested. Cybercriminals never physically enter the territory where they commit their crimes; no one observes their appearance, and they leave no traces of their physical existence at the crime scene. They also eliminate the need to flee a physical crime scene; they terminate their involvement with the digital scene of their crime by shutting down their computer or simply moving on to the next victim.

My purpose is to illustrate a simple, yet foundational, principle: cyberspace is a criminal tool of unprecedented complexity and potential. As a result, lawmakers and law enforcers are waging a losing battle against cybercrime because cyberspace lets cybercriminals evade the laws and tactics nation-states have devised to deal with unlawful conduct. In the chapters that follow, we will review precisely how and why cyberspace is such an exceptional criminal tool and what lawmakers and law enforcers are doing in an effort to nullify its utility in this regard.

A Framework for Examining Cybercrime and the Law

The discussion of cybercrime in the following chapters utilizes a distinct conceptual framework that was developed as a tool for analyzing cybercrime.[29] "Cybercrime" is the term lawyers and law enforcement officers use to refer to crimes the commission of which involves the use of computer technology. This conceptual framework divides cybercrimes into three categories: (1) a computer is the target of the crime (often a new cybercrime); (2) a computer is a tool used to commit a traditional crime such as theft or fraud; and (3) a computer plays an incidental role in committing one or more crimes.[30]

A computer is the target of criminal activity when the perpetrator attacks the computer by breaking into it, introducing code that damages it, or bombarding it with data. Here, the computer is essentially the victim of the crime. Access target crimes involve accessing a computer without being at all authorized to do so (the outsider cybercrime) or by exceeding the scope of one's authorized access to a computer (the insider cybercrime). U.S. cybercrime statutes usually define "access" as "to instruct, communicate with, store data in, retrieve data from or otherwise make use of any resources of a computer, computer system or network."[31] Access can be an end in itself or it can be used to commit another crime, such as damaging or stealing data from the computer. Access target cybercrimes are examined in chapter 1.

Code target crimes involve creating, disseminating, and using malware, computer viruses, worms, and other malicious code that damages a computer system or extracts data from it.[32] Data target crimes involve blasting a computer linked to the Internet with so much data it essentially goes off line in what is known as a distributed denial of service (DDOS) attack; the target computer receives so many malicious signals from the attacker that no legitimate traffic can reach it.[33] Code and data target crimes are examined in chapter 2.

A computer can also be a tool to commit a traditional crime, such as theft or fraud. Here, the computer's role is analogous to the role a telephone plays when a fraudster uses it to trick victims into parting with their money or property. In both instances, the use of a particular technology facilitates the commission of the crime but does not alter the nature of the offense. Computers can be used to commit most traditional crimes, including fraud, embezzlement, theft, arson, forgery, riot, assault, rape, and homicide. Tool cybercrimes are examined in chapters 3 and 4.

Finally, a computer can play an incidental role in the commission of a crime. This alternative encompasses a variety of activity, such as blackmailers using computers to e-mail their victims and drug dealers using computers and Excel to track their inventory and drug transactions. In these and similar instances, the computer's role in the crime is as a source of evidence, nothing more. That role, however, can be important; computers can, in effect, become the crime scene. The evidence investigators find on drug dealers' computers may play an essential role in convicting them of the crimes. This aspect of cybercrimes is examined in chapter 5.

This trichotomy plays two roles in analyzing cybercrimes: Investigators use it to assess how they should draft search warrants and otherwise incorporate computer technology into their investigative process. And judges and legislators use it to determine if existing law is adequate to criminalize how a computer was used in a given instance; if it is not, then judges and legislators may need to extend the reach of existing law or adopt new law.

>chapter 1

HACKING

The term "hacker" and much of what would become hacker culture emerged at the Massachusetts Institute of Technology's (MIT) Artificial Intelligence Laboratory in the late 1950s.[1] At the time, the only computers were mainframes—behemoths one interacted with via a cumbersome process involving punch cards. This created a problem for a group of MIT students who were interested in computers and programming: only faculty and other "important" users were authorized to use MIT mainframes. A sympathetic computer technician eventually let the students use a special mainframe on loan to MIT, one they could directly interact with instead of having to use the punch card process. By working with this computer, the students learned programming—learned how to make a computer "do" things (such as converting Arabic numbers to Roman numerals).

More precisely, they learned to "hack," but hacking did not have the negative connotation it has today. At MIT, a hacker was "someone who does . . . interesting and creative work at a high intensity level."[2] An MIT hack was originally a clever practical joke, like elevator hacking: the buttons on an elevator were rewired so that, say, pushing the button for the second floor sent the person to the twentieth floor.[3]

From this beginning, a culture of computer hacking grew up at MIT and spread to academic computing centers across the country. It was based on an informal ethos. According to one source, the hacker code of ethics was based on these principles:

- Access to computers . . . should be unlimited and total. . . .
- All information should be free.
- Mistrust Authority—Promote Decentralization.
- Hackers should be judged by their hacking, not bogus criteria such as degrees, age, race, or position.
- You can create art and beauty on a computer.
- Computers can change your life for the better.[4]

As the principles indicate, the early hacker culture was based on intellectual inquiry: hackers explored computer systems and shared what they learned. When a hacker created a program, he (they were usually "he" in this era) would distribute it to others, to be used and improved. This ethos of exploring and sharing evolved at a time when computers were closed systems, that is, were not accessible by outsiders, and software had not become a commercial product. Since computers were only available to a very few, hacking was still a niche activity.

That began to change in 1969 when the ARPANET went online.[5] The ARPANET linked mainframes in hundreds of universities, research laboratories, and defense contracting companies. It also linked hackers all over the United States: "Instead of remaining in isolated small groups each developing their own ephemeral local cultures, they discovered . . . themselves as a networked tribe."[6] That led to the standardization of the hacker ethos; the first version of the *Hacker's Dictionary*, which helped standardize hacker jargon, appeared in the early 1970s.[7] As an early version of the *Dictionary* noted, the "special vocabulary of hackers" bound them together by expressing "shared values and experiences."[8] This second-stage hacker culture evolved over the next decade; since the ARPANET could link a maximum of 256 computers,[9] the culture was still limited to a relatively small group until the 1980s, when the networked personal computer brought it to a much wider audience and eventually led to the corruption of what had been a pristine hacker ethos.

The popularization of hacking was the result of two innovations: One was the Internet, a new network that could support an unlimited number of computers and was available to anyone who could log on. The first versions of the Internet went online in the early 1980s and quickly replaced the ARPANET, which was shut down in 1990. The other innovation was the personal computer: though the term first appeared in print in 1962, personal computers did not become a reality until the end of the 1970s.[10] Three personal computers—the Apple II, the PET 2001, and the TRS-80—hit the market in 1979; "over half a million . . . were sold," and computing ceased to be a niche activity.[11] The era of the *WarGames* hacker had begun.[12]

In 1983, the *New York Times* noted that the number of "young people roaming without authorization through" the country's computer systems was in the thousands and was growing "hand-in-hand with the boom in personal computers."[13] The *Times* article also explained that these "electronic explorations" were being carried out by teenagers who used personal computers "in their bedrooms and basements" and the electronic bulletin boards that were a precursor of the true Internet.[14]

The *Times* article was one of many stories about hackers that appeared in 1983, most prompted by the FBI's arresting the members of a Milwaukee hacker group known as the 414s (after the local area code).[15] The 414s were six males aged sixteen to twenty-two who used personal computers and dial-up modems to hack over sixty computer systems, including the Los Alamos National Laboratory and the Security Pacific Bank in Los Angeles. They destroyed data in at least two of the systems they hacked. The 414s were caught because they returned to the same computers, over and over; a system administrator figured out what was happening and called the FBI. Only two were prosecuted (for making harassing phone calls); the other four agreed to stop hacking and pay restitution for the damage they caused. The two who were prosecuted pled guilty and were sentenced to probation.

One of the 414 hackers told Congress the group was inspired by the movie *WarGames*. In 1984, four teenagers suspected of hacking into NASA's Marshall Space Flight Center reportedly told police they used techniques they learned from the same film.[16] These were not the only instances in which life imitated art. Markus Hess, a German hacker the KGB recruited to spy on U.S. military systems, was inspired by *WarGames*;

he vowed that he, like the movie's protagonist David Lightman, would hack the North American Air Defense Command (NORAD) in Colorado.[17] Hess was not able to hack NORAD, but he hacked four hundred U.S. military computers, including a Pentagon database.[18]

In addition to accurately depicting how a hacker accessed a remote system, *WarGames* romanticized hackers.[19] As *Wired Magazine* noted twenty-five years later, it was the "geek-geist classic that legitimized hacker culture" and "minted the nerd hero."[20] *WarGames* brought the concepts of "hacking" and "hackers" to the attention of American society. It initially popularized the image of hackers as creative but benign, but that image rather quickly began to change. The arrests of the 414s and others engaged in similar activity indicated hackers were anything but benign. The image of hackers was further tarnished by a wave of publicity about the FBI's efforts to deal with their online depredations.

In 1984, a hacker-turned-FBI-informant estimated hackers stole one hundred million dollars a year in long-distance service, pirated the same amount of software, and were responsible for two hundred million dollars a year in credit card fraud.[21] In the mid-1980s, news stories said hacking had become "an epidemic" among high school students.[22] The essentially innocent image of *WarGames'* David Lightman hacking a system to find a new game morphed into the image of hacker-as-criminal, the image that still persists.

In the post-*WarGames* 1980s, a number of hacker groups arose to exploit the opportunities available in what was now known as "cyberspace," a term introduced in William Gibson's novel *Neuromancer*.[23] Some of this activity was innocuous, the type of innocent intellectual exploration associated with the original MIT hackers, but hacking also began to involve crimes that were committed for profit.[24]

As the 1980s turned into the 1990s, hacking was changing. Personal computers and software were more common—and so were targets: in the 1970s and most of the 1980s, it was a challenge "to find a system to hack"; but by the 1990s, the Internet was beginning to link everything, which meant hackers had thousands, and soon millions, of targets.[25] Since most organizations did not realize the need to secure their computers, many targets were wide-open, easy pickings. At the same time, hackers had to deal with a new phenomenon: law enforcement. In the aftermath of several high-profile hacking cases, law enforcement was becoming very aggressive in pursing notorious hackers like Los Angeles' "Dark Dante."

Kevin Poulsen was Dark Dante.[26] Born in 1965, Poulsen began hacking after his parents bought him a TRS-80 computer and modem for his sixteenth birthday. He left high school a year before graduating and became Dark Dante. Poulsen and another hacker, Ron Austin, broke into various computer systems, including systems involved in classified research for the Department of Defense. In 1983, the FBI arrested Austin, who was tried as an adult, convicted of "malicious access" to computers, and sent to jail. Since Poulsen was still only seventeen, he could not be tried as an adult and therefore was not criminally charged for his part in the hacks he and Austin carried out. He was, instead, hired by one of the entities he hacked—SRI International—to teach the military how to safeguard its computer systems. At SRI, Poulsen worked on various projects, including the Strategic Air Command's computer systems. In 1988, the FBI began investigating him for hacking classified systems and selling U.S. secrets abroad. In November 1989, a grand jury indicted Poulsen on eighteen counts of computer and telecommunications fraud, but he fled before FBI agents could arrest him.

While he hid out in Los Angeles, Poulsen used his expertise to hack a radio station's give-away contests and ensure that he won; he lived on the money from the radio station hacks. Poulsen was finally captured on April 11, 1991, after the FBI got a tip that he was seen at a grocery store in Van Nuys; an agent arrested him when he showed up there. On June 14, 1994, Poulsen pled guilty to computer fraud, mail fraud, money laundering, wiretapping, and obstructing justice. On February 9, 1995, he was sentenced to serve fifty-one months in prison and pay almost fifty-eight thousand dollars in restitution for the radio station hacks.[27] At the time, it was the "longest prison sentence ever received by a hacker."[28] Poulsen was released on June 4, 1996; in all, he spent over five years in prison, the "longest any computer hacker" had served to that point.[29]

One journalist called Poulsen "the last hacker," because his career began when hacking was still seen as a playful intellectual exercise and ended when it was morphing into something much darker: cybercrime.[30] The term appeared around the time Poulsen pled guilty[31] and was used with increasing frequency as Americans began to realize that online crime was a very real, and potentially serious, threat.[32] By the end of the 1990s,

Attorney General Janet Reno was calling for a multilateral "crackdown on cybercrime."[33] "Hacker" became, and remains, synonymous with "cybercriminal."

Hacking and Criminal Law

By the mid-1970s, existing criminal law was not adequate to deal with computer crime. If hackers like the members of the 414s were charged at all, it was with traditional crimes such as making harassing phone calls.[34] While hacker activity could usually be shoehorned into some existing crime, this often resulted in charges that did not adequately encompass the damage hackers inflicted.[35]

In an effort to address this deficiency, Senator Abraham Ribicoff of Connecticut introduced the Federal Computer Systems Protection Act into Congress in 1977.[36] The act would have created four new crimes: introducing fraudulent data into a computer; accessing a computer without authorization; altering or destroying data; and electronically stealing money, services, or "valuable data."[37] Anyone convicted of committing one of these cybercrimes could be sentenced to serve up to fifteen years in prison, pay a fifty-thousand-dollar fine, or both.

Two of the crimes the Ribicoff bill sought to create targeted hacking and hackers: accessing a computer without being authorized to do so (e.g., hacking); and altering or destroying data stored on a computer (often the proximate result of hacking into a system). The others were tool crimes. The bill was probably ahead of its time: it died in committee even though Ribicoff revised it and reintroduced it in 1979,[38] and his effort to see that computer crimes were added to the federal criminal code ended when he retired from Congress in 1981.[39]

While Ribicoff's bill was not adopted, it influenced legislation that was adopted at the state and federal levels. Between 1978 and 1986, forty-five states adopted computer crime legislation: twenty-three "modeled their statutes" after Ribicoff's bill; twenty adopted statutes that were "less closely related to the proposed federal legislation."[40] And Ohio and Massachusetts simply redefined "certain terms in their criminal codes" so their basic criminal statutes "covered computers and computer-related property."[41] The remaining five states soon passed their own cybercrime laws, with Vermont being the last to do so.[42]

States that adopted cybercrime-specific legislation followed the Ribicoff bill's example by treating hacking as a form of trespass. His bill made it a crime to access a computer without being authorized to do so. This is the cyber equivalent of trespass, which the law defines as "wrongful entry on another's real property."[43] More precisely, the Model Penal Code— an influential template of criminal laws[44]—defines criminal trespass as follows: "A person commits an offense if, knowing that he is not licensed or privileged to do so, he enters . . . any building or occupied structure."[45] The offense of criminal trespass is completed when the offender enters an area to which he does not have a lawful right of access; there is no requirement that he intend to commit an offense once the entry is complete. (If individuals intend to commit a crime once they enter an area to which they do not have a lawful right of access, they have committed the separate crime of burglary.[46])

This is the conduct that the U.S. states, the U.S. federal government, and the governments of many nations would criminalize as "simple" hacking. Simple hacking consists of gaining access to a computer without being authorized to do so; it is the functional analogue of criminal trespass, the notable difference being that a criminal trespasser invades a physical space while a simple hacker invades a virtual "space." Simple hacking in a networked world is an evolved version of the computer hacking that emerged at MIT in the 1960s and 1970s, that is, it is usually the product of simple curiosity. Simple hackers are usually motivated by intellectual curiosity—a desire to see if they can break into a system and explore what it contains.

In 1999, for example, fifteen-year-old Jonathan James hacked thirteen computers used by the National Aeronautics and Space Administration at the agency's Marshall Space Flight Center in Huntsville, Alabama.[47] James was caught, pled guilty to hacking in violation of federal law, and was sentenced to serve six months in a detention facility.[48] Before he began serving his sentence, James did an interview with PBS's *Frontline*, in which he argued that hacking was an "intellectual challenge."[49] When asked if what he did was a serious crime, James said, "Not at all. This is just harmless exploration. It's not a violent act or a destructive act. It's nothing." He put part of the blame for his actions on the government ("they should be responsible enough to provide adequate security") and claimed jail was an excessive sanction. James suggested that a more appropriate sanction "would be perhaps to take my computers away" and possibly "tell me that I can't use the Internet for a while, to teach me a lesson."

James's view of simple hacking was common in the hacker community in the 1990s and early years of the twenty-first century. Those who subscribed to this view often claimed hackers were performing a public service by alerting government agencies and private entities to the inadequacy of the measures they relied on to secure their computers. And they, like Jonathan James, tended to argue that simple hacking— accessing a computer system without being authorized to do so—should not be a crime (1) because the hacker was motivated by intellectual curiosity, rather than criminal intent, and (2) because simply "accessing" a system did not cause the type of harm that justifies the imposition of criminal liability.

Those proponents of this view claimed hacking should be a crime "only when information is stolen or systems vandalized."[50] Others pointed out that, like one who trespasses on physical property, the hacker caused harm merely by "entering" property without being authorized to do so.[51] They also pointed out that any other approach would "openly invite hackers to break into computer systems, safe in the knowledge that . . . they commit no crime."[52]

The view that simple hacking should be criminalized because it is analogous to criminal trespass ultimately prevailed. The sections below examine how states and the federal system went about doing this.

FEDERAL HACKING LAW

In the 1970s, concern about hackers led to the adoption of computer crime legislation in many states and the introduction of "more than a dozen computer crime bills" into Congress.[53] But Congress did nothing until 1984, apparently because "no House or Senate committee could be convinced that the federal government should play a specific role in controlling computer crime."[54] Congress's skepticism was in large part due to a belief that existing federal statutes could be used to prosecute hackers.[55]

By 1983, "twenty-one states had enacted computer crime legislation" and the adoption of similar legislation in the remaining states was "imminent."[56] The proliferation of state computer crime legislation, the movie *WarGames*, and a series of high-profile hacks eventually "overshadowed the concerns" that had prevented Congress from acting earlier and resulted in the adoption of the Counterfeit Access Device and Computer Fraud and Abuse Act of 1984, Pub. L. No. 98–473, Title II, section 2102(a), 98 Stat. 2190 (1984) ("the 1984 act").[57]

The 1984 act, which was codified as section 1030 of Title 18 of the U.S. Code, created four new federal crimes:

- Section 1030(a)(1)—Knowingly accessing a computer without authorization to obtain classified information in order to or with cause to believe such information would be used to harm the United States
- Section 1030(a)(2)—Knowingly access a computer without authorization or "having accessed a computer with authorization" and use such access for purposes to which the authorization does not extend to obtain information contained in a financial record belonging to a financial institution or in a consumer file belonging to a consumer reporting agency
- Section 1030(a)(3)—Knowingly access a computer without authorization to use, modify, destroy, or disclose information in, or prevent authorized use of, a computer operated for or on behalf of the United States if such conduct would affect the U.S. government's use of the computer
- Section 1030(b)(1)–(2)—Knowingly attempt or conspire to commit any of the three crimes outlined above

The 1984 act was very much a hacking-as-computer-trespass statute in that it focused only on unauthorized access crimes. This meant no one violated the statute unless he or she accessed a computer without being authorized to do so.

It is a basic principle of criminal law that criminal statutes must not be "void for vagueness," that is, must be understandable.[58] Most criminal statutes therefore define the terms they use in outlawing certain conduct, especially if the terms are not familiar to the average person. But while the 1984 act was predicated on concepts and activity that had not been the subject of federal criminal legislation and were probably not familiar to the average person, it only defined one term. It defined a "computer" as

an electronic, magnetic, optical, electrochemical, or other high speed data processing device performing logical, arithmetic, or storage functions, and includes any data storage facility or communications facility directly related to or operating in conjunction with such device, but such term does not include an automated typewriter or typesetter, a portable hand held calculator, or other similar device.[59]

After the act went into effect in October 1984, some "hailed [it] as an important first step," but "legislators and industry leaders" agreed that it "was incomplete"—that its criminal provisions were too limited.[60] Many legislators and business analysts believed section 1030 needed to be expanded so that it also protected "private sector computers used in interstate commerce."[61] Many in law enforcement criticized it as "structurally flawed and difficult to use."[62] Others criticized the act for not defining "access," "authorization," and a few other critical terms.[63]

The Department of Justice, which would prosecute the crimes created by the 1984 act, argued that the section making it a crime to use, destroy, or disclose information in or prevent authorized use of a computer operated for or on behalf of the United States if such conduct affected the government's use of the computer should be made a "strict trespass provision."[64] The department felt that, because "unauthorized access to a government computer was analogous to physical trespass onto government property," prosecutors should not be required to "show any additional elements, such as destruction of information, to gain a conviction."[65] The department also wanted two new crimes added to section 1030: a computer fraud crime and a destruction of property crime.[66]

1986 Revision

Congress responded by adopting the Computer Fraud and Abuse Act of 1986, Pub. L. 99–474, section 2, October 16, 1986, 100 Stat. 1213 ("the 1986 act"). The 1986 act made several changes to 18 U.S. Code section 1030:

- ▸ It modified section 1030(a)(3) into a strict trespass provision by making unauthorized access itself a criminal offense.
- ▸ It repealed the use exemption that had limited the application of sections 1030(a)(2) and (a)(3).
- ▸ It addressed a concern that section 1030(a)(3) might discourage whistleblowers by deleting a proviso in the subsection that prohibited "disclosure" of information.

- It changed the intent requirement of sections 1030(a)(2) and (a)(3) from "knowingly" to "intentionally."
- It eliminated the conspiracy provision created in section 1030(b)(2).

The 1986 act also added three new crimes:

- Section 1030(a)(4) made it a crime "knowingly and with intent to defraud," to access a "federal interest computer" without authorization to further the fraud and obtain "anything of value, unless the object of the fraud and the thing obtained consists only of the use of the computer";
- Section 1030(a)(5) made it a federal crime to alter, damage, or destroy information stored in a "federal interest computer" or prevent authorized use of "such computer or information"; and
- Section 1030(a)(6) made it a federal crime to traffic in computer passwords "knowingly and with intent to defraud."

The 1986 act has several definitions: for example, it defined a "federal interest computer" as (1) a computer used exclusively by "a financial institution or the United States Government" or "used by or for a financial institution or the United States Government" if the "conduct constituting the offense" affected that use or (2) "one of two or more computers used in committing the offense, not all of which are located in the same State."

Congress used the requirement that the conduct criminalized by the new fraud and property damage crimes target a "federal interest computer" to limit the applicability of the new legislation.[67] It had included similar limiting language in the 1984 act for the same purpose. The Congress of this era believed computer crime should generally be dealt with at the state and local levels, and therefore sought to "limit Federal jurisdiction over computer crime to those cases in which there is a compelling Federal interest,"[68] that is, to cases in which the targeted computer was used by the financial institutions or the federal government or to cases in which the crime involved interstate activity.

1994 Revision

The Computer Abuse Amendments Act of 1994, Pub. L. No. 103–322, 108 Stat. 1796, 2097, made two significant changes to section 1030: it expanded the section 1030(a)(5) property damage crime so that it (1) applied to computers used in interstate commerce, as well as federal interest computers, and (2) applied to both reckless and intentional conduct.[69] The 1994 act also created a cause of action for those who suffered "damage or loss" as the result of a violation of section 1030. The new civil remedy—codified as 18 U.S. Code section 1030(g)—allowed victims of such a violation to "maintain a civil action against the violator to obtain compensatory damages" and other relief.

1996 Revision

The next major revision of section 1030 came in October 1996, with the adoption of the Economic Espionage Act of 1996, Pub. L. 104–294, Title II, section 201, Title VI, section 604(b)(36), 110 Stat. 3491, 3508. The act made three notable changes to section 1030:

- It expanded the statute's scope by replacing its focus on "federal interest computers" with a focus on "protected" computers. The 1996 act defined a "protected computer" as a computer that was either (1) used exclusively for the benefit of a financial institution or the U.S. government or used by or for a financial institution or the U.S. government and the conduct constituting the offense affected that use; or (2) used in or in a manner affecting interstate or foreign commerce. This definition is still in effect.[70]
- It expanded the scope of section 1030(a)(2), which had originally targeted only unauthorized access that obtained financial records from financial institutions or consumer reporting agencies. The revised version of section 1030(a)(2), which is still in effect, encompasses unauthorized access and exceeding authorized access by which the perpetrator obtains (1) financial records from financial institutions or consumer reporting services; (2) information from any federal agency or department; or (3) information from "any protected computer." Since the legislative history of section 1030 established that "obtaining" included "mere observation of the data,"[71] the revised section 1030(a)(2) had an expansive reach. Since it now encompassed protected computers, the statute could conceivably be used to prosecute anyone who read information on a computer without being authorized to do so.
- It added an extortion crime: new section 1030(a)(7) made it a crime for someone acting with the intent to extort "any money or . . . other thing of value" from a person, government entity, or

other legal entity to transmit "in interstate or foreign commerce any communication containing any threat to" damage a protected computer.

The Economic Espionage Act also expanded section 1030's definition of "damage," which is an essential element in establishing federal jurisdiction over certain conduct and in sentencing. The act defined "damage" as including "any impairment to the integrity or availability of data, a program, a system, or information" that

- caused loss aggregating at least five thousand dollars in value during any one-year period to one or more individuals;
- modified or impaired, or potentially modified or impaired, the medical examination, diagnosis, treatment, or care of one or more individuals;
- caused physical injury to any person; or
- threatened public health or safety.[72]

2001 and 2002 Revisions

The 2001 and 2002 revisions were for the most part minor. The 2001 legislation—the USA PATRIOT Act—did make a notable change in section 1030(e)'s definition of a "protected computer." It added this language at the end of the definition quoted above: "including a computer located outside the United States that is used in a manner that affects interstate or foreign commerce or communication of the United States."[73] This language, which was in part prompted by the 9/11 attacks, was added to ensure that the U.S. government had jurisdiction to prosecute "international computer crime cases."[74]

2008 Revision

The Identity Theft Enforcement and Restitution Act, Pub. L. 110–326, Title II, sections 203, 204(a), 205 to 208, September 26, 2008, 122 Stat. 3561, 3563 ["the 2008 act"] made a number of changes in section 1030, including a substantial change to section 1030(a)(5).

Prior revisions had divided section 1030(a)(5) into two subsections: (A) and (B). Subsection (A) was divided into three sub-subsections because it created three crimes: One—section 1030(a)(5)(A)(i)—encompassed disseminating malware or launching distributed denial of service (DDOS) attacks, both of which we will examine in the next chapter. The others were hacking crimes:

- ▸ Section 1030(a)(5)(A)(2) made it a crime to intentionally access a protected computer without authorization and, "as a result of such conduct, recklessly" cause damage;
- ▸ Section 1030(a)(5)(A)(3) made it a crime to intentionally access a protected computer without authorization and, "as a result of such conduct, cause damage."

The 2008 act renumbered the sub-subsections of what was section 1030(a)(5)(A). The three crimes are now codified as section 1030(a)(5) (A) (malware or DDOS attacks); section 1030(a)(5)(B) (intentional access with reckless damage); and section 1030(a)(5)(C) (intentional access with damage).

Until 2008, subsection (B) specified that to be liable for any of the section 1030(A) crimes, the perpetrator must have caused at least one of the following:

- ▸ loss to one or more persons during any one-year period (and, for purposes of an investigation, prosecution, or other proceeding brought by the United States only, loss resulting from a related course of conduct affecting one or more other protected computers) aggregating at least five thousand dollars in value;
- ▸ the modification or impairment, or potential modification or impairment, of the medical examination, diagnosis, treatment, or care of one or more individuals;
- ▸ physical injury to any person;
- ▸ a threat to public health or safety; or
- ▸ damage affecting a computer system used by or for a government entity in furtherance of the administration of justice, national defense, or national security.

These subsections limited the use of section 1030(a)(5). Under the pre-2008 version of the statute, prosecutors could not charge someone with committing a section 1030(a)(5)(A) crime unless they could prove the case involved one of these jurisdictional requirements. The 2008 act moved the requirements to section 1030(c)(4)(A), where they are factors to be considered in sentencing someone for committing what is now a section 1030(a)(5)(B) offense.

What is the significance of this change? To understand that, it is necessary to understand why the five-thousand-dollar element was included in the prior version of the statute. When Congress transformed the Counterfeit Access Device and Computer Fraud and Abuse Act of 1984 into the Computer Fraud and Abuse Act of 1986, it created section 1030(a)(5) to "penalize those who . . . alter, damage, or destroy certain computerized data belonging to another."[75] But because Congress did not want the new provision used "against every individual who modified another's computer data," it included a damage requirement limiting its applicability.[76] The new section 1030(a)(5) criminalized the alteration, damage, or destruction in two circumstances: One was when the damage totaled one thousand dollars or more in a single year. The other circumstance was altering, damaging, or deleting data relating to medical care and treatment.

In 1996, Congress increased the damage requirement to five thousand dollars. In 2001, the USA PATRIOT Act kept the five-thousand-dollar requirement while adding the other requirements noted above, that is, modifying or impairing medical data, physical injury to a person, threatening public health or safety, or damaging a computer used by a government entity in the administration of justice, national defense, or national security.[77] The three section 1030(a)(5) crimes were moved to new section 1030(a)(5)(A), and the jurisdictional damage requirements were codified in the new section 1030(a)(5)(B).[78] As the Department of Justice explained, then-section 1030(a)(5)(A) "prohibit[ed] certain acts when accompanied by particular mental states, while section 1030(a)(5)(B)" required the government to prove "a specific kind of harm resulted from those actions."[79]

The 2008 act deleted section 1030(a)(5)(B) and moved its harm requirements to section 1030(c), where they are now factors to be considered in sentencing someone for violating what is now section 1030(a)(5)(B). Why did Congress eliminate them from the section 1030(a)(5) crimes? There were earlier efforts to eliminate the jurisdictional limitations, but until 2008 Congress declined to do so. In 2000, Senator Patrick Leahy explained why he was opposed to this: "Federal laws do not need to reach . . . every minor, inadvertent and harmless computer abuse—after all, each of the

50 states has its own computer crime laws. Rather, our federal laws need to reach those offenses for which federal jurisdiction is appropriate."[80]

Congress's view changed, no doubt because of the vast increase in cybercrime between 2000 and 2008. The requirements formerly included in section 1030(a)(5)(B) barred prosecutors from bringing charges in instances involving egregious conduct that did not demonstrably inflict any of the varieties of harm codified in that subsection. As one author noted, while "spyware may 'damage' a computer by altering data, the damage is unlikely to meet the requisite $5,000 damage threshold necessary for federal criminal jurisdiction."[81]

A Department of Justice representative testifying before Congress on legislation that would become the 2008 act called upon Congress to revise section 1030(a)(5) so that it "would appropriately penalize the use of malicious spyware, botnets, and keyloggers."[82] He explained that identity thieves obtain personal information by installing malicious "spyware on numerous individual computers. Whether or not the programs succeed in obtaining the . . . financial data, these . . . programs harm the 'integrity' of the computer and data. Nevertheless, it is often difficult or impossible to . . . prove that the total value of these many small losses exceeds $5,000."[83] Congress presumably decided it was advisable to eliminate the jurisdictional strictures that prevented federal prosecutors from using section 1030(a)(5) in appropriate instances. Congress probably also assumed they would exercise their prosecutorial discretion to avoid abusing the expanded power this gives them.

The 2008 act also made two other notable changes in section 1030. The relevant change to federal hacking law was not made at the behest of the Department of Justice. The 1984 act added a conspiracy provision to section 1030, and the 1986 act deleted that provision. The 2008 act restored it, so section 1030(b) now states that anyone who "conspires to commit or attempts to commit an offense under [section 1030(a)] shall be punished as provided in [section 1030(c)]."

It is not clear why Congress took this step, which was a return to the past. The 1984 act made it a crime to conspire to commit a substantive violation of section 1030(a). The legislative history for the 1984 act does not explain why Congress did this. The 1986 act eliminated the conspiracy offense then codified as 18 U.S. Code section 1030(b)(2). The legislative history for this revision merely notes that the Senate Judiciary Commit-tee intended "that such conduct be governed by the general conspiracy offense" codified as 18 U.S. Code section 371. Since the legislative history for the 2008 act offers no explanation for Congress resuscitating the con-spiracy provision, we can only assume it acted out of a general concern for expanding prosecutorial tools against cybercriminals.

STATE HACKING LAW

Every U.S. state criminalizes hacking (accessing a computer without being authorized to do so) and the related crime of exceeding one's au-thorized access to a computer. Many states use a two-tiered approach that criminalizes (1) basic unauthorized access to a computer (simple hack-ing) and (2) unauthorized access that involves additional criminal activity such as copying or destroying data (aggravated hacking). States that use this approach generally define simple hacking and aggravated hacking as distinct crimes and make simple hacking a misdemeanor and aggravated hacking a felony.[84]

Some states use a single statute to criminalize both activities.[85] Others have separate provisions. Hawaii has one of the more complicated statu-tory structures; its penal code creates three distinct intrusion crimes and two different damage crimes.[86]

The substance of the simple hacking statutes tends to be consistent, but there is a fair degree of variation in how they characterize the crimes. Some refer to simple hacking as "unauthorized access," while others refer to it as "computer trespass," "unauthorized use," or "computer tampering." At least one state has a "criminal mischief" statute that makes it a misde-meanor to knowingly access a computer while "having no right to do so or reasonable ground to believe the person has such right."[87]

The substance of the statutes targeting aggravated hacking are also generally consistent, but these statutes vary more in structure than the simple hacking provisions. They all prohibit unauthorized access that results in the copying, alteration, or deletion of data or damage to a com-puter system. A number also outlaw the use of a computer to engage in other criminal acts. New York has a cyberburglary statute that makes it a crime to break into a computer or computer system intending "to commit or attempt to commit or further the commission of any felony."[88]

Unlike 18 U.S. Code section 1030, many state hacking statutes do "access." The most commonly used definition is that access "means to approach, instruct, communicate with, store data in, retrieve data from, or otherwise make use of any resources of a computer, computer system, or computer network."[89] This is the definition that was at issue in *State v. Allen*, the first and still most important decision to parse the meaning of access in cybercrime statutes.[90]

Anthony Allen was charged with using a telephone modem to gain unauthorized access to a Southwestern Bell computer system. According to the prosecution, Allen "used his computer ... to call various Southwestern Bell computer modems. The telephone numbers for the modems were obtained by random dialing. If one of Allen's calls were completed, his computer determined if it had been answered by voice or another computer."[91] When a call was answered, Allen hung up.

Allen claimed he had not "accessed" the computers because the prosecution "presented no evidence" that showed he had ever "entered any Southwestern Bell computer system." The prosecution argued that what Allen did constituted "access" under a Kansas statute that was then identical with the current Florida statute; more precisely, the Kansas prosecutor argued that Allen had, at a minimum, "approached" the Southwestern Bell computer system.

The Kansas Supreme Court disagreed. It noted that, in a 1989 publication, the Department of Justice said that predicating unauthorized access crimes on the concept of merely "approaching" a computer could be unconstitutional.[92] The Justice Department explained that if the word "approach" were taken literally, "any unauthorized physical proximity to a computer could constitute a crime."[93] In other words, basing criminal liability on approaching a computer would make the statute unconstitutionally vague, since it would not provide reasonable notice as to what conduct was forbidden. The Kansas Supreme Court therefore held that the trial court correctly dismissed the charges against Allen.

In the wake of the *Allen* decision, some states deleted "approach" from their definitions of what it means to access a computer. The issue has seldom arisen since the *Allen* case.

There have been, and continue to be, prosecutions under state antihacking laws, though they are far from common. While some of these cases involved traditional, outsider hacking, many involved the insider crime—exceeding authorized access to a computer system.

U.S. Hacking Law: An Assessment

The federal government and all of the states have laws in place that adequately criminalize hacking. In most instances, these laws have been in effect for well over a decade. The general adequacy of U.S. hacking laws is no doubt attributable to the attention hacking gained in the late 1980s and early 1990s, in the wake of the movie *WarGames* and the publicity surrounding a number of high-profile hacking episodes. Surprisingly, these laws are rarely used, at both the state and federal levels.

This *might* be attributable to a national awareness of the need to prevent hackers from gaining access to computers, but that does not, in fact, seem to be the case. While both the general public and organizational users appear to have some appreciation for the need to secure computers, anecdotal evidence indicates that this appreciation tends to be honored more in the breach than in its observance.

That reality is due to a number of factors, two of which are the time and expense involved in maintaining computer security. Unlike real-world threats, online threats are moving targets: a bank, for example, can invest in an expensive vault to secure its assets for years; neither the aspirations nor the efforts of bank robbers have changed appreciably over the last century. The same bank cannot simply hire computer staff members, provide them with equipment and the best available security software, and assume it has protected its systems from online criminals for the foreseeable future. As chapter 1 demonstrated, modern bank robbers operate in a malleable environment, one in which those who are responsible for securing computer systems find themselves in an arms race with those who are determined to undermine security and infiltrate the systems.

The relative paucity of hacking prosecutions is probably a function of several factors, one of which is that many corporate victims of hacking do not report the crimes to law enforcement for fear of negative publicity. Online crimes targeting corporate entities are more likely to be reported to law enforcement when the attack on the entity harmed one of its customers, as when the Bullitt County thefts were reported to law enforcement.

Another factor that contributes to the relative paucity of hacking prosecutions is a lack of computer crime expertise among local investigators and prosecutors. Many local police departments have few, if any, trained computer crime investigators; even if a department has an investigator, the process of collecting and analyzing digital evidence is time consuming, which means a department cannot pursue every case that comes to its attention. Law enforcement's computer crime resources are currently targeted toward cases involving online crimes against children. Given the very limited resources available, this can erode a police department's ability to pursue hacking cases.

It may also be that hacking cases are not seen as a high priority. A few years ago, I was chatting with a computer crime investigator who had established an online sting operation that targeted pedophiles who were using the Internet to seduce children into having sex with them. He said he mentioned the operation to an officer who headed a nearby city police department's vice unit and suggested that they establish a similar operation in the vice unit. The officer I spoke with said the vice unit officer declined, saying "I have *real* crimes to deal with." The implication, of course, was that what happens online is less of a concern than what happens in the real, physical world. That attitude might—or might not—contribute to the relative paucity of hacking prosecutions.

>chapter:2

MALWARE AND DDOS ATTACKS

Not all cybercrimes are physically carried out by a human being—a cybercriminal. Unlike traditional crimes, certain types of cybercrime can be automated, that is, they can be carried out by computer code that has been created and designed to attack a computer system. This chapter examines the two types of automated cybercrime that have so far arisen: malware, that is, the use of computer viruses, worms, and other programs to damage or steal data from a system, and DDOS attacks, the use of computer code to take over "innocent" computers and incorporate them into a cyberarmy that then attacks websites and other online systems.

Malware

"Malware" is a portmanteau—a word created by blending "malicious" and "software."[1] It denotes software that is designed to infiltrate or damage a computer without the owner's knowledge and consent. There are many types of malware,[2] but most people are only familiar with two: viruses and worms.

COMPUTER VIRUSES

A computer virus is a program that can copy itself and infect computers, much as a biological virus infects people.[3] Like biological viruses, computer viruses need a host to spread to other computers; they use computer code as their host. Computer viruses infect program code in one system and use that host—plus their capacity for replication—to infect other systems.[4]

Computer viruses are far from new: in 1975, John Walker created Pervading Animal, a virus that infected UNIVAC mainframes via files transferred between systems on magnetic tape.[5] Seven years later, a Pittsburgh ninth-grader, Rich Skrenta, created the first virus to infect personal computers.[6] His Elk Cloner virus, which was spread by infected floppy disks, targeted Apple II computers. The infected computers shut down or performed a "trick" every fifth time they booted up, and displayed a poem every fiftieth time.[7] The virus—which was apparently intended as a practical joke—caused little damage, but removing it was time consuming.

In 1984, computer scientist Fred Cohen was the first to use the term "virus" to refer to self-propagating code.[8] Two years later, Pakistani brothers Amjad and Basit Farooq Alvi released the Brain virus—the first to infect IBM personal computers.[9] The virus infected boot sectors on IBM floppy disks; among other things, infected sectors displayed a cryptic message that included the phrase "Welcome to the Dungeon."[10]

Over the years, more viruses appeared: About two hundred were in circulation by the end of 1990. By 2003, the number of viruses in circulation had jumped to seventy thousand;[11] by 2008, it was over one million;[12] and by 2010, experts estimated that millions of computer viruses were in circulation around the globe.[13]

COMPUTER WORMS

Like a virus, a computer worm is a self-replicating computer program.[14] Unlike a virus, a worm does not need to attach itself to a host to spread to other systems.[15] A worm uses a network to send copies of itself to other computers on that network; worms can therefore replicate on their own, without any assistance from computer users.[16]

The term "worm" comes from a 1975 science-fiction novel: John Brunner's *The Shockwave Rider.*[17] It is set in a "dystopian early 21st century America dominated by computer networks";[18] the hero is a fugitive from the sinister government think tank that educated him. The government wants to find him because he can program networks "using only a touch-tone telephone."[19] The plot is convoluted but at one point involves the hero's using a network worm—a "computer tapeworm"—to disable the programs the government uses to lock down its network and ensure that its nefarious activities remain secret.[20]

In the early 1980s, computer scientists at Xerox's Palo Alto Research Center began experimenting with benign "worm" programs such as the "vampire" worm that put computers to work at night, when they would otherwise be idle.[21] This research ended when it became apparent that worms could be dangerous; a worm developed at Xerox malfunctioned one evening and repeatedly crashed computers at the research center.

In 1988, Robert Morris was a graduate student in computer science at Cornell University.[22] He developed a worm either to gauge the size of the Internet or to test the level of security on the Internet.[23] It is, however, clear that whatever Morris's motive was for creating the worm, he did not mean for it to cause harm.[24]

Morris designed the worm to spread through the Internet once it was released; it was supposed to be unobtrusive and not interfere with the operation of the computers it infected. To prevent the worm from reinfecting computers—which would make it easier to detect, as well as cause computers to crash—Morris programmed it to "ask" a computer if it had been infected. If it said "yes," the worm would not reinstall itself. And if Morris had stopped there, no one might ever have heard of his worm. But he went a step further: to ensure that programmers could not defeat the worm by programming computers so that they falsely answered "yes" when asked if they were infected, Morris set the worm to duplicate itself every seventh time it received a "yes." Unfortunately, he "underestimated the number of times a computer would be asked the question, and his one-out-of-seven ratio resulted in far more copying than he had anticipated."[25]

Morris released the worm "into the wild" at 5:00 p.m. on November 2, 1988, releasing it from MIT to hide its connection with Cornell. It quickly became apparent he had made a terrible error: the feature he included to prevent the worm from reinstalling itself had the opposite effect; the 14 percent replication rate proved disastrous, as the worm raced through computers, reinfecting them every seventh time it received a "yes" to its query about infection. According to one analyst, it took less than ninety minutes for the worm to shut down a computer system.[26] It disabled an estimated six thousand computer systems;[27] and experts estimated that the cost of dealing with the worm at each infection site ranged from two hundred to over fifty-three thousand dollars.[28]

When Morris realized what was happening, he consulted a friend at Harvard, and they eventually sent an anonymous e-mail telling programmers how to kill the worm and prevent it from reinfecting computers.[29] Since the worm had clogged the Internet, the message did not reach programmers until it was too late; by the time they received it, they had come up with their own approaches. Programmers across the country spent the next two days cleaning up after the worm and reviving their systems.[30]

Blame became the issue in the worm's aftermath. Many demanded that Morris be prosecuted for what he had done, but there was a problem: it was clear he had not intended for the worm to cause damage, and it had not destroyed or altered data in the systems it attacked. But it had caused other types of damage: programmers spent fifty or sixty hours disabling the virus and getting their systems back up and running; and universities (and taxpayers) lost research time worth millions of dollars.[31] The difficulty lay in quantifying the damage. The Computer Virus Industry Association estimated that it cost "nearly $100 million in lost computer time and manpower to eradicate the worm and restore" the victimized systems.[32] Other estimates were lower but were still in the millions.

It was inevitable that Morris would face criminal charges. In July 1989, a federal grand jury in Syracuse, New York, indicted him on one count of gaining unauthorized access to university and military computers.[33] Morris was the first person to be indicted under the federal Computer Fraud and Abuse Act. If convicted, he faced five years in prison and a $250,000 fine. Morris entered a not guilty plea and went to trial. He was convicted on January 23, 1990, and sentenced on May 5.[34] After noting that prison "did not fit the crime," the federal judge sentenced Morris to pay a ten-thousand-dollar fine, spend three years on probation, and do four hundred hours of community service.[35] He served his sentence, received a PhD from Harvard in 1999, and became a professor at MIT.[36]

Over the next twenty years, computer worms would evolve in sophistication. In July and August of 2001, three versions of the Code Red worm appeared, in sequence; each spread rapidly, defacing web pages and resulting in a general slowdown in Internet traffic.[37] One of the Code Red versions was designed to launch what would have been a massive, crippling attack on the White House's computer system; experts were able to prevent the attack from succeeding by altering the White House's Internet protocol (IP) address, which deflected the traffic the worm directed toward its intended target.[38] In September 2001, the Nimda worm was released a week after the 9/11 attacks, causing concern that it was linked to terrorist activity. Nimda spread rapidly and caused a general slowdown in Internet traffic but proved not to be terrorism related.[39] Two years later, the SQL Slammer worm appeared; fifteen minutes after it hit its first victim, "huge sections of the Internet began to wink out of existence."[40]

Like viruses, worms increased in sophistication as the years passed: In 2008, the Conficker worm infected six to seven million computers.[41] Successive versions of the worm emerged later, and Conficker iterations were still infecting computers in 2010.[42] What unnerved experts was that by 2010 Conficker had infected and taken control of millions of computers but done nothing more; some predicted that the world had yet to see how destructive Conficker would become.[43]

But Conficker was eclipsed by an even more sophisticated worm. Stuxnet, which was discovered in the summer of 2010, takes control of the computer systems used to operate critical infrastructure components.[44] Malware analysts concluded that Stuxnet was written to target the SCADA (supervisory control and data acquisition) systems that are used to operate power plants, water treatment and distribution systems, oil and gas pipelines, transportation systems, communication systems, and other infrastructure components.[45] In other words, Stuxnet attacks the systems on which nation-states rely for their prosperity and survival.

Experts who have analyzed Stuxnet say it represents a shift from malware deployed for profit to malware that is deployed to "bring down critical infrastructure."[46] And as analysts learned more about Stuxnet, they speculated that it was developed by a nation-state—possibly by Israel, which may have had support from the United States.[47] The inference that Stuxnet was created and deployed by these nation-states was in part based on the fact that it "wiped out roughly a fifth" of Iran's nuclear centrifuges, thereby delaying Iran's nuclear program.[48] The complexity and targeting structure of Stuxnet led many to conclude that it was a "game changer for critical infrastructure protection."[49]

The Morris worm and the increasingly sinister varieties of malware that followed revealed what no one realized in the early years of the Internet: when computers are linked to a network, they become vulnerable to hostile programs in ways that were not possible when computers were freestanding mainframes. In the 1990s and in the early years of the twenty-first century, it became increasingly apparent how serious, and how intractable, this threat is. It also became apparent that this was an area of activity law needed to address.

MALWARE AND CRIMINAL LAW

Malware laws are second-generation cybercrime laws, that is, they were adopted after a jurisdiction had criminalized hacking. This is primarily because the dangers of malware did not become apparent until the 1990s, years after citizens and legislators discovered the existence of and the risks associated with hacking.

Federal Malware Law

Neither the 1984 nor the 1986 version of the Computer Fraud and Abuse Act addressed malware, an issue Senator Patrick Leahy raised in a 1992 article.[50] He noted that the "importance of such legislation was recently underscored" by the appearance of a series of destructive computer viruses.[51] And he explained why the current version of the Computer Fraud and Abuse Act was inadequate in this regard:

> Crimes under the current statute must be predicated on the violator's gaining "unauthorized access" to the . . . computers. However, . . . the most severe forms of computer damage are often inflicted on remote computers to which the violator never gained "access." . . . Instead, . . . those computers are damaged when a malicious program or code is replicated and transmitted by other computers or diskettes already infected by a violator's earlier transmission of a virus.[52]

Senator Leahy was not the first to recognize this problem.

In 1989, Representative Wally Herger of California introduced the Computer Virus Eradication Act into the House of Representatives.[53] The bill would have added a section to the Computer Fraud and Abuse Act that made it a crime "to knowingly insert a harmful code into a computer or a computer program and then knowingly distribute that program to others."[54] Herger's bill never came up for a vote in the House or the Senate, perhaps because Senator Leahy's legislation—then known as the Computer Abuse Amendments Act of 1991—was also pending at the time.

It was five years before a malware offense was added to the Computer Fraud and Abuse Act. The Computer Abuse Amendments Act of 1994 added a section to section 1030(a)(5) that made it a crime to knowingly or recklessly cause "the transmission of a program, information, code, or command" and thereby "damage" a computer.[55] This section has been part of the act ever since but was revised in 1996. The 1996 revision eliminated the mens rea of recklessness; ever since, this provision has imposed liability only on those who knowingly disseminate malware intending to cause damage.[56]

The deceptively simple language of the Computer Fraud and Abuse Act's malware provision has proven quite effective in dealing with those who disseminate viruses and worms; it has the advantage of not tying liability to particular technology or particular techniques. Some state malware statutes take a similar approach, while others tend to craft their malware prohibitions in language that is more complex.

State Malware Law

Basically, U.S. states take two approaches to criminalizing malware: one makes it a crime to disseminate a "computer contaminant"; the other approach makes it a crime to disseminate a computer virus.

California is one of the states that fall into the first category. California Penal Code section 502(c)(8) makes it a crime to knowingly introduce "any computer contaminant into any computer, computer system, or computer network." The statute defines a computer contaminant as

> any set of computer instructions that are designed to modify, damage, destroy, record, or transmit information within a computer, computer system, or computer network without the intent or permission of the owner of the information. They include, but are not limited to, a group of computer instructions commonly called viruses or worms, that are self-replicating or self-propagating and are designed to contaminate other computer programs or computer data, consume computer resources, modify, destroy, record, or transmit data, or in some other fashion usurp the normal operation of the computer, computer system, or computer network.[57]

Unlike the federal statute, the California provision only requires that the perpetrator "knowingly" introduce malware into a computer system; it does not require that he or she do so with the intention of damaging that computer or other computers. The statute may, however, reach that result indirectly, by defining a computer contaminant as a code that is, at least in part, designed to damage a computer, computer network, or the data contained in such a system. Since there are no reported cases involving prosecutions under the statute, it appears no court has addressed this issue.

A number of other states also follow this approach: using essentially the same definition of computer contaminant and making it a crime to knowingly introduce such a contaminant into a computer or a network.[58] Other states take the other approach, basing their malware prohibitions on defining and then outlawing the use of what they refer to as computer viruses.[59] Their definitions of a computer virus are often broad enough to also encompass computer worms.[60]

Since there are, as of this writing, no reported cases involving prosecutions under any of these statutes, it appears states have made little, if any, effort to target the use of malware. This may explain why a number of states do not appear to have criminalized the use of computer viruses, worms, or other types of malware.

The apparent lack of legislation criminalizing malware and prosecution for such crimes at the state level may also be a function of a basic reality: the dissemination of malware is almost inherently a transborder crime, that is, when a computer virus or worm is released it will almost certainly not respect state or national jurisdictional boundaries. Given that, it would probably be unrealistic to expect U.S. states to adopt and attempt to rigorously enforce malware legislation.

This is a task more suited to the capabilities of the federal system, though even federal law enforcement finds it challenging to pursue cybercriminals whose activities transcend U.S. borders.

U.S. Malware Law: An Assessment

The malware provisions of section 1030(a)(5)(A) are quite adequate for prosecuting those who release malicious code into cyberspace. The malware prohibitions adopted by U.S. states also seem adequate to this task.

The difficulty involved in bringing such prosecutions lies not in the adequacy of the law but in the fact that malware has become a far more complex phenomenon than it was when the first viruses appeared in the early 1980s. As a report explains, between 2005 and 2006, "malware production transformed from a hobby of malevolent computer geeks into a major source of money for organized crime."[61]

The Zeus Trojan horse program used to carry out the bank theft examined in the introduction is a product of offshore organized crime. A report on the program noted that it is "the handiwork of Eastern European organized criminals."[62] While the leaders of the organizations that use tools like Zeus tend to be located in Eastern Europe, they are a small part of the transnational network that implements the Trojan, collects the funds it siphons from bank accounts and other sources, and moves those funds into accounts that can be accessed by the leaders of the particular cybercrime group involved.[63]

The offshore, usually multinational character of these organized cybercriminal groups means that investigating the use of particular malware and apprehending those responsible for its implementation will almost certainly be beyond the capabilities of U.S. state law enforcement personnel. It is also a daunting task for federal law enforcement officers. For the purposes of this discussion, it is sufficient to note that adopting adequate malware laws is but the first step in dealing with this expanding area of criminal activity.

DDOS Attacks

Distributed denial of service (DDOS) attacks differ from hacking and malware. Hackers and malware both have to access a computer in order to complete their respective missions. Both involve activity that takes place in the attacked system: the hacker enters the target computer system to explore, copy data, cause damage, or for any of several other purposes; malware infects the target computer in order to copy data, interfere with its functioning, or use the targeted computer to replicate itself and send the copies to other computers.

DDOS attacks do not involve the perpetrator's gaining entry into—or access to—a computer. They are in that sense analogous to wartime attacks involving bombs dropped from airplanes or delivered by airborne missiles. Bombs eradicate their targets, thereby preventing the country to which they belong from utilizing them in defensive or offensive maneuvers. Like bombs, DDoS attacks inflict harm externally, without ever entering the target of the attack. Unlike bombs, DDoS attacks inflict harm in a nonphysical environment.

In a DDoS attack, the attacker tries to prevent the legitimate users of computers "from accessing information or services. By targeting your computer and its network connection, or the computers and network of the sites you are trying to use, an attacker may be able to prevent you from accessing e-mail, websites, online accounts (banking, etc.), or other services that rely on the affected computer."[64]

As a federal agency explains, the most common type of a DDoS attack occurs when "an attacker 'floods' a network with information. When you type a URL for a particular website into your browser, you are sending a request to that site's computer server to view the page. The server can only process a certain number of requests at once, so if an attacker overloads the server with requests, it can't process your request. This is a 'denial of service' because you can't access that site."[65]

The effect of a DDoS attack is functionally analogous to what would happen if someone used an automated dialing system to repeatedly call a pizza delivery company that relied entirely on telephone orders for its revenue. The automated calls would tie up the company's phone lines and prevent legitimate customers from placing orders. The company would lose business for as long as the attack continued and might also lose some residual business, if once regular customers decided to abandon the company.

It is difficult to pinpoint precisely when DDoS attacks emerged. News stories noting the use of a primitive form of the attack date back at least to the mid-1990s.[66] According to one expert, the tools used to launch the more sophisticated attacks that are common today were "developed in the underground" in mid-1998, with the first reported DDoS attack occurring in August 1999.[67] What is clear is that the public—and the government —only became aware of DDoS attacks in 2000.

On Monday, February 7, 2000, something strange began happening at Yahoo! Its computers began to slow down: "Instead of loading pages in 1.7 seconds, the computers were taking over 6 seconds to load web pages and 6 seconds is a long time in Internet Time."

From there things got worse. By 10:30 a.m. Pacific time, almost half the users who tried to log on to Yahoo! were shut out—getting error messages. Engineers discovered that a "huge tidal wave of data" was overwhelming the computers.[68]

Yahoo! engineers were eventually able to redirect traffic to backup computers, so by the middle of the afternoon things were back to normal.[69] The attack ended around the same time, but the next day new attacks "slowed or crippled" high-profile websites such as eBay, Amazon, Dell, and CNN.[70] On Wednesday, DDOS attacks targeted ZDNet.com, E-Trade, Datek, and Excite.[71] Then attorney general Janet Reno held a news conference and announced that the FBI was investigating and would catch the person or persons responsible for the attacks.[72]

On February 11, a market research firm estimated that the attacks caused $1.2 billion in global economic damages.[73] A week after the attacks, then president Bill Clinton "held a cyber-summit with high-tech executives and academics . . . to discuss Internet security" in the wake of the new threat.[74] He warned against calling the attacks "an 'electronic Pearl Harbor'" but said they "served as a wakeup call" to the need to ensure security on the Internet.[75]

Meanwhile, the FBI's investigation focused on a "15-year-old high school student from a posh Montreal suburb" who used the Internet alias "Mafiaboy."[76] Agents began investigating Mafiaboy "almost immediately" after the DDOS attacks because he claimed responsibility for some of them "on Internet Relay Chat [IRC], a public chat system."[77] After an investigator at an Internet security firm heard Mafiaboy was claiming responsibility for the attacks, he recorded IRC chats in which Mafiaboy threatened to shut down the CNN and E-Trade sites, both of which "went down five to 10 minutes" after he made the threat.[78] Investigators traced the IP address used in Mafiaboy's posts to his Internet service provider in Canada, which gave them his home address.[79] U.S. and Canadian investigators then spent several weeks analyzing the digital trail that led to Mafiaboy and linking him to the attacks; their goal, in part, was to ensure that he was not being framed by someone who had used his IP address to launch the attacks.[80]

On April 15, Canadian investigators arrested Mafiaboy at his home and searched the residence, seizing computer equipment they found there.[81] Canadian prosecutors initially charged him with "two counts of 'mischief to data,'"[82] but added sixty-three more counts, which brought the total to sixty-five.[83] In January 2001, Mafiaboy pled guilty to fifty-six of the counts,[84] and in September 2001, he was sentenced to serve "eight months in a juvenile detention facility," spend another year on probation, and pay a fine of $165.[85]

In the wake of Mafiaboy's conviction, other adolescent hackers launched similar, though less dramatic, attacks.[86] But within a few years, DDOS attacks, like hacking and malware, had become the province of adult cybercriminals.[87] And as they moved into the adult world, the tactics used in such attacks changed.

Mafiaboy personally orchestrated his DDOS attacks, using his own computer skills. This changed as DDOS attacks increasingly became a tool of professionals. The processes of organizing and launching such attacks evolved into what one observer referred to as "a mature service industry."[88]

In modern DDOS attacks, the attackers use a network of compromised computers—known as "zombies"—to send massive bursts of data at the targets of the attack. The zombies are computers that have been taken over by "bots"—software that subtly and invisibly infiltrates a computer.[89] The compromised computers belong to legitimate users, for example, individuals, businesses, government, and educational and other agencies. The bot software gives the person—the "bot herder"—who infected the computers the ability to control them; the person uses that ability to integrate the computers into a command-and-control structure, that is, a zombie army.[90] These zombie armies are known as "botnets." The owners of the compromised computers that are recruited into such an army usually have no idea their equipment is moonlighting as a minion of some more or less sinister force. The computer will operate almost normally: the user may notice it is running a little slower than usual, but that may well be the only indication it has become a zombie.

Botnets have become huge: botnets encompassing millions of compromised computers are now common, and at the end of 2010, the Dutch National Crime Squad took down Bredolab—a "massive botnet consisting of around 30 million" zombies and "150+ command and control servers spread across Italy, Spain, South Africa, the U.S. and the U.K."[91] According to news stories, the Bredolab botnet was "directly linked to the spread of spam e-mails and malicious file attachments and to identity theft, including banking account compromises and stolen credit cards."[92] One source pointed out that, "at its height," the botnet was capable "of sending 3 billion e-mails every day."[93]

Bredolab, like many botnets, seems to have been used primarily to generate revenue. Other botnets are used primarily, if not exclusively, for other purposes.

In November 2010, hactivists from the "Anonymous collective" used DDOS attacks to shut down "the two main Recording Industry Association of America (RIAA) websites . . . as revenge for the organisation's long-running legal offensive against [peer-to-peer file-sharing service] Limewire," an effort that eventually led to "the closure of the controversial" service.[94] That same month, unknown perpetrators "severed" Myanmar from the Internet by targeting the country with "10 days of distributed denial of service attacks that culminated in a massive flood of data that overwhelmed the . . . country's infrastructure."[95]

Nation-states are not the only targets of DDOS attacks. In April 2010, an unidentified "multinational financial institution in Australia" was shut down for several hours by a "China-based" DDOS attack on its systems.[96] And in 2009, Twitter was taken off line twice in two weeks by DDOS attacks.[97] It would be an exaggeration to describe these and similar attacks as the norm, but DDOS attacks are far from unusual, which is not surprising given the ease with which they can be launched.

While Mafiaboy was a talented amateur, contemporary DDOS attacks are for the most part launched by professionals. A 2010 report described "a malware ecosystem designed to maintain the operations of botnets,"[98] including the botnets used in DDOS attacks. This ecosystem not only maintains the operation of botnets but also rents them to cybercriminals who use botnets for spamming, fraud, and other crimes.

As one security expert noted, various issues "are taken into account when setting the price of a botnet rental," such as "the size of the botnet; type of attack (e.g., spam, DDOS . . .); target (military, private organizations . . .); plus . . . the length of attack."[99] According to this expert, a "24-hour DDOS attack" can cost anywhere "from $50 to several thousand dollars for a larger network attack" and sending a million spam e-mails "ranges between $150–200."[100]

For those who prefer not to rent botnets, the malware ecosystem offers tools they can use to create their own. In 2010, for example, a tool called TwitterNET Builder was available online for free.[101] TwitterNET Builder let anyone with minimal computer skills "build a botnet using a Twitter account as a command and control center."[102] This "toy" let technical novices create a botnet "with only a couple of mouse clicks" and use it to launch DDOS attacks.[103] Fortunately, TwitterNET Builder was so poorly constructed it never became a serious threat.[104]

Unfortunately, the same has not been true of the Zeus Trojan horse that was used in the bank attack examined in the introduction. Zeus is used to build botnets,[105] as well as to access financial accounts and steal passwords and other personal information.[106] In 2010, the "basic ZeuS builder kit" cost three to four thousand dollars on the malware market, but a cyber-criminal could also buy "modules" to customize the basic version of the tool.[107]

Given all this, it is not surprising that a report issued at the end of 2010 predicted that the increasing proliferation and sophistication of botnets would be one of the major cybersecurity concerns in 2011.[108] It noted, among other things, that targeted botnet, including attacks launched "on the U.S. Federal government,"—are on the rise.[109] The report also expressed concern about attacks that will be directed at physical targets, such as "critical infrastructure" components and "information technolo-gies deployed in the healthcare sector."[110]

DDOS ATTACKS AND CRIMINAL LAW

Like malware laws, DDOS laws have been a relatively late addition to the arsenal of cybercrime laws.

Federal DDOS Law

The review of malware law noted that the Computer Abuse Amend-ments Act of 1994 added a section to section 1030(a)(5) that made it a crime to knowingly or recklessly cause "the transmission of a program, information, code, or command to a computer or computer system" and thereby damage a computer, computer network, data, information, or a program.[111] This section—which is currently codified as 18 U.S. Code section 1030(a)(5)(A)—has been part of the Computer Fraud and Abuse Act ever since.

This section can be used to prosecute those who launch DDOS attacks, as well as those who use or distribute malware, because a DDOS attack in-volves transmitting the code used to turn computers into zombies and transmitting the code that is used to direct the zombies to attack a given target.

The first such prosecution was brought in 2006, when federal prosecutors in California charged James Ancheta with renting botnets he used in launching DDOS attacks.[112] According to a Department of Justice press release, Ancheta pled guilty to violating 18 U.S. Code section 1030(a) both by hacking into computers to commit fraud and by "selling access" to botnets that were used to launch DDOS attacks. Ancheta was sentenced to fifty-seven months in prison for his crimes.

In 2007, federal prosecutors in California indicted Greg King with violating section 1030(a)(5)(A) by creating a botnet of "over seven thousand" bots and using it to "conduct multiple" DDOS attacks "against websites of two businesses."[113] In 2003, he pled guilty to two counts of violating section 1030(a)(5)(A) and was sentenced to two years in prison.[114]

According to the Justice Department, King used his botnet to attack websites operated by Killanet, a "forum where members share advice on graphic design," and Castlecops, an "Internet security community."[115] He was one of eight cybercriminals nabbed as part of the FBI's Operation Bot Roast II.[116] Operation Bot Roast II was a successor to an earlier FBI initiative. According to the FBI, its 2006 Operation Bot Roast resulted in the indictment, guilty pleas, and sentencing of thirteen offenders involved with the use of botnets.[117]

While there does not appear to have been an Operation Bot Roast III, federal authorities have continued to prosecute U.S. citizens who launch DDOS attacks for profit or other motives. In May 2010, for example, federal prosecutors in Ohio charged Mitchell Frost, then twenty-two, with creating a botnet and using it to attack "various websites."[118] Frost was accused, among other things, of using his botnet to attack websites belonging to conservative commentators Bill O'Reilly and Ann Coulter and a website operated by then presidential candidate Rudy Giuliani.[119]

As these examples indicate, most federal DDOS prosecutions have targeted U.S. citizens operating from within the United States. There have, on occasion, been federal prosecutions that involved perpetrators from outside the United States, but they tend to involve conduct that was based in or somehow originated in the United States.

In 2008, for example, a man from Britain and a man from Germany were charged with launching DDOS attacks against "U.S. retail websites."[120] They were allegedly "hired by Saad Echouafni, former head of satellite communications company Orbit Communications" to launch the attacks against "Echouafni's retail competitors."[121] Both Orbit Communications and the companies targeted by the DDOS attacks were in the United States.[122] As the alleged instigator of the attacks, Echouafni was charged with aiding and abetting violations of section 1030(a)(5)(A) and conspiring to commit violations of the statute.[123] So while the two men involved in carrying out the DDOS attacks were from Europe, the attacks themselves were conceived in, and their targets were located in, the United States. So while this case involved some foreign participation in DDOS attacks, it did not encompass the primarily extraterritorial criminal activity that is typical of DDOS attacks and malware crimes.

State DDOS Law

Many states have laws criminalizing malware, but the laws seem to be seldom, if ever, used. It is therefore somewhat surprising that only four U.S. states appear to have laws that criminalize DDOS attacks or preparing to launch such attacks.

Georgia makes it a crime to "knowingly, willfully, or with conscious indifference or disregard cause computer software to be copied" onto a computer and use the computer "as part of an activity" that includes but is not "limited to, launching a denial of service attack."[124] This provision was added to the Georgia Code in 2005 but, as I write this in mid-2011, does not seem to have been used in any prosecutions.

Ohio has taken a somewhat similar approach. States sometimes use the term "computer contaminant" in legislation criminalizing malware. Ohio is one of those states. But unlike most of the computer contaminant states, Ohio defines computer contaminant as also including a "group of computer programs commonly known as 'zombies' that are designed to use a computer without the knowledge and consent of the owner . . . and that are designed to send large quantities of data to a targeted computer network for the purpose of degrading the targeted computer's or network's performance, or denying access through the network to the targeted computer or network, resulting in . . . 'Denial of Service' or 'Distributed Denial of Service' attacks."[125] Like the other states that use computer contaminant statutes to criminalize malware, Ohio makes it a crime to "introduce a computer contaminant into a computer."[126] That approach is reasonable for *malware*; the problem with the Ohio statute is that it seems to equate botnets and DDOS attacks with malware.

States make it a crime to introduce malware into a computer system because that inflicts the particular types of harm it is designed to produce. In other words, introducing malware into a computer is analogous to providing a would-be robber with a likely victim: it creates the circumstances needed for the consummation of the crime. But that analogy does not apply to botnet-facilitated DDoS attacks. The botnet aspect of the Ohio statute makes it a crime to *assemble* a botnet, but not to use it. The act of creating a botnet, in and of itself, does not inflict the harm produced by DDoS attacks; it is mere preparation. As we saw earlier, the DDoS harm is inflicted when a botnet is used to launch a DDoS attack on a target that effectively takes it off line.

The Ohio statute at most criminalizes an attempt to commit a DDoS attack; the law of criminal attempts allows prosecutors to hold someone liable for preparing to commit a crime they never actually carry out.[127] The advantage of Ohio's approach is that it means someone who is preparing to launch DDoS attacks could be prosecuted if their preparations were discovered before they actually began the attacks. For this approach to be effective, of course, law enforcement officers would have to be able to ascertain when someone has introduced botnet software into a computer system prior to the point at which they actually use it to launch DDoS attacks; while this is possible, it is unlikely that the preuse installation of botnet software will come to the attention of law enforcement personnel. It is consequently not particularly surprising that the Ohio statute does not seem to have been used in any prosecutions.

South Carolina's approach to DDoS attacks is essentially identical to Ohio's approach. South Carolina also uses the concept of computer contaminant in outlawing malware. And like Ohio, it defines computer contaminant as including "a group of computer programs commonly known as 'zombies'" that are used in a "Denial of Service" or "Distributed Denial of Service" attack.[128] And like Ohio, South Carolina makes it a crime to introduce a computer contaminant into a computer or computer system but does not appear to make it a crime to use a botnet to launch DDoS attacks.[129] Like the Ohio statute, the South Carolina statute does not appear to have been used in any prosecutions.

Pennsylvania, on the other hand, has a very straightforward and quite adequate prohibition on DDoS attacks. The Pennsylvania statute makes it a crime to "intentionally or knowingly" engage "in a scheme or artifice, including, but not limited to, a denial of service attack" on a computer or computer system "that is designed to block . . . or deny the access of information . . . by users of that computer" or computer system.[130] A related statute defines "denial of service" attack as an "attempt to prevent legitimate users of a service from using that service" by, among other things, "flooding a network, thereby preventing legitimate network traffic."[131]

Pennsylvania's definitional statute has the virtue of clearly defining a DDOS attack (at least as the attacks currently manifest themselves). And its substantive statute is clearly intended to criminalize the launching of DDOS attacks on computers and computer systems, but there is a certain ambiguity in the way the statute prohibits that conduct.

Pennsylvania's substantive DDOS statute makes it a crime to engage in a scheme or artifice that *includes* a denial of service attack, which at least inferentially suggests that, absent a scheme or artifice, launching a DDOS attack does not violate this provision. The ambiguity the reference to "scheme or artifice" introduces into the statute is exacerbated by the fact that this statute does not define what constitutes a "scheme or artifice" within its prohibitions. Another Pennsylvania computer crime statute makes it an offense to gain unauthorized access to a computer "with the intent to . . . execute any scheme or artifice to defraud."[132] This usage of the phrase is consistent with how it is used in federal criminal statutes and criminal statutes adopted by other states;[133] the phrase "scheme or artifice" is, as a result, usually associated with fraudulent activity.

It is therefore reasonable to infer that the reference to "scheme or artifice" in Pennsylvania's substantive DDOS statute was intended to restrict its applicability to conduct that is designed to further fraud. While that is a reasonable interpretation of the statute's language, it is an interpretation that has a puzzling effect on the scope of the statute's prohibitions. It is difficult to understand why Pennsylvania would have wanted to narrow its substantive DDOS statute's scope so that it only criminalizes DDOS attacks when they are part of a scheme or artifice the presumptive purpose of which is to defraud someone or something. Since the statute has, unfortunately, yet to be used in a prosecution, we are left with no resolution of these issues. If and when the statute is used to prosecute someone, it will probably be necessary for a court to determine what, if any, impact the reference to "scheme or artifice" has on the scope of its prohibitions.

These are the only state criminal prohibitions that target DDOS attacks, but one state—Texas—has a noncriminal statute that targets botnets. Section 324.055 of the Texas Business and Commerce Code provides as follows:

> (b) A person who is not the owner or operator of the computer may not knowingly cause or offer to cause a computer to become a zombie or part of a botnet.
>
> (c) A person may not knowingly create, have created, use, or offer to use a zombie or botnet to:
>   (1) send an unsolicited commercial electronic mail message . . . ;
>   (2) send a signal to a computer system or network that causes a loss of service to users;
>   (3) send data from a computer without authorization by the owner or operator of the computer;
>   (4) forward computer software designed to damage or disrupt another computer or system;
>   (5) collect personally identifiable information; or
>   (6) perform an act for another purpose not authorized by the owner or operator of the computer.
>
> (d) A person may not:
>   (1) purchase, rent, or otherwise gain control of a zombie or botnet created by another person; or
>   (2) sell, lease, offer for sale or lease, or otherwise provide to another person access to or use of a zombie or botnet.[134]

A related Texas statute defines botnet as "two or more zombies" and defines zombie as "a computer that . . . has been compromised to give access or control to a program or person other than the computer's owner or operator."[135]

The two Texas statutes are clear enough: combined, they prohibit creating, using, buying, renting, or selling a botnet. What is peculiar about the statutes is that they are part of the Texas *Business and Commerce* Code, rather than the Texas Criminal Code. As such, they do not authorize imposing criminal liability on one who violates their provisions. Instead, section 324.055 authorizes the imposition of *civil* liability on violators. Section 324.055(e) states that an Internet service provider (ISP) whose network was used "to commit a violation" of the statute or a person "who has incurred a loss or disruption of the conduct of the person's business, including for-profit or not-for-profit activities" as the result of such a violation can bring a civil suit for damages. The ISP or person bringing such a suit can seek an injunction against the bot herder and (1) actual damages resulting from the violation or (2) "$100,000 for each zombie used to commit the violation."[136]

It is perplexing that state legislature decided to impose civil, rather than criminal, liability on bot herders. It is not unknown for legislatures to create a civil cause of action for those who have been injured by criminal activity; 18 U.S. Code section 1030(g) does precisely this. It is, however, unusual for a legislature to decide to impose only civil liability on those who engage in what other jurisdictions regard as criminal activity.

That decision is particularly puzzling since the perpetrators are very likely to be operating from outside the United States. This means that a business that has been injured by a violation of this statute and decides to seek civil redress would have to track the perpetrators down in another country, ascertain what it would have to do to serve them with notice of the suit and otherwise ensure that a Texas court would have jurisdiction over them, and then pursue the lawsuit in an effort to obtain a judgment in its favor. Having done that, the business would then have to embark on the tortuous and probably impossible task of enforcing the judgment against individuals who might have disappeared into another country, never to be heard of again. It seems, to say the least, unlikely that the Texas statutes will be used successfully against offshore bot herders.

U.S. DDOS Law: An Assessment

Federal law is adequate for use in prosecuting bot herders and others involved in launching DDOS attacks, should they be apprehended. State DDOS law, on the other hand, is almost nonexistent. Three states apparently criminalize the processes of preparing to launch DDOS attacks. These statutes could be used to prosecute aspiring DDOS perpetrators if they were apprehended before they could launch the attacks. It is peculiar that these states only chose to criminalize DDOS attempts; it is surprising that, haven taken this initial step, they did not proceed and adopt statutes that criminalize launching DDOS attacks.

Pennsylvania has at least partially criminalized DDOS attacks but apparently only if they are part of a fraudulent scheme. If that is the correct interpretation of the Pennsylvania statute, its utility will depend upon how broadly the Pennsylvania courts interpret the concept of a scheme or artifice to defraud. If, for example, they interpret it as encompassing a scheme to launch DDOS attacks that "defraud" victims by depriving them of the use of computer resources for some period of time, the statute could be used generally against those who launch such attacks. If, as seems more reasonable, they interpret the concept of a scheme or artifice to defraud as it has traditionally been interpreted—as an effort to trick someone out of money or property—then the statute will have a very limited application to DDOS attacks.

It may seem surprising that so few states have attempted to address the problem of DDOS attacks, but that is probably a function of two unrelated factors. One concerns the nature of the problem: state law is unlikely to be an effective tool in pursuing DDOS perpetrators.

The other factor is that DDOS attacks are not perceived as a problem state legislatures need to address, at least not at this time. DDOS attacks received a great deal of attention in 2000, when Mafiaboy attacked high-profile websites. Since then, there has been little publicity about DDOS attacks, which is probably in part because they have become a tool of the online criminal underground. Except in rare instances, DDOS attacks generally go unnoticed by the public and, I submit, by most state legislators. If and when one or more DDOS attacks on U.S. civilian targets receives the media attention that was devoted to the 2010 WikiLeaks attacks, we may see state legislatures adopting statutes that address this problem.

>chapter:3

CYBERCRIMES AGAINST PROPERTY

Instead of being the target of a cybercrime, a computer can be a tool that is used to commit a cyberanalogue of a traditional crime, such as theft or fraud. In tool cybercrimes, the computer's role is analogous to either the gun used to rob a bank or the implements a burglar uses to break into a building. In either instance, the computer is merely a device the cybercriminal employs to commit a crime involving computer technology but not directed at a computer "victim." In tool crimes, then, the computer plays a lesser but still far from insignificant role in the criminal activity.

Law has approached target and tool cybercrimes differently. Target cybercrimes generally required the adoption of new laws because the conduct involved and the harm inflicted by a target cybercrime was not encompassed by traditional criminal law. Tool cybercrimes generally have not required the adoption of new, cybercrime-specific laws because they involve using computer technology to commit what is already a crime . . . which might lead one to wonder why they should require *any* new law.

The extent to which a particular tool cybercrime requires modifying existing law or adopting new law is a function of the particular crime at issue. This chapter analyzes the extent to which traditional criminal law is adequate to deal with the various tool cybercrimes. But first, it is instructive to examine a tool cybercrime that was committed a decade ago but still illustrates how the use of computers can challenge existing law.

Theft? Fraud? . . .

In 2001, someone accessed the servers used by two online casinos and manipulated the gambling software to alter the poker and video slot games.[1] The games were set so that, for anyone playing, "every roll of the dice in craps turned up doubles, and every spin on the slots generated a perfect match." During the "few hours" the manipulation was in effect, 140 gamblers won $1.9 million, which the casinos dutifully paid out.

No one was ever prosecuted for the manipulation, probably because the casinos could not identify the perpetrator or did not want to give the event any more publicity than necessary. For the purposes of analysis, though, it is useful to assume that the casinos were able to identity the perpetrator—whom we will call Robin Hoode—and law enforcement was able to apprehend him. The question this fictional scenario then presents follows: what, if anything, can Hoode be charged with?

One possibility is theft, because it appears, at least at first glance, that the casino lost something of value ($1.9 million, to be exact). In criminal law, theft is the "taking and carrying away of the personal property of another with intent to steal the same."[2]

The problem with characterizing what Robin Hoode did as theft is that he did not "take and carry away" personal property belonging to the victimized casinos. People commit theft to enrich themselves; they take someone's property so they can use it or sell it. Robin Hoode did not do either of these things; he never took possession of the money the casino paid out and therefore never personally benefited from the payouts.

The fact that Robin Hoode did not personally benefit from manipulating the software is the primary *legal* obstacle a prosecutor would face in convicting him of theft. But there is also an evidentiary issue: how could the prosecutor prove beyond a reasonable doubt that those who won when the manipulation was in effect would not have won had it not been in effect? The odds in casinos favor the casinos, but people still win in honest games, and it is reasonable to assume these casinos ran honest games. It could, therefore, be difficult for a prosecutor to convince a jury, beyond a reasonable doubt, that what happened *could not* have happened but for the manipulation of the software. If a prosecutor could not prove this, then Hoode would have to be acquitted.

Fraud is another possible charge. Like theft, fraud is a property crime; both involve the unlawful acquisition of property belonging to another. The difference between the crimes lies in how the perpetrator (thief or fraudster) obtains the property: The thief takes the property from the victim without his or her consent; in aggravated theft (or robbery), the thief uses force to take the property. The fraudster uses deception to persuade the victim to hand the property over willingly; the crime of fraud was originally known as "false pretenses" because the victim gives money or property to the perpetrator under the misapprehension that certain circumstances (e.g., it is being used to buy the Brooklyn Bridge) exist when they, in fact, do not. Centuries ago, English common law developed fraud as a separate crime because those who tricked a victim into handing over property voluntarily could not be prosecuted for theft.[3]

Fraud is to some extent an appropriate charge for what Hoode did because the casinos voluntarily paid out the money but did so under a misapprehension. The misapprehension was that the games were functioning correctly; had the casinos known the games had been altered to guarantee payouts, they would certainly have halted play—and payouts—in the poker and video slots sections of their websites. Since the casinos paid because they assumed the games were legitimate, the facts establish the deception needed for fraud. The critical issue is whether the facts otherwise establish the traditional fraud dynamic, in which the trick is used to convince the victim to give her or his property to the fraudster.

Fraud implicitly assumes that the person who uses the trick to persuade the victim to part with property and the person who obtains the property are one and the same. Fraud implicitly incorporates this assumption because it is derived from theft. Since fraud, like theft, implicitly assumes that the perpetrators act to benefit themselves, the prosecutor encounters the same difficulty in charging Robin Hoode with fraud as he did with theft. There is no evidence that Hoode manipulated the casinos' software to benefit himself; he does not appear to have profited from the manipulation. The lack of evidence establishing that element would probably make it impossible to charge Robin Hoode with fraud.

Another issue might also be an impediment to charging Hoode with fraud: In 1997, a British defendant was sued for fraud based on his alleged role in a scheme to defraud the car company Renault, which was offer-ing discount purchases to British airline pilots.[4] According to the civil complaint, the scheme resulted in Renault's providing 217 new cars at the discount prices, only three of which were purchased by British airline pilots; the others were sold to regular customers for a profit. The defen-dant's attorney moved to dismiss the suit, arguing that even if the facts were as the plaintiff claimed them to be, there was no fraud because no fraudulent misrepresentation was made by one human being to another. In other words, the defense argued that fraud, whether civil or criminal, necessarily involves one human being's tricking another.... And here the trick—the fraudulent misrepresentation—was "made not to a human being but to a machine."

Robin Hoode might make a similar argument if he were charged with fraud, pointing out that he manipulated software, not individuals. The ar-gument might, or might not, succeed. In the British case, the judge saw no problem with "holding that a fraudulent misrepresentation can be made to a machine acting on behalf of the claimant . . . if the machine is set up to process certain information in a particular way in which it would not process . . . if the correct information were given."[5] This issue does not ap-pear to have arisen in any reported U.S. cases, but it will probably be raised at some point. If and when it is raised, its likelihood of succeeding will depend to a great extent on whether the fraud crime at issue is phrased in terms of defrauding an individual or whether it is phrased more generally, that is, in terms of executing a scheme to defraud.

If Robin Hoode cannot be prosecuted for theft or fraud, would he face no criminal liability for what he did? Hoode could still be prosecuted but not for a tool crime: his manipulating the casinos' software without being authorized to do so clearly constitutes hacking, or gaining unauthorized access to a computer. The statute 18 U.S. Code section 1030(a)(5)(B) makes it a crime to access a computer without being authorized to do so and cause damage. Section 1030(e)(8) defines damage as "any impairment to the integrity . . . of data, a program, a system, or information."

Robin Hoode clearly accessed the casinos' computers because he was able to modify the software each used; since he had no authority to access either casino's computers, prosecutors would have no difficulty proving his access was without authorization. And since his manipulation of the software impaired the integrity of the casinos' computer systems or programs, thereby causing damage under section 1030(a)(5), Robin Hoode would clearly be liable for violating section 1030(a)(5)(B).

The real question is whether convicting Robin Hoode of violating section 1030(a)(5)(B) would be enough to constitute justice. There is no doubt he committed this crime, but many might find this charge inadequate, on the premise that Hoode did much more than simply access the computers without being authorized to do so and impair the integrity of their software. The concern here is with the consequential effects of his unauthorized access: It cost the casinos $1.9 million. It probably also cost them the money they paid to have the manipulations corrected and, perhaps, to analyze their systems to determine how Hoode was able to access them.

A court could, of course, take the consequential effects of Hoode's unauthorized access into consideration in sentencing him for the section 1030(a)(5) offense, but that still may not be enough to sanction him for the harm he inflicted. The need to address that possibility is one reason tool cybercrimes can play an important role in pursuing cybercriminals.

Target cybercrimes are primarily concerned with harm to a computer or computer system; tool cybercrimes are concerned with the *other* harms criminals can inflict by exploiting computer technology. More precisely, they are concerned with the harms cybercriminals like Robin Hoode inflict on persons or property. The problem is that, while traditional crimes such as fraud and theft address the harm caused to persons or property, they may not apply when the harm is inflicted digitally— which means the Hoodes of the world face no consequences for inflicting such harm.

If, as seems likely, that outcome is not acceptable, legislators could (1) revise the existing definitions of theft and fraud so that either or both encompasses what Robin Hoode did or (2) create a new crime that encompasses such activity. The first option is preferable as a general matter because it merely updates existing crimes to incorporate the use of new tools. The other option should only be used when absolutely necessary, to avoid an undesirable expansion of criminal law. Unfortunately, when disconnects arise between the scope of existing criminal law and the infliction of harms in novel ways, legislatures often have a tendency to adopt new criminal laws that often prove flawed, duplicative, or even counterproductive.

Theft

The law defines theft as taking someone's personal property with the intent to steal it. Many, if not all, U.S. states have statutes that define theft: Alabama, for example, defines it as knowingly "obtain[ing] or exert[ing] control over the property of another, with intent to deprive the owner of his or her property."[6] A few U.S. states also have statutes that define the term "steal"; for example, Iowa's statute says it "means to take by theft."[7]

Since theft is defined as taking or carrying away property belonging to another with the intent to deprive the rightful owner of that property, theft crimes have historically targeted the misappropriation of personal property, rather than real property.[8] Real property is "land and any improvements upon or connected with land,"[9] while personal property is "any tangible or intangible property, goods, services, chattels, merchandise, commodities, or any item of value in any form or type, other than real property."[10]

In common law, theft only encompassed the misappropriation of tangible personal property, such as gold, jewels, and currency.[11] Common law limited theft to tangible property because intangible personal property, as such, did not yet exist. Today, many, if not most, U.S. states define theft in terms of misappropriating tangible or intangible personal property. But many states have not updated their theft laws so they explicitly criminalize the copying of valuable data.

CYBER BANK THEFT

The introduction examined the Bullitt County case, in which unknown perpetrators siphoned nearly half a million dollars from the county's bank account. The Bullitt County episode is useful for illustrating how cybercriminals operate, but since no one has been—or is likely to be—apprehended and charged with stealing the county's funds, it is not particularly useful in analyzing theft as a tool cybercrime.

Perhaps the best example of theft as a tool cybercrime is the Citibank case. In August 1994, Carlos Arario, head trader at the Argentinian firm Invest Capital, came to work one morning and discovered that more than two hundred thousand dollars had disappeared overnight from his firm's account with Citibank.[12] Four anonymous wire transfers had been made from the Invest Capital account to four unknown accounts. Arario called Citibank executives in New York to tell them what had happened. Unfortunately, notwithstanding that call, it continued to happen: over the next months, someone siphoned almost ten million dollars from twenty Citibank accounts.

Citibank executives assembled a war room of experts to try to stop the extraction of funds from Citibank accounts, but they could only watch as money was transferred from client accounts to accounts in California, Tel Aviv, Rotterdam, Athens, Latin America, Finland, and Israel. The experts launched a global investigation in an effort to track the transfers and prevent more from occurring. They got a break when the unknown cyberthief transferred $218,000 from an Indonesian businessman's account to a Bank of America account in San Francisco. Citibank experts and federal agents traced the account to Evgeni and Erina Korolkov, Russian nationals who had come to the United States from St. Petersburg; Erina was arrested when she tried to make a withdrawal from the San Francisco account. (She and Evgeni had allegedly opened this and other accounts in order to launder the funds being stolen from Citibank.) Federal agents flew to St. Petersburg and were given access to records that showed the Citibank accounts were being accessed from a computer at AO Saturn, a software company in St. Petersburg.

By December, Erina was cooperating with federal authorities and also encouraged her husband to help them identify the Citibank thief. After the FBI promised Evgeni they would treat him leniently if he cooperated, he identified Vladimir Levin, who worked at AO Saturn, as the cyberthief. Levin was then a twenty-nine-year-old computer programmer who allegedly used a laptop computer at the AO Saturn offices to carry out the Citibank fund transfers. As these agents were identifying Levin, other FBI agents were arresting Russian mules in the Netherlands and other countries; the mules' role was to collect the funds that had been transferred from Citibank accounts to foreign accounts. Citibank ultimately claimed it had recovered all but four hundred thousand dollars of the stolen funds.

Since the United States and Russia did not have an extradition treaty, Levin was safe as long as he stayed in Russia. For some reason, he flew to London in 1995, where British authorities arrested him on behalf of the United States; Levin spent eighteen months in a British jail, fighting extradition. He was finally sent to the United States and indicted on federal charges of theft and hacking; in 1998, he pled guilty and was sentenced to three years in prison.[13]

Many do not believe Levin was the sole architect of the Citibank thefts (or almost thefts). Many found it difficult to believe Levin could have developed and implemented the complex international network of bank accounts and mules to launder the proceeds. Many also did not believe he had the computer skills needed to hack the Citibank accounts. Various theories emerged to explain what really happened. According to one, a Russian hacker group known as Megazoid figured out how to access the Citibank computers; one of them sold that information to Levin—or to someone working with Levin—for one hundred dollars and two bottles of vodka.[14] As to how Levin implemented the network of international bank accounts and mules, some, including then U.S. attorney general Janet Reno, suggested he was working for the Russian mafia, which was, and is, involved in cybercrime.[15]

We will probably never know what happened with the Citibank crimes: whether Citibank did recover most of the money; whether Levin acted alone in hacking the Citibank system and transferring the funds from the accounts; and whether the Russian mafia was involved, either at the outset or as a broker for the stolen funds. At the time, Citibank confessed that its experts had never quite figured out how the crimes—or frustrated crimes—were executed. All of that, though, is irrelevant to the point at hand: whoever he was, the architect of the Citibank thefts was a post-twentieth-century bank robber; instead of using a mask and a gun to steal from a bank, he used computers. He used a new tool to commit a very old crime.

NON-ZERO-SUM THEFT

Vladimir Levin's crime was simply a high-tech version of bank robbery. As such, it had what was missing in Robin Hoode's casino exploits: the perpetrator directly takes property (cash) from its rightful owner without the owner's consent.

That type of computer theft is straightforward, as far as law is concerned. It is the only type of theft known in the physical world because real-world assets are tangible (e.g., cash, jewels, electronics, etc.). The theft of tangible items is a zero-sum transaction: the possession and use of the items moves entirely from the rightful owner to the thief. Since this is the only type of theft that can occur in the real world, theft laws tend to assume zero-sum theft.

It is not the only type of theft that can occur once property becomes intangible. Certain types of computer data have great value, but data is intangible; unlike property in the real world, digital property is not an either-or commodity. That is, it does not, by definition, exist in only one place at a time; digital property can be duplicated, which means it can exist in two (or more) places at the same time.

That aspect of digital property was at issue in an Oregon case: *State v. Schwartz*.[16] Randal Schwartz was an independent contractor working for Intel Corporation. At one point, he began working in Intel's Supercomputer Systems Division (SSD), which created "large computer systems" that were "used for applications such as nuclear weapons safety." Everyone who worked at SSD had to use a unique password to gain access the SSD computers and the data stored on them. The data was stored "in an encrypted or coded fashion."

After he had worked there for a while, Schwartz had a disagreement with a systems administrator that led to the termination of his contract with SSD. (Schwartz later said he "hadn't left SSD on the best of terms.") Intel disabled his passwords for all but one of the SSD computers; it inadvertently failed to disable his password for the computer known as Brillig. Schwartz continued to work as a contractor for a different Intel division and accessed the Brillig computer without being authorized to do so. About a year and a half after he quit working for Intel's SSD division, Schwartz downloaded a password-guessing program called Crack. When he ran Crack on Brillig, he discovered the password for

"Ron B.," one of Brillig's authorized users. Although he knew he did not have the authority to do so, [Schwartz] used Ron B.'s password to log onto Brillig. From Brillig, he copied the entire SSD password file onto another Intel computer, Wyeth. Once the SSD password file was on Wyeth, [he] ran the Crack program on that file and learned the passwords of more than 35 SSD users, including . . . the general manager of SSD. Apparently, [Schwartz] believed that, if he could show SSD's security had gone downhill since he left, he could reestablish the respect he had lost when he left SSD. Once he had cracked the SSD passwords, however, [he] realized . . . he had . . . "stepped out of my bounds." Instead of reporting what he had found to anyone at ssd, [Schwartz] did nothing and simply stored the information while he went to teach a class in California.[17]

Intel system administrators discovered what Schwartz had been doing and called the police. The investigation resulted in his being charged with "computer crime," which in this instance consisted of accessing or using a computer for the purpose of committing "theft of proprietary information." Schwartz was convicted and appealed, arguing that the prosecutor did not prove he "took property," which is an essential element of a theft charge.

An Oregon statute states that someone commits theft when "with intent to deprive another of property . . . the person . . . takes, appropriates, obtains or withholds such property from" its owner.[18] Schwartz argued that he could not have

> "taken, appropriated, obtained or withheld" the password file and individual passwords because, even though he moved them to another computer and took them in the sense that he now had them on his computer, the file and passwords remained on Intel's computers. . . . The individual users whose passwords [he] obtained could still use their passwords just as they had before. Intel continued to "have" everything it did before . . . and consequently, [Schwartz] reasons, he cannot be said to have "taken" anything away from Intel.[19]

The prosecutor argued that, by copying the passwords, Schwartz "stripped them of their value." The prosecution contended that "like proprietary manufacturing formulas, passwords have value only so long as no one else knows what they are." According to this theory, once Schwartz copied the passwords they became "useless for their only purpose, protecting access to information in the ssd computers. The loss of exclusive possession of the passwords . . . is sufficient to constitute theft."

The prosecutor won. The court of appeals found that since the statute under which Schwartz was charged criminalized the theft of "proprietary information," it was broad enough to encompass what he had done:

> Proprietary information, like the passwords and password files at issue here, is not susceptible to exclusive possession; it is information that, by

definition, can be known by more than one person. Nevertheless, the legislature indicated that it could be subject to "theft." ... We conclude that the state presented sufficient evidence to prove that, by copying the passwords and password file, [Schwartz] took property of another, namely Intel, ... for the purpose of theft.[20]

Schwartz lost because, instead of being charged under a regular theft statute, he was charged with violating a statute that made the theft of *information* a crime. The court of appeals was able to use the fact that this statute was designed to protect information to rationalize what was problematic: the notion of non-zero-sum theft of property. If the charge had been brought under the regular theft statute, it would have been difficult, if not impossible, for the court of appeals to uphold Schwartz's conviction.

Oregon's theft statute, like other theft statutes, defines the crime in terms of "depriving" someone of their property.[21] "Deprive" is defined as "to deny ... possession" of something.[22] This notion of theft as a complete transfer of property has its roots in English common law, which is the basis of U.S. criminal law. In common law, theft was defined as "the felonious taking and carrying away of the personal goods of another."[23] The "taking and carrying away" element of the crime required that the possession of the goods be completely transferred from the rightful owner to the thief. It would therefore have been more difficult for the Oregon Court of Appeals to uphold the conviction if it had involved a traditional, zero-sum theft charge.

The *Schwartz* case illustrates not only how theft can become a tool cybercrime but also why governments need to revise their laws so they encompass new variations of old crimes. One approach some states have taken is to expand the definition of "deprive" as the word is used in theft statutes. In Delaware theft statutes, for example, deprive means "to withhold property of another person permanently or for so extended a period or under such circumstances as to withhold a major portion of its economic value or benefit."[24] The last option captures the kind of non-zero-sum data theft that was at issue in the *Schwartz* case.

THEFT OF TRADE SECRETS

The federal criminal code approaches the theft of proprietary information —or trade secrets—as economic espionage. The Economic Espionage

Act of 1996 (EEA) criminalized two types of trade secret theft: Section 1831 of Title 18 of the U.S. Code makes it a crime to steal a trade secret to benefit a foreign government; this offense is analogous to the traditional crime of espionage, since it is committed on behalf of another nation-state. Section 1832 of Title 18 of the U.S. Code criminalizes the theft of trade secrets that is "carried out for economic advantage," regardless of whether it benefits a foreign government or foreign agent.[25]

The EEA defines "trade secret" as (1) "financial, business, scientific, technical, economic, or engineering information, . . . whether tangible or intangible" (2) that is "stored, compiled, or memorialized . . . electronically, graphically, . . . or in writing" (3) if the owner took "reasonable means" to keep the information secret and (4) if it "derives independent economic value" from not being "generally known to" or "readily ascertainable" by the public.[26] When the act was adopted in 1996, online economic espionage was not a notable concern, but it has become a major concern in the years since, as a New York prosecution illustrated.

On February 11, 2010, Sergey Aleynikov was charged with theft of trade secrets in violation of 18 U.S. Code section 1832(a)(2).[27] He moved to dismiss the charge, claiming it was legally inadequate. This is how the economic espionage prosecution against Aleynikov arose:

> Aleynikov was a computer programmer employed by Goldman [Sachs & Co.] as a Vice President in its Equities Division. . . . [He] was responsible for developing and maintaining some of the computer programs used to operate Goldman's high-frequency trading system. Aleynikov resigned . . . to work for Teza Technologies, LLC . . . [as] "Executive Vice President, Platform Engineering," . . . responsible for developing Teza's own high-frequency trading business that would compete with Goldman.
>
> High-frequency trading . . . involves the rapid execution of high volumes of trades in which trading decisions are made by sophisticated computer programs that use complex mathematical formulae known as algorithms. The algorithms use statistical analyses of past trades and current market developments. Goldman used a proprietary system . . . [called] the "Platform," to rapidly obtain information on the latest market movements, process that information into a form that can be analyzed by the algorithms, and execute the trading decisions reached

by the application of the algorithms to that information. Together, the trading algorithms and Platform comprise Goldman's trading system (the "Trading System"). . . .

Aleynikov was a member of a team of programmers responsible for developing and improving aspects of the Platform. . . . On his last day of employment at Goldman, [he] copied, compressed, encrypted, and transferred to an outside server in Germany hundreds of thousands of lines of source code for the Trading System. . . . In the days that followed, Aleynikov accessed the German server and downloaded the source code to his home computer, and from there to other home computers and to a portable flash drive. . . .

Aleynikov [then] flew to Chicago . . . to meet with Teza. He brought a laptop and the flash drive containing source code for Goldman's Trading System.[28]

Aleynikov was charged with violating 18 U.S. Code section 1832(a)(2), which makes it a crime for one acting with the "intent to convert a trade secret, that is related to or included in a product that is produced for or placed in interstate or foreign commerce, to the economic benefit of anyone other than the owner thereof" to copy, duplicate, deliver, transmit, or otherwise convey such information without being authorized to do so. Aleynikov claimed the charge was legally insufficient because it did not allege that the source code for Goldman's Trading System is

related to or included in a "product" that is "produced for or placed in interstate and foreign commerce." According to Aleynikov, a "product" . . . must be a tangible item of personal property distributed to and used by the commercial public. Because Goldman has never licensed or sold the Trading System . . . Aleynikov contends that the Trading System is not a "product produced for or placed in" commerce within the meaning of section 1832.[29]

In response, the prosecution argued that the Trading System is, in fact, a product that

has an "obvious and indisputable connection" to interstate and foreign commerce. The Government thus agrees . . . that the trade secret at issue . . . is the source code, and the relevant "product" is the Trading System. . . . The Government . . . expects to prove at trial that there are high-frequency trading systems that may be purchased by securities trading firms, and that Goldman maintains computers in the United States and elsewhere in the world that use its Trading System to conduct trading on world markets.[30]

In ruling on these arguments, the judge to whom the case was assigned found that, since the EEA, of which section 1832 is a part, does not define "product," she was required to give the term its "ordinary meaning."[31] The judge therefore used the ordinary meaning of the term "product" in analyzing the charge and found there was no doubt that the Trading System was a product within the meaning of the EEA because it

> is "comprised of different computer programs." . . . The only difference between the Trading System and other computer software, like Microsoft Windows, is that Goldman does not presently intend to sell or license the Trading System. This . . . does not, however, render the Trading System any less of a "product" within the meaning of the EEA.[32]

The judge also found that the Trading System was produced for interstate commerce:

> The sole purpose for which Goldman purchased, developed, and modified the computer programs that comprise the Trading System was to engage in interstate and foreign commerce. . . . Goldman's high-frequency trading activity, which is uniquely made possible by the Trading System, undoubtedly qualifies as interstate and foreign commerce. As such, the Trading System was "produced for" interstate and foreign commerce within the meaning of the EEA.[33]

She therefore denied Aleynikov's motion to dismiss the EEA charge, which meant the case went to trial. Aleynikov was tried, convicted, and sentenced to serve ninety-seven months in prison; the case is currently on appeal.[34]

The *Aleynikov* case illustrates how easy it can be for an employee to copy data that may be essential to the survival of an employer's business. Theft of trade secrets—particularly online theft—is considered such a significant threat to the economic viability of the United States that the Office of the National Counterintelligence Executive submits an annual report on foreign economic espionage to Congress.[35]

To understand why online economic espionage is such a concern, it is only necessary to imagine a slightly altered version of the facts alleged in the *Aleynikov* case: assume, for the purposes of analysis, that Aleynikov copied the Goldman Sachs source code and transferred the data to the German server.

Now assume that instead of staying in the United States to take a position with Teza (or some other company), Aleynikov immediately went to the airport and boarded a flight for Russia. The United States does not have an extradition treaty with Russia; therefore, Russia would not be obliged to turn him over to U.S. authorities so he could be returned to the United States and tried on the economic espionage charge. In this scenario, Aleynikov would be safely ensconced in a foreign country, immune from U.S. justice—and the source code would become a commodity that could be sold to the highest bidder.

THEFT OF SERVICES

Data theft is not the only tool cybercrime involving theft, at least not according to some. In a number of instances, people have been charged with theft based on their using wireless Internet networks provided by businesses libraries and other institutions. In 2006, twenty-year-old Alexander Eric Smith of Battle Ground, Washington, was charged with theft after he parked his truck in the parking lot of a coffee shop (Brewed Awakenings) and used its wireless network.[36] Smith was charged after Brewed Awakenings employees called the police to report that he had been using the shop's wireless network for three months (without ever buying anything).

Smith—and other wireless freeloaders—are charged with "theft of services," a crime that until recently only encompassed obtaining telephone, electricity, cable, and professional services without paying for them.[37] Theft of services is a relatively new crime. In common law, "time or services" were not "recognized as a subject" of theft because there can be no "taking and carrying away" of either.[38] The criminalization of the theft of services in the United States began in the 1960s as a result of the American Law Institute's Model Penal Code.[39] The Model Penal Code—which, as its name implies, is a template for drafting criminal statutes—appeared in 1962 and introduced a new theft of services crime.[40]

Under the Model Penal Code, one commits theft of services if he obtains services "he knows are available only for compensation" without paying for them. Services include "labor, professional service, transportation, telephone or other public service, accommodation in hotels, restaurants or elsewhere, admission to exhibitions, [and] use of vehicles or other movable property." The Model Penal Code's theft of services crime—which has been adopted by most, if not all, states[41]—differs slightly from traditional theft crimes. Traditional theft is a zero-sum event in which the possession and use of property is transferred from one person (the owner) to another (the thief); if the thief succeeds, the victim is completely deprived of her or his property. In theft of services, the victim's property is the ability to offer services in exchange for pay. When a theft of services occurs, the victim is completely deprived of some quantum of the services she or he offers—or, more accurately, of the remuneration that should have been paid for those services—but is not deprived of the ability to offer such services. This difference is irrelevant to the applicability of traditional principles of criminal liability because the victim has still been deprived of a commodity that lawfully belonged to her or him.

When the Model Penal Code was written, there was no Internet and no wireless Internet access. But there is no reason the theft of services crime cannot apply to freeloading on a wireless network; if nothing else, the theft of wireless services comes within the Model Penal Code's definition of services as including "telephone or other public service." The only real difficulty with applying theft of services to wireless freeloading comes with another aspect of the crime: the requirement that the person being charged knew the services were "available only for compensation." When someone taps an electric line to get free electricity, she or he *has* to know that the service is legally available only to those who pay for it; if nothing else, we can infer the person's knowledge from the fact that she or he surreptitiously tapped into the electric company's lines and that it is common knowledge one must purchase electricity, just as they purchase other commodities. The same logic applies when someone obtains other services—such as telephone or television cable service—because he or she cannot obtain those services without doing something to bypass conduits or other devices intended to make the service available only to those who pay for it.

The problem that can arise in applying theft of services to wireless freeloading is that wireless Internet service, unlike other services, is sometimes given away for free. In the Smith case, the coffee shop was intentionally giving free wireless access to its customers. The same has been true in most, if not all, of the cases in which people have been prosecuted for wireless freeloading. Some, therefore, claim it is not theft of services to use an open wireless network to check e-mail or surf the web. As one person put it, "Complaining to the police about someone 'stealing' your unsecured internet access is like complaining that your neighbours are 'stealing' from you when the smell of your rose bushes wafts into their windows."[42] Or, as another said, "If you advertise your unsecured wireless network to people by broadcasting its name and the fact that it's unsecured, you're inviting them to use it."[43]

As these comments illustrate, some point out that wireless freeloading is only possible when the owner of a network has left it unsecured and therefore open for public use; they say this distinguishes wireless freeloading from the activity at issue in traditional theft of services cases. Traditionally, theft of services cases arose when someone bypassed measures meant to keep people from obtaining services they had not paid for. Wireless freeloaders do not bypass any kind of security; the networks they use are unsecured and available to be used by anyone in that area. Many argue that the theft of wireless services cannot occur unless the network was secured; they claim theft of wireless services only occurs when the wireless thief bypasses password or other protection on a network. Some also point out that in many cases the owner of the network has done more than simply leave it unsecured: he or she left it unsecured for the express purpose of providing free wireless service; those who take this view argue it is impossible to steal what is being given away. As one noted, "If I stick a tap outside my gate with a sign on it saying 'Drinking Water' I wouldn't expect the police to arrest anyone drinking from it. Why is wireless any different?"[44]

The response to that argument is that when a commercial establishment —a coffee shop, say—gives away free wireless, it intends to provide the service to its customers—and only its customers. In the Brewed Awakenings case, the coffee shop reported Smith because he used their network for months of time but never bought anything. The problem is that free wireless service bleeds outside the immediate area of the restaurant or other establishment that provides it, making it possible for nonpatrons to use it along with patrons. And the same is true when the unsecured wireless network belongs to an individual; as I write this in my home study, there are three unsecured wireless networks, each coming from a home near my own, that pop up whenever I log onto my laptop. I can just as easily access those networks as I can my own (which is safely encrypted and therefore secured from use by others). My neighbors who own the networks are not intentionally offering free wireless service, but that is, in fact, what they are doing.

How should we resolve these issues? It would be difficult to prosecute someone for theft of services under statutes based on the Model Penal Code's version of the crime because the prosecution would have to show that the alleged thief *knew* he was getting something he was supposed to pay for. A Maryland legislator—Delegate LeRoy Myers Jr.—introduced a bill that seemed to resolve this issue: it made wireless freeloading a crime only if the freeloading was intentional, that is, if the freeloader meant to steal wireless service.[45] Unfortunately, Myers's bill only compounded the problem. In criminal law, the mens rea element of a crime defines the mental state—the evil mind—someone must have to commit that particular offense. Someone acts knowingly when he or she is *aware* of committing a particular act (obtaining a service without paying for it), but to act intentionally the person must not only be aware of committing a particular act but also *want* to commit that act.[46] Myers's bill raised the standard a prosecutor would have to meet to convict someone of stealing wireless services. While that seems to have been Myers's goal, his bill would have not only protected inadvertent freeloaders but also made it almost impossible to prosecute those who knew what they were doing. In the end, the issue was moot; Myers's bill failed, apparently because it was opposed by other Maryland legislators and by the state's public defenders.[47]

There do not seem to have been many—if any—other efforts to criminalize wireless freeloading. Most lawyers and computer security experts think the solution lies not in law but in technology. If the owners of wireless networks would secure their networks, freeloading would no longer be a problem (or, at least, no longer be a widespread problem). Securing wireless networks would be a somewhat more complicated process for institutions and establishments that offer free wireless to a particular constituency, but even that is possible.

Some say this approach misses the point because A can be prosecuted for trespass if A enters B's house without B's permission, even though B left the door unlocked.[48] The crime of trespass forbids entering someone's property without permission; it does not require that the owner secure the property in an effort to prevent others from entering it. The premise is that people should be able to assume their property is safe from intrusion by outsiders. Some say the same should be true for wireless networks. The problem with this argument is that, to trespass in a building or on undeveloped property, the trespasser has to take affirmative action to enter onto the property. Someone has to go into a house or onto property to commit criminal trespass; the property does not approach the person. But that is precisely what an unsecured wireless network does; the owner of the network has lost control of the property, which, as a result, approaches computer users to offer them its services.

The debate over whether legal or technical solutions are the appropriate approach for a particular cybercrime is not limited to the wireless free-loading context. It arises in other areas, as well.

Fraud

Fraud derives from theft: the thief takes property from you without your consent; the fraudster tricks you into handing over your property voluntarily by making you believe you will receive something of equal or greater value in return. The fraudster, of course, lies; the victim receives nothing (or, at least, nothing of equivalent or greater value) in return. Since the victim acts under a misapprehension, law does not regard the transfer of the property as valid. Instead, law has treated this type of flawed transaction as the crime of fraud.

Fraud has always been a persistent aspect of human society, but it has exploded in cyberspace. One website lists twelve different kinds of online fraud.[49] While that list may be accurate for the moment, new varieties are inevitable because the Willie Sutton effect is particularly influential in this context.

In the 1930s and 1940s, Willie Sutton was a notorious bank robber who was eventually captured. According to legend, when a reporter asked Sutton why he robbed banks, he said, "Because that's where the money is."[50] As the 1990s ended and the twenty-first century began, criminals realized the Internet was increasingly where the money was, and went after it. Fraud has been one of the most popular activities for the new breed of the online Willie Sutton.

Online fraud is so prevalent and so complex, it would be impossible to review all of the variations in this chapter. Fortunately, there is no need for such a review because each type of online fraud is simply a version of the basic fraud dynamic—tricking someone into handing over money or property. The sections below therefore concentrate on the more common types of Internet fraud, beginning with the 419 scam.

419 FRAUD

This variation is known as 419 fraud because many of the scams originate in Nigeria and section 419 of the Nigerian Criminal Code criminalizes fraud.[51] While certain aspects of 419 fraud are novel—such as the use of e-mail to contact victims who are in other countries—the scheme itself is not. It is a variation of what is known as advance fee fraud. In advance fee fraud, "the victim pays money to someone in anticipation of receiving something of greater value—such as a loan, contract, investment, or gift—and then receives little or nothing in return."[52]

Online 419 fraud is an updated version of the Spanish Prisoner, an advance fee scam that dates "back as far as 1588."[53] In the original version of the fraud, the victim receives a letter from the scammer, in which the latter says he or she "is in contact with a very important, and wealthy, person who has been imprisoned in Spain"; the person is using an alias, so his jailers have "no idea of his true value or importance."[54] The letter says his jailers can be bribed (relatively cheaply) to release the prisoner, who will give the victim a handsome reward and "his beautiful daughter's hand in marriage."[55] This begins a correspondence in which the victim initially sends money to bribe the jailers, only to be advised that problems continue to arise that "require more and more funds to overcome."[56] The process continues until the victim runs out of money or realizes he or she has been duped.[57]

The Spanish Prisoner has gone through many iterations since it first appeared, the most recent of which is the 419 scam. The 419 version of the Spanish Prisoner uses an e-mail—rather than a letter—and usually purports to be from someone who knows of a large amount of unclaimed gold or money the scammer cannot access directly because of some more or less minor legal obstacles. The amount of money involved is always in the millions, and the recipient of the e-mail is promised a large share of the money if he or she will help the author of the e-mail get it out of the country or bank account in which it resides.[58] If the recipient of the e-mail agrees to help, he or she will be required to send an initial amount of money for expenses; and as in the original version of the Spanish Prisoner, there will be successive requests for more money as complications arise in extracting the gold or money from its current location.

People fall for this scam, as they have always fallen for versions of the Spanish Prisoner scam. No one knows how many people respond, but a conservative estimate is that a 419 fraudster will receive "two interested replies for every thousand e-mail messages" he or she sends out;[59] since 419 scammers send millions of e-mails, that would be an eminently satisfactory return rate. It means a fraudster receives up to two thousand interested responses for every million e-mails sent out. If even 5 percent of those who respond go on to participate in the scam, it will, at the least, have been worth the time. After all, 419 scammers have essentially no overhead; they often operate from Internet cafes, so their primary expenditure is the effort they put into composing the initial e-mails and responding to those who become victims.

The victims—who come from various countries—are encouraged to wire funds to the fraudster, and many do. Estimates of how much they send vary; a 2006 report from Britain estimated that the average UK victim lost thirty-one thousand pounds.[60] A few victims go completely overboard: in 2007, Thomas Katona, former treasurer of Alcona County, Michigan, was charged with embezzlement after he siphoned over $1.2 million of the county's money and wired it (plus seventy-two thousand dollars of his own money) to "overseas bank accounts . . . linked to the Nigerian Advance Fee Fraud Scheme."[61]

And in 2008, Janelia Spears, a nurse in a small town in Oregon, wound up sending four hundred thousand dollars to a Nigerian con man.[62] It began with an e-mail promising her twenty million dollars left by her grandfather, with whom her family had lost touch years before; Spears said the fact the e-mailer knew her grandfather's name piqued her interest and convinced her there must be something to the story. She started by sending just one hundred dollars but kept responding to the scammer's escalating demands for money; by the time she was done, she had mortgaged the house she and her husband lived in, put a lien on their car, and spent his retirement money.[63]

The Katona and Spears cases are extreme examples of the personal havoc 419 scams can inflict, but that is not the only reason governments are concerned about these frauds. They also inflict significant economic losses: in 2006, a British report estimated that this type of fraud cost the UK economy £150 billion a year,[64] and estimates put the losses to U.S. citizens in the hundreds of millions of dollars.[65] Any estimate of the amount lost to 419 fraud is likely to be understated, though, because most victims do not report the crime to the police, usually out of embarrassment at having been taken. The one point on which everyone agrees is that online fraud is a booming industry—a criminal enterprise that has so far had very little to fear from law enforcement.

IDENTITY FRAUD (AKA IDENTITY THEFT)

While there are many types of online fraud, identity fraud (or identity theft) is one of the most common. This section uses two cases to illustrate what this crime targets and what it does not.

The first case is *United States v. Godin*: Cori Godin was prosecuted for identity theft in violation of federal law.[66] She defrauded eight banks and eight credit unions out of forty thousand dollars by opening accounts using Social Security Numbers she fabricated

> by altering the fourth and fifth digits of her own social security number. Godin's social security number is 004-82-xxxx. Of the seven fabricated numbers, only one, number 004-44-xxxx, belonged to another person. Godin opened an account at Bank of America with the fabricated 004-44-xxxx number but provided the bank with her . . . name, address, date of birth, driver's license number, and telephone number.[67]

Godin defrauded the victims by opening accounts with a fabricated Social Security Number, closing some of them and then depositing checks drawn on those accounts into the still open accounts. She withdrew money from these falsely inflated accounts, leaving the banks and credit unions with losses of forty thousand dollars.

Godin was charged with identity fraud under 18 U.S. Code section 2018(A)(a)(1), which makes it a crime to knowingly use, "without lawful authority, a means of identification of another person" in perpetrating a felony. The prosecution said she used "a means of identification of another" in committing bank fraud because she used fake Social Security Numbers to trick the banks and credit unions into giving her money to which she was not entitled. Godin pled guilty to the bank fraud charges that were also brought against her; she was tried and convicted of the section 2018(A)(a)(1) charge.

On appeal, Godin argued that, to convict her, the government had to prove beyond a reasonable doubt that she knowingly used the identity of another person, but the government did not prove this. Godin argued that this was not a case in which the perpetrator misappropriated "a means of identification" (like Social Security Numbers) that belonged to someone else; Godin cloned her Social Security Number to create new numbers. She said that, as far as she knew, none of the cloned numbers belonged to a real person; more precisely, she said she did *not* know any of them belonged to a real person. At trial, the government called two witnesses to prove Godin had knowingly used a means of identification of another:

> The first was employed by Bank of America and testified that Godin used number 004-44-xxxx to open an account but gave the bank her correct name, address, phone number, driver's license number, and date of birth. The government then called a Special Agent for the Social Security Administration [who] testified that by searching a secure and password-protected Social Security Administration database, he determined that social security number 004-44-xxxx was assigned to a man who resided in Maine. The Agent also testified that he could not tell by looking at the number that it belonged to another person because there are millions of unassigned numbers.[68]

The issue the court of appeals had to decide was whether "knowingly" applied to the fact that this means of identification belonged to another person. At trial, the district court instructed the jury that the government was "not required to prove that she knew the means of identification actually belonged to another person."

In ruling on the issue, the court of appeals noted that the language of the statute is ambiguous as to whether "knowingly" applies to the means of identification belonging to someone else. It explained that, if "a statute contains a 'grievous ambiguity,'" it must be resolved in the defendant's favor. So the court held that "knowingly" applies to the means of identification belonging to another person, which meant that the district court instructed the jury incorrectly.[69] The court of appeals went on to review the evidence presented at trial—the testimony of the witnesses described

above—and held that a "rational fact-finder could not find beyond a reasonable doubt that Godin knew the false social security number was assigned to another person."[70] It therefore reversed her conviction and re-
manded the case to the district court, instructing it to dismiss the section
2018(A)(a)(1) count against Godin.

The *Godin* case points up the inherent ambiguity in how law concep-
tualizes identity fraud or identity theft. Identity theft is not theft in the
traditional sense because the victim is not completely deprived of his or
her identity. Theft was historically a zero-sum phenomenon, and law has
expanded its conception of theft to encompass the copying of data. So
it has in some instances moved beyond zero-sum theft; the question is
whether that is appropriate in this context or whether law should approach
what Godin did as a type of fraud.

In its analysis of section 2018(A)'s legislative history, the *Godin* court
found that Congress meant the statute to be a theft statute—that it was intended "to punish 'thieves,' or those who knowingly use another's identification." The prosecution seems to have implicitly recognized that in the
Godin case because it only charged her with one count of identity theft—
since, coincidentally, one of the Social Security Numbers she cloned happened to belong to a real person.

The issue the *Godin* decision implicitly raises is whether identity theft is
meant to be a theft crime (which means no charge can be brought unless
the defendant misappropriated a real person's identifying information)
or a fraud crime. If it is meant to be a fraud crime (and some states call it
identity fraud), it would not matter whether the identification documents
someone like Godin used belonged, or did not belong, to a real person. All
that would matter is that she used information that did not belong to her
to trick companies or others out of money or property. (As noted earlier,
fraud is simply theft by trick.)

It seems the best argument for construing the unauthorized use of another's means of identification as a theft crime instead of a fraud crime
is that both the federal system and the states already have fraud statutes
(like the bank fraud statutes used to charge Godin) and do not really need
more. When someone is charged with fraud, the victim is the person or
entity who was tricked out of money or property—the banks and credit
card companies in this case. When someone is charged with theft, the
victim is the person who lost some quantum of property. According to

this argument, in the *Godin* case and cases like it, the government already has the tools it needs to seek justice for the fraud victims; the identity theft statutes let it seek justice for the indirect victims, for those whose identities were misappropriated and used to commit fraud. As to the harm the indirect victims suffer, their credit ratings may be impaired or they may discover they are responsible for thousands of dollars in debt run up by the person who misused their identity.

The *Godin* case is a good example of a traditional identity fraud (or identity theft) crime. There are, though, other permutations of identity fraud (or identity theft), one of which involved the infliction of a particularly egregious harm.

The case is *State v. Baron*, and it is from Wisconsin.[71] Christopher Baron was an emergency medical technician (EMT) for the city of Jefferson, Wisconsin. Mark Fisher was the director of Jefferson's emergency medical service (EMS) program and Baron's boss. According to the criminal complaint filed against Baron, he hacked into Fisher's work computer and forwarded e-mails he found in Fisher's e-mail account to about ten people.

Since Baron was using Fisher's account, the e-mails he forwarded appeared to come from Fisher. They were e-mails Fisher had sent to a female EMT, and they suggested the two were having an affair. The content consisted primarily of sexual innuendoes between Fisher and the female EMT, as well as attempts to set up meetings to engage in the affair. The e-mails also indicated Fisher was using an apartment owned by the EMS department to conduct the affair. Baron sent the e-mails to various local and county EMS workers, as well as to Fisher's wife. The day after Baron sent the e-mails, Fisher committed suicide.

Baron told the officers investigating the matter that he sent the e-mails to get Fisher in trouble. He knew Fisher's password because he had helped Fisher with his computer. Baron used his home computer to access Fisher's work computer and forward the e-mails. He said he originally intended to send them only to Fisher's wife but then decided to send them to others so they could see that Fisher was not "golden."

Baron was charged with computer crime for hacking Fisher's e-mail account and with identity theft under Wisconsin Statutes section 943.201(2)(c). The identity theft statute makes it a crime to use any "personal identifying information" of another without authorization and, "by representing that he" is the other person, to "obtain credit, money, goods, services, employment, or any other thing of value or benefit" or "harm the reputation, property, person or estate of the individual." This is an unusual identity theft (or fraud statute) because most jurisdictions define the crime solely in terms of using another's identity for profit. For some reason, Wisconsin's legislature added the "harm the reputation" provision to what is otherwise a standard identity theft statute. Had it not been included, there probably would not have been any crime Baron could be charged with that captured the most serious harm he inflicted: using Fisher's identity to destroy his reputation and, in so doing, cause him to destroy himself.

The *Baron* case illustrates how cyberspace can be used to harm people, as well as property. The next section examines two crimes that often involve the infliction of both types of harm; the next chapter examines tool cybercrimes that specifically "harm" people.

Extortion and Blackmail

In common law, extortion consisted of a public official's using his office to coerce someone into paying him money.[72] The term "black-mail" also originated in England, where it referred to a similar practice in which "freebooting chiefs" extorted money from villages in exchange for not attacking them.[73] Both crimes have evolved over the years.

In modern U.S. law, extortion consists of using a threat to obtain "the property of another, with intent to deprive him of the property."[74] As that definition suggests, extortion is a type of theft; the extortionist forces the rightful owner of property to surrender it to avoid certain consequences. Under the Model Penal Code, one commits extortion if "he purposely obtains property of another by threatening to" do any of the following:

(1) inflict bodily injury on anyone or commit any other criminal offense; or

(2) accuse anyone of a criminal offense; or

(3) expose any secret tending to subject any person to hatred, contempt or ridicule, or to impair his credit or business repute; or

(4) take or withhold action as an official, or cause an official to take or withhold action; or

(5) bring about or continue a strike ... or other collective unofficial action, if the property is not demanded ... for the benefit of the group ... ; or

(6) testify or provide information or withhold testimony or information with respect to another's legal claim or defense; or

(7) inflict any other harm which would not benefit the actor.[75]

The Model Penal Code provision expands the common law definition of extortion and, in so doing, makes blackmail a subset of extortion. The distinctive characteristic of blackmail lies in the nature of the threat; traditionally, blackmail involved the third alternative quoted above, that is, threatening to expose a secret that exposes the victim to ridicule or otherwise damages his or her reputation. Under the Model Penal Code, which influenced U.S. law, blackmail is informational extortion; while extortion can involve essentially any kind of threat, blackmail is limited to threats to reveal information the victim would prefer not to have revealed.

Both blackmail and extortion have migrated into cyberspace, though extortion is far more common than blackmail. It is more common because of the Willie Sutton principle: most cybercrime is driven by greed, and an extortionist by definition acts to enrich himself.

CYBEREXTORTION: THE TERESHCHUK CASE

Generic definitions of extortion like the one quoted above are usually broad enough to encompass online extortion, but specialized computer extortion statutes sometimes are not. The case that best illustrates this is Myron Tereshchuk's improbable attempt to extort seventeen million dollars from an intellectual property company.[76] Because he believed MicroPatent had wronged him, Tereshchuk hacked its network and obtained confidential proprietary information. He then used alias e-mail accounts to send MicroPatent e-mails in which he demanded it pay him seventeen million dollars or he would release the information publicly. Federal agents spent weeks investigating the source of the threats; their task became much easier when Tereshchuk demanded the money be paid via check and sent an e-mail telling MicroPatent to "make the check payable to Myron Tereshchuk and deliver it" at an address he provided (which was his parents' home).[77]

Federal prosecutors wanted to charge Tereshchuk with computer extortion under 18 U.S. Code section 1030(a)(7), but they had a problem. While he clearly engaged in an extortion attempt under a general definition of the crime, the method he used did not fit within the language of section 1030(a)(7) as it existed when he threatened MicroPatent. At that time, section 1030(a)(7) made it a crime to send a "communication containing any threat to cause damage to a protected computer" with the "intent to extort" money. Tereshchuk did not threaten to damage a computer; he threatened to release confidential information. Since section 1030(a)(7) —the computer extortion statute—did not apply to what Tereshchuk had done, he was prosecuted under a generic extortion statute: 18 U.S. Code section 1951. Section 1951(a) makes it a federal crime to obstruct, delay, or affect commerce by engaging in extortion. Section 1951(b)(2) defines "extortion" as obtaining property "from another, with his consent, induced by wrongful use of actual or threatened force, violence, or fear." Since Tereshchuk sought to induce MicroPatent to surrender property—money—by inducing fear that he would release confidential proprietary information, his conduct fell under this provision.

In 2008, Congress revised section 1030(a)(7) so it encompasses threats other than those directed at a computer.[78] The revised statute makes it a crime for someone who acts with the intent to extort "money or other thing of value" to transmit a communication that contains a threat (1) to damage a protected computer, (2) to obtain information from a protected computer without being authorized to do so, or (3) to impair the confidentiality of information obtained from a computer without authorization. Tereshchuk *could* be prosecuted under the revised version of section 1030(a)(7), since it includes threats based on compromising the confidentiality of information improperly obtained from a computer. And he could be prosecuted even though he never got his seventeen million dollars; as courts have noted, since extortion criminalizes the act of making the threat, the crime is complete when the threat has been sent to the victim.[79]

Tereshchuk's unsuccessful extortion effort is not typical of contemporary cyberextortion. Financially motivated extortion predicated on distributed denial of service (DDOS) attacks and directed at online casinos and other businesses is the most common, and most successful, type of cyberextortion.

SEXTORTION

In the real world, blackmail is usually a property crime, that is, usually involves threatening to reveal information unless the victim gives the perpetrator money or other items of value. Blackmail also tends to be a property crime in the cyberworld,[80] but it can take on an additional aspect, something akin to a crime against persons. The relatively new phenomenon known as "sextortion" is an example of this type of cyberextortion.

A 2008 case from Kentucky illustrates the dynamic, and the harm, involved in sextortion.[81] On October 1, a female student at the University of the Cumberlands went to the police and told them someone was trying to force her to make a video of herself masturbating and send it to him. She said she had received an e-mail from an unknown male who said he had webcam clips of her having sex with a young man; the unknown e-mailer said that unless she made the video he wanted (which he described in great detail), he would send the clips to her friends and professors. The woman said she had made the videos with her boyfriend several years before. Federal agents identified Sungkook Kim, a South Korean student, as the sextortionist. Kim told a federal agent he found the clips after he noticed a student fail to log off of a computer in the university's computer lab; he found the webcam clips on that computer and saved them to a portable flash drive, which he took with him.

Kim's sextortion scheme shows how blackmail can morph online. The tactic he used qualifies as blackmail because he threatened to reveal information that would expose the victim to contempt or ridicule, but it is not at all clear that he used the threats in an attempt to obtain property. Kim did not demand money; the video he wanted would constitute property once it came into existence, but Kim was not demanding property that already existed. He demanded that his victim create a video to his specifications. That could present a problem if blackmail statutes, like extortion statutes, *only* criminalized threats designed to obtain property.

Under the Model Penal Code and Model Penal Code–influenced blackmail statutes, the threat must be to obtain money or property, but contemporary blackmail statutes tend to be phrased more broadly.[82] Kansas, for example, defines blackmail as "gaining or attempting to gain anything of value or *compelling another to act against such person's will*" by threatening to reveal information that would subject the person to "public ridicule, contempt or *degradation*."[83] Kim's conduct constitutes blackmail under a statute like this: he sought to use his threats to compel his victim to do things she did not want to do, things that would certainly subject her to public degradation if she had made his video and it had come to public light.

Kim's actions may seem extraordinary, but unfortunately they are not. Financially motivated extortion still tends to be the most common, but there are an increasing number of cases in which males use threats to force victims to create sex videos for them. In one case, a nineteen-year-old Maryland man captured the images three teenaged girls left online when they "flashed their breasts" at a webcam in a chat room; he began sending threatening e-mails to one of the girls, telling her he would post the images "to her MySpace friends unless she pose for more explicit pictures and videos for him."[84] She complied on at least two occasions before law enforcement became involved and tracked the perpetrator down.

In another sextortion case, a thirty-one-year-old California man "hacked into more than 200 computers and threatened to expose nude photos unless their owners posed for more sexually explicit videos"; forty-four of his victims were juveniles.[85] And in a variation on the male-female sextortion cases, an eighteen-year-old Wisconsin boy "posed as a girl on Facebook and tricked more than 30 male classmates" into sending him sexually explicit photos of themselves.[86] He then contacted at least seven of the boys who had sent him photos and, "posing as a girl, threatened to post" their compromising photos online or send them to their friends "unless they engaged in sexual activity with a friend of 'hers.'"[87] The sextortionist was arrested after victims contacted law enforcement and then prosecuted, convicted, and sentenced to fifteen years in prison.

So far, those who engage in this type of activity and are apprehended tend to be prosecuted for child pornography offenses (since child pornography involves using minors to create sexually explicit material). Prosecutors are probably relying on child pornography rather than extortion because of a concern as to whether this type of activity qualifies as extortion, even under the Model Penal Code's definition of the crime. Under the Model Penal Code, extortion consists of using a (1) threat to compel the victim (2) to give property to the extortionist. This formulation expands the types of threat that can be used to commit extortion far beyond what the common law offense encompassed. Under the Model Penal Code, the threats used by cyberextortionists should qualify as threats to "expose a secret" or to inflict "other harm which would not benefit the" victim.[88]

The problem lies not with the threat but with the need to prove the sextortionist sought property. In common law, extortion only applied if the perpetrator sought to compel the victim to surrender tangible property, such as money. The drafters of the Model Penal Code rejected that approach in favor of a broader definition of the property that can be the focus of extortion. Section 223.0(6) of the Model Penal Code defines property as "anything of value, including . . . tangible and intangible personal property." The photos and videos a sextortionist compels the victim to produce have value to the extortionist, who seeks them for his own gratification, and at least arguably have a type of value—a negative value (e.g., the interest in not being humiliated)—to the victim. Logically, then, prosecutors should be able to use extortion statutes to prosecute sextortion. The possibly insurmountable difficulty with doing so is that existing extortion statutes were clearly intended to encompass only extortion that targets property that has value in the traditional, financial sense. Existing statutes probably cannot, therefore, be used to prosecute sextortionists. If legislators decide sextortion needs to be prosecuted, they could accomplish this by either (1) adopting new, sextortion-specific statutes or (2) revising existing extortion statutes so they encompass the type of harm inflicted in sextortion cases.

In a peculiar variation on the typical sextortion cases, a St. Charles, Illinois, mother was accused of using nude photos in an attempt to force her daughter's ex-boyfriend to resume his relationship with her daughter.[89] According to reports, before the thirteen-year-olds broke up, they exchanged nude photos of each other via their cell phones. After they broke up, her forty-two-year-old mother threatened to post the thirteen-year-old boy's nude photos online unless he started dating her daughter again; she apparently sent him hundreds of e-mails and text messages trying to coerce him into doing what she wanted. The district attorney referred the matter to the unit of his office that handled online crimes, calling it "an odd situation." It is very unlikely that any criminal charges were filed in this case because, while it could constitute blackmail under modern statutes, a prosecution would only have compounded the humiliation, ridicule, and other pain this incident must have caused the two children.

Property Damage: Arson and Vandalism

Arson and vandalism target conduct that damages or destroys property. While both crimes have historically been associated with damaging or destroying real property (such as homes, businesses, and other structures), the modern versions of the offenses encompass damaging or destroying personal, as well as real, property.

ARSON

The use of fire generally distinguishes arson from vandalism. Under California's arson statute, for example, one commits arson "when he or she willfully and maliciously sets fire to or burns or causes to be burned . . . any structure, forest land, or property."[90] The statute divides arson into four categories based on the nature and degree of harm inflicted: arson that "causes great bodily injury"; arson of an inhabited structure; arson of a structure or forest land; and a residual category that encompasses other property, including personal property. The penalties decrease as the severity of the harm decreases, though each of the crimes is a felony punishable by at least two years in prison. Other U.S. states have similar statutes.

Many states have updated common law arson (which *only* involved the use of fire) by incorporating the use of explosives into their arson statutes. Under Colorado's arson statute, for example, someone who "knowingly sets fire to, burns, causes to be burned, or by the use of any explosive damages or destroys . . . any building or occupied structure of another without his consent commits . . . arson."[91] Other states have similar provisions.

Existing U.S. law, therefore, criminalizes burning a structure and using explosives to inflict the same harm. The question is whether arson has, or is likely to, become a cybercrime, that is, whether cyberspace can be used to inflict the harm targeted by the crime of arson. If it can be used to inflict that harm, existing law will no doubt need to be updated to encompass this new version of arson.

As this is written in mid-2011, there do not appear to be any reported cases, news stories, law review articles, or other sources that cite instances of cyberarson. Since this chapter is examining how computers can be used to commit updated versions of traditional crimes, it is appropriate to consider whether arson can make the transition to cyberspace and become a cybercrime.

For it to become a cybercrime, cyberspace will have to become the tool one uses to inflict the harm targeted by arson statutes, that is, damaging or destroying homes, offices, and other structures. Logically, then, a cyberarson offense could take either of two forms: in one, the crime consists of using cyberspace to damage or destroy a structure by triggering an incendiary or explosive device; in the other alternative, the crime consists of using cyberspace itself to damage or destroy a structure. The first alternative targets what is probably the only role cyberspace can play in arson;

while the second alternative is a logical possibility, it is almost certainly not a realistic one.

It is not realistic because, unlike incendiary and explosive devices, cyberspace itself has absolutely no capacity to directly inflict physical harm on tangible property, a state of affairs that seems inevitable given the disconnect between the virtual world of cyberspace and the physical world humans inhabit. DDoS attacks, in which a cybercriminal uses bits and bytes to bombard a website and effectively shut it down, are a destructive force in cyberspace because they are directed at virtual targets. DDoS attacks, in and of themselves, cannot directly harm physical targets because they cannot transcend the border between the conceptual world of cyberspace and the empirical world in which people, and their buildings and other property, exist.

DDoS attacks might be used to harm physical targets indirectly by, say, interfering with the operation of the systems that control a dam's water levels, causing the dam to overfill and flood a nearby area.[92] The same dynamic could come into play with cyberarson under the first alternative outlined above: A cyberarsonist could use cyberspace to hack into the system that controlled the heat in a building and manipulate the system so it overheated and started a fire. Logically, this would inflict the harm proscribed by traditional arson statutes (setting a structure on fire); if the cyberarsonist hacked into the system and manipulated it so that it exploded, this would inflict the harm proscribed by the evolved arson statutes described above.

While cyberarson does not seem to have manifested itself yet, there is no reason to believe it will not do so. As the world's experience to date with cyberspace illustrates, criminals are quick to realize the advantages it offers in committing certain crimes. There is no reason to believe they will not, at some point, realize cyberspace can be used to infiltrate and compromise control systems and use them to trigger fires or explosions. Aside from anything else, this approach offers at least one notable advantage to an aspiring arsonist: it eliminates the possibility that arson investigators will find accelerants or explosive devices in the targeted structure, which alerts them to the fact that the fire or explosion was not inadvertent. A clever cyberarsonist might be able to disguise arson as an accident, thereby eliminating any investigation and the possibility of being held criminally liable for the harm he or she inflicted.

If cyberspace does become a tool used to commit arson, there should be no need to adopt new, cyberarson statutes to address the activity. States did not adopt new, explosive-arson-specific statutes when the use of explosive devices became another way to inflict the harm targeted by traditional arson statutes. Instead, they incorporated the use of this new criminal tool into their existing arson statutes. This is appropriate. Because criminal law is concerned with controlling the infliction of certain harms, the statutes that define various crimes focus on the harm, not on the method by which the harm is inflicted. Every U.S. state has statutes that criminalize homicide, which is taking the life of another human being. States divide homicide into degrees, based on the culpability involved in the crime; purposely causing another's death is murder, knowingly doing so is manslaughter, doing so recklessly is reckless homicide, and negligently killing someone is negligent homicide.[93] Since the concern is with the harm involved in the crime, homicide statutes focus on that harm and not on the method by which it is inflicted. Jurisdictions do not have murder-by-gun, murder-by-poison, murder-by-stabbing, murder-by-strangulation statutes; the method is, for the most part, irrelevant.

If that principle is applied to cyberarson, there should be no need for a new crime. States would need to review their arson statutes to determine if they are flexible enough to encompass cyberarson; if they are not, states would need to do precisely what they did when they added the use of explosives as an alternative means of committing arson. That is, they would have to ensure that the language of their arson statutes either (1) explicitly incorporated the use of cyberspace to commit the crime or (2) focused on the harm proscribed. States that elected the second approach would need to craft arson statutes that made it a crime to damage or destroy structures without regard to the means employed to do so.

VANDALISM

The modern crime of vandalism evolved from the common law's "malicious mischief."[94] Malicious mischief was defined as "the malicious destruction of or damage to the tangible property (either real or personal) of another" person.[95] Real property consists of land and "improvements" to land, such as buildings, while personal property essentially consists of mobile items, that is, cell phones, cars, furniture, clothing, jewelry, and so forth.

Vandalism statutes define the crime in terms almost identical to those used in the common law's definition of malicious mischief. California's statute, for example, says anyone "who maliciously commits" certain acts "with respect to any real or personal property not his or her own" is "guilty of vandalism."[96] The proscribed acts are defacing "with graffiti or other inscribed material," damaging, and destroying property.

No states seem to have adopted cybervandalism statues, even though vandalism is common in cyberspace. Perhaps the most common type of online vandalism is the defacement of a website, either for personal or political motives. Politically motivated website defacement is one of several activities associated with "hactivism," which has been defined as "hacking for a political cause."[97]

At the end of 2010, for example, the website belonging to India's "top investigation agency, the Central Bureau of Investigation" was "hacked and defaced" by a group "calling themselves the 'Pakistani Cyber Army.'"[98] Earlier that year, unknown activists defaced the website "of electronics manufacturer Foxconn" in an apparent attempt to draw attention "to an alarming space of worker suicides at a plant in southern China."[99] These are far from isolated events; estimates are that thousands of websites are defaced every year.[100]

There is no indication that anyone was held responsible for the Central Bureau of Investigation or Foxconn defacements, which is not surprising given that both presumably involved attackers who were outside the country in which the site was hosted. That makes it extraordinarily difficult for law enforcement officers to track down the perpetrators of website defacements and other cybercrimes.

Not all website defacements involve transnational actors. Many, at least in the United States, involve domestic perpetrators—usually someone who has a grudge against the person or entity that owns the defaced site. A case from 2008 illustrates how U.S. law and law enforcement deals with online vandalism.

Bradley Dierking was accused of defacing "the online reservations page of the Miraval Resort website" by "adding the following content to the web page: '"A.R." IS A HOMOSEXUAL' and '"L.K." IS A STUPID FUCKING JEW.'"[101] According to prosecutors, Dierking defaced the website of the "luxury resort in Arizona" as an act of revenge; he had been a programmer for Geary Interactive, an advertising company "whose largest client was Miraval Resort."[102] After Geary terminated Dierking's employment, he went to work for another advertising company, which also represented Miraval. Dierking then used his access to Miraval's website to deface it, which resulted in Geary's losing Miraval as a client.

If the allegations against Dierking as accepted as accurate, if only for the purposes of analysis, then he clearly engaged in an act of online vandalism. Vandalism statutes, like the California statute quoted above, make it a crime to deface property with graffiti or "other inscribed material," which is precisely what Dierking allegedly did to Miraval. He could, then, have been prosecuted for vandalism in violation of California law, since that is where Dierking was when he committed the defacement.

Dierking was prosecuted but not by California and not for vandalism. He was, instead, prosecuted in federal court for violating 18 U.S. Code section 1030(a)(5)(B). Section 1030(a)(5)(B) makes it a crime to access a computer without authorization and cause damage. The statute 18 U.S. Code section 1030(e)(8) defines damage as "any impairment to the integrity or availability of data . . . or information." The indictment against Dierking charged him with accessing the Miraval Resort website without being authorized to do so and causing damage to data or information contained on that site.[103]

The *Dierking* case illustrates how law is approaching online vandalism: instead of pursuing it either as traditional, real-world vandalism or as a new, cybervandalism offense, prosecutors are pursuing it as a target cybercrime. The section 1030(a)(5) crimes were created to target a variety of activities, most notably hacking computers and damaging or deleting data. But because of the way section 1030(a)(5) and similar state hacking statutes are drafted, they effectively criminalize online vandalism, as well as hacking.

Vandalizing a website cannot be done entirely from the outside. As the *Dierking* case illustrates, online vandals must gain access to a website to be able to deface it or otherwise damage it. Since federal and state hacking statutes specifically encompass this type of activity, they at least implicitly subsume online vandalism . . . which means there has been, and is, no need to create separate cybervandalism statutes.

>chapter:4

CYBERCRIMES AGAINST PERSONS

There are so many ways people can use cyberspace to injure each other it would be impossible to catalog them all in one chapter. Instead, this chapter uses some of the more common, and more egregious, online crimes against persons to illustrate the legal issues that arise in this context. It is divided into two parts: psychological harm cybercrimes and physical harm cybercrimes.

Psychological Harm Cybercrimes

Criminal law has historically not concerned itself with psychological—or emotional—harms; to the extent law concerned itself at all with these harms, they were consigned to the civil arena. So those who believed their reputations or honor or even their feelings had been damaged by what someone else did either sued the perpetrator for damages or got over it.

Criminal law historically focused on "hard" harms: physical damage to persons or property.[1] It focused on these harms because they are necessarily the first priority for a society. Societies must keep the infliction of such harms under control or they will disintegrate; as failed states demonstrate, humans cannot maintain the social and economic activities that are essential to their survival in an environment in which people are free to prey on each other. Criminal law is the device societies use to keep those who would prey on others under control; law enforcement officers implement the dictates of criminal law and, in so doing, maintain the base level of stability a society needs to survive and prosper.

In the twentieth century—especially in the latter part of the twentieth century—U.S. criminal law began to target some "soft" harms, as well as the hard harms it had always dealt with. Unlike hard harms, which involve tangible injury to persons or property, soft harms are more difficult to categorize. Essentially, they involve inflicting some type of injury to any of several interests, including affectivity (or human emotion). In the sections below we will examine two types of soft harm crimes, one old and one new.

THREATS

Threats became a crime under English law in 1754, when a statute made it a crime to send a letter threatening to "kill or murder any of his Majesty's ... subjects, or to burn their houses or other property."[2] This threat crime came to the United States with the English colonists and has been incorporated into federal law and the laws of every state.

There is some dispute as to whether threat crimes really target soft harms. Some say threat crimes fall into the category of what the law calls an inchoate crime, or incomplete, crime. Attempt is an inchoate crime; it criminalizes unconsummated efforts toward the commission of a crime. So, assume the FBI learns that John Doe intends to rob the First National Bank (FNB). The FBI observes Doe as he "cases" the FNB and makes other preparations and tracks him as he heads to the bank on the day he intends to commit the crime. FBI agents arrest him outside the bank before he is able to begin the process of robbing it. Doe will be charged with attempting to rob the bank; he cannot be charged with robbing it because he never got the chance to do that.

Modern criminal law criminalizes attempts on the theory that it protects public safety. If we did not criminalize attempts, the FBI would have to wait for Doe to rob the bank and try to arrest him afterward. Aside from letting him take money that is not his, this could expose people in the bank to the risk of death or serious injury if something went wrong in the robbery. Criminal law developed inchoate crimes like attempt to give law enforcement the ability to intervene and stop crime before it can occur.

The quid pro quo for letting law enforcement do this is that the criminal can only be charged with attempting to commit the crime; so Doe will be charged with attempted bank robbery, which carries a lower penalty than a completed bank robbery. (The penalty for attempt is lower because the perpetrator failed to inflict the harm that results from the completed crime.)

Some say threats are inchoate offenses, on the premise that a threat is the first step in an attempt to commit a target crime, for example, robbing a bank or hurting someone.[3] Others say threat crimes are not inchoate crimes but target the infliction of a completed, though soft harm; they protect the victim "from fear and disruption."[4] The U.S. Court of Appeals for the Sixth Circuit had to decide which view was correct in an early—and disturbing—cybercrime case: *United States v. Alkhabaz a/k/a Jake Baker.*[5]

In the fall of 1994, Jacob Alkhabaz, who used his mother's name and was known as Jake Baker, was an undergraduate at the University of Michigan. In October, he began submitting stories depicting the rape, torture, and murder of young women to the alt.sex.stories usenet group. One of the stories depicted—in graphic detail—the rape, torture, and murder of one of his classmates, a woman courts referred to as Jane Doe. This story, like the others Baker posted, are notable both for the extreme violence they depict (such as raping the victim with a hot curling iron or hanging her upside down, cutting her with a knife, pouring gasoline over her, and setting her on fire) and for the sadistic enjoyment the writer seems to take from the victim's pain.

A Michigan graduate who read the story and recognized the victim's name brought it to the attention of University of Michigan authorities, who contacted the police. When police searched Baker's computer, they found more stories and an e-mail correspondence he had maintained with a Canadian: Arthur Gonda. The e-mails outlined a plan by which the men would meet in real life, abduct a young woman, and carry out the fantasies depicted in Baker's stories and his e-mails to Gonda. The police apparently believed Baker and Gonda represented a threat to Jane Doe and other potential victims, so they brought in the FBI. (They may also have brought in the FBI because they were not sure whether Baker could be prosecuted under Michigan law as it existed at the time.) The FBI arrested Baker, and a grand jury charged him with sending threats via interstate commerce in violation of 18 U.S. Code section 875(c).

Baker moved to dismiss the charge, arguing that neither his alt.sex.stories postings nor his e-mails to Gonda constituted threats to kidnap or injure anyone. Baker said they were simply fantasies he was sharing with Gonda. The district court agreed and dismissed the charges; the government appealed the dismissal to the Sixth Circuit Court of Appeals.

The Sixth Circuit upheld the dismissal. Like the district court judge, these judges found that, while Baker's stories were sadistic and disturbing, they did not constitute threats. They explained that to constitute a threat, a communication must "be such that a reasonable person . . . would take the statement as a serious expression of an intention to inflict bodily harm." They also explained that, to constitute a threat, such a communication must be such that a reasonable person would perceive it as being communicated "to effect some change or achieve some goal through intimidation." The majority of the court held, therefore, that even if a reasonable person would "take the communications between Baker and Gonda as serious expressions of an intention to inflict bodily harm, no reasonable person would perceive such communications as being conveyed to effect some change or achieve some goal through intimidation."[6]

Essentially, the Sixth Circuit found that the notion of threat implicitly assumes that the communication is directed *at the victim* for the purpose of effecting change or achieving a goal through intimidation. That, after all, is how threats worked in the past, and it is how they usually work, even in an era of electronic communication. In *Irizarry v. United States,*[7] for example, Richard Irizarry was convicted of violating section 875(c) after he sent his ex-wife hundreds of e-mails in which he threatened to kill her, her new husband, and her mother. He apparently believed they were abusing his children, which was the state of affairs he sought to change with his threats.

Most believe the Sixth Circuit reached the right result in *Alkhabaz*. As that court noted, any other result would mean someone could be convicted of violating section 875(c) if they took notes at a trial in which a defendant admitted sending threats to his former spouse and e-mailed their notes to someone else. If the notes quoted the threats, the notetaker would literally be sending threats to injure another via interstate commerce; but it defies common sense to conclude that the notetaker was threatening someone.

The problem with the *Alkhabaz* decision is that it opens up possibilities for doing something new: using online communications passively, in a way that makes someone uncomfortable or even fearful but does not rise to the level of a threat. In 2001, William Sheehan, a computer network engineer who lived in Kirkland, Washington, put a website called JusticeFiles.org online.[8] It listed the home addresses, telephone, and Social Security Numbers and other personal information of local police officers; some of the entries included a map to the officer's home and, in at least one instance, a photograph of the home. The information on the site came from public sources, so Sheehan committed no crime in collecting and compiling it. Sheehan said he eventually wanted to expand the site to include information about officers from a broader geographical area.

Police were upset about the site; they saw it as providing information someone could use to retaliate against an officer or his or her family. Sheehan denied any improper motive. In an interview, he said, "The police have too much power.... In putting the information up in the fashion that I have, it makes it much easier . . . for a citizen to hold police accountable for any wrongful act that may happen."[9] Sheehan explained that, when he said police should be held "accountable," he meant they should be amenable to being sued or to being subpoenaed to testify in court; he said that, because many police officers have unlisted addresses and phone numbers, "citizens wanting to sue officers for alleged wrongdoing or call them as witnesses . . . often can't find them."[10] And he noted that his site included this disclaimer: THIS SITE DOES NOT ENCOURAGE VIOLENCE.[11]

Neither Sheehan's disclaimer nor his disavowal of any desire for revenge convinced the officers his site was not a threat to their safety and the safety of their families. Presumably at the police's behest, the Washington state legislature passed, and the governor signed a law that prohibited publishing personal information of police or other law enforcement personnel with "the intent to harm or intimidate" them.[12] Sheehan sued, claiming the statute violated the First Amendment and was therefore unconstitutional.

The First Amendment protects the right to free speech but does not protect *all* speech. Some speech can be criminalized because the harm it inflicts outweighs the value of the speech. One type of speech that can be criminalized is threats, or what the law calls "true threats." According to the Supreme Court, true threats are statements in which "the speaker means to communicate a serious expression of an intent to commit an act of unlawful violence" against a person or persons.[13] In the *Sheehan* case, the police argued that releasing their personal information was itself a true threat, but the federal judge disagreed. He noted that the police cited "no authority for the proposition that truthful lawfully-obtained, publicly-available personal identifying information constitutes" a threat.[14] He also found that "disclosing and publishing information obtained elsewhere is precisely the kind of speech the First Amendment protects," and therefore held that the statue was unconstitutional.[15]

This result is correct as a matter of law. Sheehan, and those who have created similar websites, point out that, as long as they are posting information that is publicly available, they are, in effect, simply publishing a phone book. Telephone directories do much the same thing as sites like the JusticeFiles; they provide information that can be used to find someone, which is why many police officers have unlisted numbers.

The First Amendment therefore bars the adoption of laws criminalizing the mere posting of "lawfully-obtained, publicly-available" personal information as the material being published does not rise to the level of a true threat. That, of course, leaves room for manipulation. Perhaps no website better illustrates this than Who's a Rat, a website that describes itself as the "largest online database of informants and agents."[16] The site lets people "post, share and request any . . . information that has been made public . . . prior to posting it on this site pertaining to local, state and federal Informants and Law Enforcement Officers."[17] The information on Who's a Rat comes from court documents (which are public records and often describe how someone cooperated with police to get a reduced sentence) and from anonymous posters who accuse someone of being an informant or an undercover police officer. Those who pay a small membership fee can access this information,[18] which is a matter of great concern to law enforcement.

Police often try to keep informants confidential to protect their safety and to encourage others to come forward with information; the online outing of informants not only endangers the safety of a prior informant but also can discourage others from cooperating with police. The outing of undercover police officers obviously puts their lives in danger, as do postings that falsely identify someone of being an informant. Who's a Rat and defense lawyers argue that the site performs a valuable service for defense attorneys who need to be able to identify those who played a role in the investigation that resulted in their client being charged with a crime.

Who's a Rat seems to have been inspired by a website Leon Carmichael, a defendant in a federal drug case, created in 2003.[19] After he was indicted, Carmichael created a website to seek information on the federal agents and informants involved in the investigation of his case. As a judge noted, "The site displayed the word 'Wanted' in large, red letters, beneath which are the words 'Information on these Informants and Agents.'"[20] It asked those with information about these informants and agents to contact Carmichael's attorneys, whose names and telephone numbers were listed on the site.

The government filed a motion asking the court to shut down Carmichael's site, claiming it was intended to intimidate and harass the agents and informants. One of the informants told the court that Carmichael's site "changed his life dramatically. He . . . is scared to let his children leave his house."[21] And a federal agent testified that three witnesses who had agreed to testify at trial changed their minds after the site appeared; none, though, cited it as their reason for refusing to testify.

The federal judge rejected the government's attempt to have the site shut down. While she noted there were legitimate concerns about the site, she found "that the following statement on the web-page could be reasonably construed as negating any criminal intent: 'Only public records will be published on this site.'"[22] Both she and another federal judge rejected the government's repeated efforts to have the site shut down; both judges found that the information solicited by and displayed on the site did not constitute a true threat and was therefore protected by the First Amendment.[23]

The rulings in the *Carmichael* case probably also apply to Who's a Rat, which may explain why the Department of Justice has apparently not asked a court to shut it down. Instead, the Justice Department and agencies involved in the administration of the federal courts have been investigating ways to purge sensitive information from publicly accessible court records while ensuring that the public still has access to its court system.[24]

As these incidents illustrate, anyone with access to a website can become a publisher and can publish whatever they like, as long as what they publish does not take on the character of a true threat. The obvious solution to the publication of publicly accessible information is to shield the information and limit—or eliminate—its status as public. That can work for certain types of information, such as the records kept by businesses and educational institutions; it becomes more problematic when the information is compiled by a government agency. Democratic government requires a level of accessibility; accessibility helps to ensure accountability, while secrecy tends to have the opposite effect.

Until recently, accessibility to information—such as information in court records—was not a matter of particular concern for two reasons. One was that except for lawyers and judges, few bothered to review court records; the other was that, even if someone rummaged through court records, there was little he or she could do to publicize what was found. Newspapers and other media might review records for details of a pending case, but they would be careful about what they published; newspapers, for example, have traditionally declined to publish the names of rape victims, to protect the privacy of someone who has already been harmed. Now, though, anyone who accesses such information can publish it online; the expense of online publishing is minimal, and the exposure is at least potentially global.

STALKING AND HARASSMENT

Stalking and harassment are the only offenses in U.S. law that unambiguously target soft harms. They are, as a result, relatively new crimes.

Harassment is the older of the two, at least in its original form. In the United States, the criminalization of harassment began a century ago, when it became clear that telephones could be used for less than legitimate reasons. The initial problem came from callers who used "vulgar, profane, obscene or indecent language."[25] Concerned about the harm being done to the women and children who received such calls, states adopted statutes that created the crime of "telephone harassment."[26] Initially, telephone harassment tended to focus on obscene or threatening calls, but some states broadened their statutes to encompass more general conduct, such as "anonymous or repeated telephone calls that are intended to harass or annoy."[27] But as a 1984 law review article noted, the harassment statutes then in effect generally failed to encompass more problematic conduct, such as touching someone, insulting them, or following them.[28]

That began to change in 1989, when actress Rebecca Schaeffer was stalked and killed by an obsessive fan.[29] Shocked by the Schaeffer murder and five similar murders, California legislators passed the nation's first criminal stalking law in 1990. By 1993, forty-eight states had followed suit,[30] and in 1999, New York became the final state to adopt a criminal stalking statute.[31]

Most of the early statutes followed the California model, which criminalized harassment culminating in a "credible threat." The original statute had two elements: "First, [it] requires willful... and repeated following or harassment.... The statute defines 'harasses' as requiring a course of conduct, which is a series of acts over a period of time that shows a continuity of purpose.... Second, the statute requires a 'credible threat'... intended to cause the victim to reasonably fear death or great bodily injury."[32] California's approach led some to characterize stalking as an inchoate crime, on the premise that the harm it addresses is the "murder, rape or battery" the stalking "could ultimately produce."[33] In this view, stalking crimes are analogous to threat crimes, that is, are concerned not with a soft harm but with preventing a hard harm. Others argued that stalking is not an inchoate crime because its concern is with the infliction of a distinct, soft harm. As one law review article noted, the harm stalking laws address is "a product of potential future harm. Stalking is wrongful because the threat of future violence causes emotional injury to the victim."[34]

Florida took a different approach. It created two crimes—basic and aggravated stalking. Basic stalking required that the stalker intend to inflict emotional harm on the victim and willfully engage in repeated following or harassment of the victim.[35] The aggravated stalking crime tracked the California provision by requiring that the stalker make a "credible threat" with the intent to cause the victim to fear for her safety. Basic stalking was a misdemeanor, while aggravated stalking was a felony.[36]

As societies became more familiar with the nuances of the conduct involved in and the harm inflicted by stalking, states expanded their statutes. As one article noted, modern stalking statutes encompass conduct that not only can be seen as threatening but also would cause a reasonable person to "suffer severe emotional distress."[37]

The emotional distress stalking statutes go beyond the concept of stalking as a crime concerned with the infliction of physical harm to encompass a purely soft harm. Missouri's stalking statute, for example, says that one "who purposely and repeatedly harasses... another person commits the crime of stalking" and defines "harasses" as engaging "in a course of conduct directed at a specific person that serves no legitimate purpose, that would cause a reasonable person to suffer substantial emotional distress, and that actually causes substantial emotional distress to that person."[38] The Missouri statute does not define "emotional distress," but other statutes do. Michigan's stalking statute, for example, defines it as "significant mental suffering or distress that may, but does not necessarily, require medical or other professional treatment or counseling."[39]

Other states have similar provisions, and some courts have noted that stalking statutes are intended to prevent "emotional harm to victims."[40] A few states have gone further, adopting cyberstalking statutes that make it a crime "to communicate, or to cause to be communicated, words, images, or language by or through the use of . . . electronic communication, directed at a specific person, causing substantial emotional distress to that person and serving no legitimate purpose."[41]

While a number of states incorporate harassment into their stalking statutes to define stalking or a lesser-included offense of stalking,[42] some have harassment offenses that also make it a crime to cause someone emotional distress. For example, Massachusetts makes "criminal harassment" a crime and defines the conduct involved in the offense as engaging "in a knowing pattern of conduct . . . directed at a specific person, which seriously alarms that person and would cause a reasonable person to suffer substantial emotional distress."[43]

Cases of Stalking and Harassment

Online stalking is often a form of revenge, a way to punish someone for breaking up with the stalker or refusing to date him or her. An Ohio case, for example, began when James Cline met

> Robin Rabook, Betty Jean Smith, and Sonja Risner in internet chat rooms. After several dates with each of the three women, they declined further contact with him. . . . In an apparent attempt to take revenge . . . Cline used his knowledge of computers and the internet, along with the women's personal information, to create havoc in their personal lives. For example, Cline locked the women out of their internet accounts, and he scheduled dates for the women, unbeknownst to them. He used their names to send vulgar messages to others, and he sent vulgar messages about the women to others.[44]

The conduct attributed to Cline would not constitute a threat because he did nothing that would make a reasonable person believe he was going to harm them physically. He instead did things online stalkers often do: he disrupted their lives by locking them out of their e-mail accounts and arranging for strange men to show up for dates the women had never made. Maneuvers like this cause emotional distress by making victims feel they have lost control of their lives. Can you imagine how unnerving it would be to have a strange man or strange woman show up at your house ready for a date you knew nothing about?

Cline targeted his victims directly, but other stalkers act indirectly. Can someone be convicted if he or she uses innocent people to cause emotional distress to the victim? A few cases have dealt with this issue, one of which is *State v. Parmelee.*[45]

When Renee Turner married Allan Parmelee, she found out he corresponded with "incarcerated people"; Allan himself had at one point been incarcerated in an Illinois federal prison. After three years and a child, Renee sought a divorce, which became contentious; at one point, Allan created a website and posted "highly offensive material" to her on it. She got a protective order that barred him from doing certain things; when Allan sent her printouts of the material on the site, which apparently violated the order, she called the police. He was charged with violating the protective order and incarcerated until the case was resolved.

Renee then began receiving letters from prisoners at the institution where Allan was being held; one "was a letter like you want to be a pen pal," but others were "very graphic and described the sexual acts the prisoner wanted to perform with" her. She gave the letters and the ones that followed to the police. They discovered Parmelee had not only encouraged particular inmates to contact his wife (who, he said, liked "nasty" sex) but also had this flyer copied and posted around the prison:

Renee Turner, 2315–41st Avenue East, Seattle, Washington, 98112, age 48, height 5 foot 8, weight 135, hair red, dark, race white, recently divorced ex-husband in jail for long time, likes ex-cons, loves sex, wants men to come live with her, will send money if requested with photo, likes you to talk dirty to her, say you saw her ad in the prison magazine.

Allan was charged with stalking based on his inducing prisoners to contact Renee for sex. His conduct is at least arguably distinguishable from the conduct usually involved in stalking cases in that Allan used third parties as pawns in his campaign to inflict emotional distress on Renee. He did not engage in any of the usual acts involved in stalking, like posting false information about her or publishing true information she would like to keep private (such as the code to her security system). Allan therefore *might* have argued that, since he did not engage in any activity that directly affected Renee, he could not be charged with stalking her.

He apparently did not, and for good reason. Criminal law long ago recognized that a clever perpetrator can use innocent dupes as a way to avoid being held liable for the crimes he or she instigates. It therefore treats a guilty person (Allan) who convinces innocents (the prisoners) to engage in conduct that constitutes a crime as the real perpetrator of the crime.[46] The prisoners did not stalk Renee; the letters they sent caused her emotional distress, but that was not their purpose. They had no idea this was what they were doing because they believed what Allan told them. Since they lacked the guilty mind, or mens rea, for stalking, they committed no crime. To ensure the truly guilty person is held accountable, criminal law imputes the prisoner's conduct (guilty acts) to Allan, who did have the guilty mind needed to commit the crime of stalking.

The *Parmelee* case is not an *online* stalking case; though Allan posted offensive material on a website at one point, his stalking primarily involved the use of the mail to cause Renee emotional distress. The case is instructive, though, because it illustrates how stalkers can manipulate others to achieve their own ends. In one cyberstalking case, a security guard whose interest in a woman was not reciprocated retaliated by posting ads online that said she "was seeking to fulfill fantasies of being raped. On six occasions, men showed up at her door in response to the ads."[47] The victim became so desperate she put a note on her apartment door that said the online ads were fakes; the stalker then updated the ads so they said the note was part of her fantasy and anyone showing up to carry out the fantasy should simply ignore it. He was finally identified and prosecuted for stalking.

In another case, the perpetrator pretended to be the victim in order to carry out his own ends. It was reported in the media as a cyberstalking case, but it really is not. Indeed, it may not fit into any of the existing crimes that target the infliction of soft harms.

The perpetrator—"Mr. X"[48]—was a twenty-three-year-old man who worked at a church in Wabash, Indiana. He apparently decided to assume the identities of two sisters—one twenty-eight, the other sixteen—whose family attended the church.[49] Mr. X created Facebook pages in each of their names and then pretended to be them online. On these Facebook pages, he posted photos of each sister, listed their addresses and phone numbers, and described their after-school activities and work places in detail. This went on for two years.

Why did he do this? If it were stalking, he would have done it to torment the women. He would have posted false (or correct) information about them to damage their reputations in the community or have used the Facebook pages to do other things that would unnerve, even terrify, the sisters. As one author noted, stalking is "a form of mental assault, in which the perpetrator repeatedly, unwontedly and disruptively breaks into the life-world of the victim, with whom he has no relationship."[50] Stalkers therefore focus their efforts *on their victims*, whether they carry out the activity in the real world or in the virtual world of cyberspace.

Mr. X did not do that. The victims learned about the fake Facebook pages after they had been up for two years. Mr. X was not interested in them; he did not directly target them in any way, whether for a "mental assault" or threats. Instead of targeting the women whose identities he used, Mr. X acted purely for his own benefit. He used these Facebook pages to "have virtual sex with men around the world."[51]

Mr. X simply used these women's identities to have a good time, in his own way. He must have had no desire for them to discover what he was doing because that would (and did) bring his online frolics to an end. Unlike a stalker, he did not *want* the victims to know what he was doing online.

How did the sisters find out about their secret lives? They did not, at least not initially. It seems the pastor of their church found the Facebook sites when he was "compiling an Internet list of his congregation" he could take with him when he left for a new post.[52]

The only news story apparently published on the case does not address this, but it is reasonable to assume that the pastor initially believed the sisters were responsible for what were presumably raunchy Facebook pages. The process of sorting things out must have been frightening and painful for the victims because it may have taken a while to figure out it was Mr. X who was responsible for the pages and for the activities they hosted. Because I got a message from one of the victims after I did a blog post on the case, I know she and her sister were terrified after they found out what Mr. X had been doing.[53] Remember, he used their names and posted their addresses, photos, and other identifying information; one of the men with whom Mr. X fraternized online could have decided to show up in Wabash at one of the sister's homes, prepared to continue the online affair in the real world.

The victim said she and her sister had tried to befriend Mr. X because they felt sorry for him since he had "had an unfortunate past."[54] I also received an e-mail from Mr. X's sister, who said his mother has "a professed addiction to sex and using the Internet to meet people and his father is a convicted child molester and molested" Mr. X when he was a child.[55] So the sisters, and others, can perhaps understand what drove Mr. X to do what he did, but it still harmed the victims. The issue in the case is not whether Mr. X did what he was accused of; rather, it is whether he committed a crime and, if so, what crime that was.

Mr. X was charged with "felony stalking and harassment."[56] Since felony stalking is essentially aggravated harassment, the analysis of the charges against Mr. X must involve the lesser charge—the harassment charge. Indiana Code section 35-45-2-2(a) defines harassment as follows:

> A person who, with intent to harass, annoy, or alarm another person but with no intent of legitimate communication:
> (1) makes a telephone call, whether or not a conversation ensues;
> (2) communicates with a person by . . . mail, or other . . . written communication;
> (3) transmits an obscene message . . . on a Citizens Radio Service channel; or
> (4) uses a computer network . . . to: (A) communicate with a person; or (B) transmit an obscene message or indecent or profane words to a person; commits harassment, a Class B misdemeanor.

On its face, the statute cannot apply to what Mr. X did. He did not make phone calls; he did not send written communications to either victim; and he did not send anything on Citizen's Radio. He did use a computer to communicate with a person and transmit an obscene message or indecent words to a person, but he *did not do either of those things* to the women who are the alleged victims of harassment.

Harassment has one characteristic in common with threats: both require that the perpetrator direct words or acts at someone for the purpose of harassing, annoying, or alarming that person. It is an implicit but integral element of harassment that the perpetrator must have sent harassing communications *to* the victim, not posted something online where the victim might see it and might find it harassing, annoying, or even alarming. That element is specifically included in Indiana's definition of harassment. Indiana Code section 35-45-10-2 defines harassment as *"conduct directed toward a victim* that . . . would cause a reasonable person . . . emotional distress and . . . causes the victim . . . emotional distress." Since Mr. X did not direct any of his activity toward either of his victims, he could not be held liable for harassment.

That leaves stalking: Indiana Code section 35-45-10-1 defines stalking as a "knowing or an intentional course of conduct involving . . . continuing harassment of another . . . that would cause a reasonable person to feel . . . frightened . . . or threatened and . . . causes the victim to feel . . . frightened . . . or threatened." Stalking is a felony, which means a conviction will result in the imposition of a higher penalty (usually more jail time) than a harassment conviction. While the stalking statute does not explicitly require conduct that is directed toward the victim, that is an implicit element of all stalking laws. It is an integral element of the notion of stalking, as we saw above. Stalking is, in fact, a kind of "mental assault"; you cannot assault someone—either physically or mentally—unless you direct your efforts at him or her.

Some might say Mr. X *did* stalk his victims because he engaged in a course of conduct involving harassment that caused them to feel frightened. The problem with this argument is mens rea: No evidence shows that Mr. X either intended or knew that what he was doing on Facebook would cause the sisters to be frightened. He may have assumed—indeed, hoped—they would never know anything about it. So even though his conduct caused the harm targeted by the crime of stalking, he cannot be convicted of stalking unless he acted with the necessary guilty mind.

What happened to Mr. X? According to the e-mail I received from his sister, his defense lawyer and the prosecutor in the case "agreed that a jury would convict if he went to trial on the original charges and he would be in prison until it was overturned (and they both agreed it would be overturned) on appeal."[57] The problem the defense saw was that Mr. X would be in prison while his case was appealed, a process that can take a year or more. The defense attorney and the prosecutor negotiated a deal, under which Mr. X pled guilty to a lesser charge of some sort; he was sentenced to serve thirty days in the local jail, spend a year on probation while attending counseling sessions, and surrender his computer.[58]

The impetus for the deal seems to have been a legitimate concern for Mr. X's safety; according to his sister, the judge commented that the plea deal probably saved his life because he would not have survived in prison.[59] The victim who contacted me—the younger sister—seemed to find the outcome satisfactory; in a remarkable display of charity and maturity, she said she and her sister "were not out for vengeance; we only wanted him to get help to stop it from happening again."[60]

Stalking and Harassment: Concluding Thoughts

The Mr. X case is an atypical soft harm case in one respect—he did not intend to cause harm to the women whose identities he appropriated—but typical in another. Like the security guard who went online and pretended to be a woman seeking to be raped, stalkers and harassers often use their victims' own identities against them. This is a new phenomenon, at least as far as criminal law is concerned.

If someone uses the victim's identity to threaten the victim or inflict emotional distress on him or her, the culprit can usually be prosecuted for making threats or for stalking or harassment. Sometimes, though, the perpetrator—like Mr. X—simply pretends to be the other person. Mr. X did this to have sex online. Some years ago, I remember reading a news story about a woman who was, and is, a distinguished commentator on online culture. She had recently had a very peculiar experience: when she went into work one day, her coworkers and other people repeatedly complimented her on the insightful comments she had posted in an online chat room the night before. However, she was not in that chat room and had no idea what everyone was talking about. She investigated and found that someone pretending to be her had been in the chat room and had posted comments that, fortunately, were not harmful. Her theory was that someone simply wanted to be her—to be an acknowledged online expert—for a night.

While that may seem a trivial use of another's identity, I do not think it is. I, for one, would be both unnerved and aggravated if someone did that to me. The harm here is the loss of control over our identity—over our "self." The soft harm and identity theft laws we have in place are all about using someone's identity to *do* something; the crime consists of using the identity to inflict a hard or soft harm on a victim. In the incident above, the imposter did not use the identity to inflict any type of harm on anyone, at least, not any type of harm the criminal law currently addresses. It seems to me we should have the right to control how our identity is used in any regard.

I believe we need a new crime—a crime of imposture. Imposture, as such, has not historically been a crime, probably because it is relatively difficult feat to pull off in the real world. As I tell my students, in the real world I cannot pretend to be a male (a judge, say), and I am likely to have difficulty pretending to be an identifiable female (a senator, say). If I am clever, I may be able to assume the identity of a male judge, just as the unknown imposter assumed the identity of the expert on online culture. In the real world, therefore, there has been little need for criminal imposture statutes. Most states make it a crime to pretend to be a police officer or a public servant, but few have statutes that could be used to prosecute someone who assumes a regular person's identity.

Yet that is precisely what happened in the Mr. X case, and it is also what happened—in a different way and for a very different reason—in *State v. Baron*, the Wisconsin case discussed in chapter 3.[61] As chapter 3 explained, Christopher Baron hacked into the computer his boss, Mark Fisher, used at work and forwarded e-mails Fisher exchanged with a woman with whom he was apparently having an affair. Baron sent the e-mails to Fisher's wife, among other people. The day after Baron sent the e-mails, Fisher committed suicide. Baron said he sent the e-mails to get Fisher in trouble.

Baron's conduct might be qualified as identity theft. It *might* also constitute stalking or harassment. Baron may have sent the e-mails intending to cause Fisher emotional distress—which he obviously succeeded in doing—but stalking and harassment also require that the perpetrator have engaged in a continuing course of conduct. That requirement is meant to ensure that Jane Doe cannot be prosecuted for stalking or harassment if she sends a nasty e-mail to her ex-boyfriend. The premise is that, while her e-mail may cause him emotional distress, and while that may have been her intention, it is neither just nor practical to criminalize every instance in which one person causes emotional harm to another.

To avoid that, stalking and harassment require a persistent, relatively prolonged course of conduct that is designed to cause emotional distress; the persistence of the activity ensures that casual slights or cruelties cannot be prosecuted. However, Baron did not engage in a persistent course of conduct; forwarding the e-mails was a single event, one that probably took less than a minute.

Wisconsin law, though, offered another alternative: a Wisconsin statute makes it a crime to intentionally use any personal identifying information of another (including his name and e-mail address) to "harm the reputation ... of the individual."[62] In effect, this is a criminal impersonation statute. And criminal impersonation seems to have been the only criminal charge that could apply to what Baron did.

Other states should adopt their own versions of a criminal impersonation offense. If nothing else, it provides a useful alternative in cases— like the Baron case and perhaps like the case of the expert on online culture—that cannot be prosecuted as stalking, harassment, transmitting threats, or any of the other crimes that currently exist. It could also be used as an additional charge in cases like the rejected security guard's using the woman's identity to set her up to be raped. That is, in cases like that, the defendant could be charged with stalking or harassment (whichever seemed more appropriate) and with criminal impersonation. That would be a good result because it is possible to stalk or harass someone without assuming that person's identity; the criminal imposture charge captures the additional harm an imposter can cause.

Physical Harm Cybercrimes

There are few reported cases in which computer technology has been used to physically injure someone. I believe it is clearly impossible to use cyberspace to commit one of the physical harm crimes: rape, at least as it is traditionally defined.[63] Rape is defined as having sexual intercourse with someone without his or her consent; it often involves the use of force to compel the victim to have sex with the perpetrator. As long as we define rape as a physical assault, I do not see how it can be committed in cyberspace.

That leaves two physical harm crimes: assault and death (homicide). Since assault is a lesser-included offense of homicide, this analysis only examines homicide, the premise being that, if cyberspace can be used to kill someone, it can also be used to inflict the lesser physical injury that constitutes the crime of assault.

The sections below analyze two ways to use cyberspace to commit homicide: One, as in the *Baron* case, is to cause them to take their own life. The other is to use cyberspace to actually kill someone.

SUICIDE

There are cases in which what one person did in cyberspace seems to have prompted another to kill himself or herself. This occurred in the *Baron* case. Prosecutions for causing individuals to kill themselves are rare because, as far as criminal law is concerned, it is difficult to hold someone liable for another's suicide.

For one thing, suicide is not a crime. It was a felony in common law, which meant individuals could be prosecuted for attempting suicide if they failed to kill themselves.[64] But by the twentieth century, lawmakers realized that criminalizing suicide was cruel (as well as futile). As the drafters of the Model Penal Code noted, "There is a certain moral extravagance in imposing criminal punishment on a person who has sought his own self-destruction, who has not attempted direct injury to anyone else, and who more properly requires medical or psychiatric attention."[65] The drafters therefore did not criminalize suicide, and their decision seems to have been influential; no U.S. state makes suicide a crime.

The drafters of the Model Penal Code realized there is a fundamental difference between committing suicide and *causing* someone to commit suicide. They noted that intentionally causing individuals to kill themselves would be a "pretty clever way" to commit murder.[66] The drafters of the Model Penal Code therefore included this provision in the code: "A person may be convicted of criminal homicide for causing another to commit suicide only if he purposely causes such suicide by force, duress or deception."[67]

This provision does not create a new crime. It only makes it clear that, if perpetrators purposely or intentionally cause individuals to kill themselves, the perpetrators can be prosecuted for murder. Notwithstanding that, no one in the United States has been prosecuted for causing another to commit suicide, thought there might be thousands of instances in which people's thoughtless or callous actions have had that effect.

There are two reasons no one has been prosecuted for causing another to commit suicide. One is intent: In the *Baron* case, Baron's forwarding Fisher's e-mails clearly seems to have prompted Fisher to take his life. But nothing suggests this was Baron's intent; he said he forwarded the e-mails to discredit Fisher. It is unlikely Baron ever though Fisher would kill himself because of the e-mails; suicide is an extraordinary step, one people do not expect. They may know they are doing something that will upset someone—they may even know they are being cruel—but they do not expect the person to kill herself or himself as a result.

There are, no doubt, cases in which a jilted lover committed suicide after being rejected; the jilted person's death is in an empirical sense attributable to being spurned. In other words, there might be what the law calls "but for" causation: but for the person's breaking up with the victim, the victim presumably would not have committed suicide when and as he or she did. The law cannot, however, hold the person who initiated the breakup liable for what ensued afterward unless we can prove beyond a reasonable doubt that the person acted intentionally—and wanted to cause the victim to kill himself or herself.

That is very difficult to do. A 2007 case illustrates why it is so difficult:[68] Thirteen-year-old Megan Meier lived with her parents in a Missouri suburb. Megan had attention deficit disorder, battled depression, and had "talked about suicide" when she was in the third grade. She had been heavy but was losing weight and was about to get her braces off. She had just started a new school and was on their volleyball team. She had also recently ended an off-again, on-again friendship with a girl who lived down the street.

Megan had a MySpace page. A "cute" sixteen-year-old boy named Josh contacted Megan via MySpace and said he wanted to add her as a friend. Megan's mother let her add him, and they corresponded without incident for six weeks. Josh told her she was pretty and gave Megan the impression that he liked her, until one day he sent her an e-mail telling her he didn't know if he wanted to be her friend because he had heard she was not "very nice" to her friends. Josh followed up with other, not very nice e-mails, such as the one that said "Megan Meier is a slut." After this had gone on for a while, Megan hanged herself in her closet and died the next day. Her father saw a final message from Josh on Megan's MySpace: a really nasty message that ended with the writer telling Megan that the "world would be a better place without her."

Megan's parents tried to e-mail Josh after her death, but his MySpace account had been deleted. Six weeks later, a neighbor told them there was no Josh, that he and his MySpace page were created by adults—a parent of the girl with whom Megan had ended her friendship. According to the police report, the girl's mother—Lori Drew—and a "temporary employee" of hers created the MySpace page so Lori could "find out" what Megan was saying about her daughter.

When all of this became public, people were outraged; many called for Lori Drew to be prosecuted for causing Megan to commit suicide. The first problem with that is intent: while Lori Drew was amazingly juvenile and irresponsible, as in the *Baron* case, there is no evidence she wanted Megan to kill herself. Unless a prosecutor can prove that Lori Drew's purpose in creating the website and sending the "Josh" e-mails was to drive Megan to kill herself, she cannot be prosecuted for homicide in the form of causing suicide.

Even if a prosecutor could somehow show this *was* Lori Drew's motive for creating Josh and his MySpace page, the prosecutor would still have to overcome the other problem in bringing a case like this to the court. The biggest problem, the probably insurmountable problem, in prosecuting someone for causing suicide is the following: how can a prosecutor prove that Lori Drew "caused" Megan Meier to kill herself? The decision to take one's life is always ultimately up to that person. There is nothing in the facts here a prosecutor could use to prove beyond a reasonable doubt that Megan's decision to commit suicide was the direct result of what Lori Drew did. The cruel trick Drew played on Megan may have contributed to her decision to commit suicide; it might even have been the tipping point, the factor that pushed her over the edge. But people—especially teenagers—play cruel pranks on others all the time without the victim committing suicide.

The drafters of the Model Penal Code sought to limit the use of the causing-suicide-as-homicide charge by requiring that defendants in such cases both (1) have intended to cause the victims to kill themselves and (2) have used "force, duress or deception" to accomplish that end. Using force would mean, for instance, that Drew held a gun on Megan and made her hang herself; using duress would mean she pointed the gun at Megan's mother or father and threatened to kill the parent if Megan did not kill herself. Clearly, neither applies here.

Lori Drew did, in a sense, use deception. She deceived Megan into believing she had a cute, older online boyfriend who thought she was pretty. However, this deception cannot be used to hold Lori Drew criminally liable for Megan's death because it is not the kind of deception the drafters of the Model Penal Code had in mind. They used deception to denote instances in which A deceives B about certain facts knowing that, by doing so, A is driving B to self-destruction. Assume, for example, that A hacks into B's medical records and creates a false report on the results of certain tests B took; in B's report, the results show A has several horrible, untreatable illnesses that will kill A after months of excruciating pain. (In reality, the tests show A is fine.) B does this because A is his wealthy uncle and B is his only heir; B devises and implements this scheme because he is in a hurry to collect his inheritance. B hacks the e-mail account A's doctor uses professionally; B sends an e-mail to A that is allegedly from A's doctor. The e-mail contains the false report on the tests A took.

B waits; if A kills himself after reading the false report, then B, at least arguably, committed homicide by causing suicide. Of course, even in this carefully constructed hypothetical, it is impossible to know whether B's trick ultimately caused A to take his own life. But the drafters of the Model Penal Code believed that, if the facts warranted, a charge such as this should be presented to a jury, which would then decide whether this was, in fact, a "pretty clever" murder.

There is no way to know if anyone will ever be prosecuted for using cyberspace to cause another person to kill himself or herself. It might happen. If it did, the fact that the case involved homicide, rather than mere suicide, might never be discovered. On the other hand, the perpetrators of cyberspace might make it easier to prove a causing-suicide case because they—like Lori Drew—left trails of digital evidence behind.

MURDER

Murder is defined as intentionally causing the death of another human being.[69] Murder is not method specific. It encompasses the use of any technique (e.g., stabbing, poisoning, shooting, etc.) that can kill someone. The focus in a murder case is on the same issue as in a causing-suicide case: the defendant's intent to kill someone and whether the defendant did, in fact, kill that person.

So far, no one seems to have been charged with using cyberspace to commit murder. This, of course, involves the killers using cyberspace as a murder weapon, not as a means of persuading victims to take their own lives. In cybermurder, the killer uses cyberspace instead of a gun or poison.

A 1994 case from the United Kingdom *might* have involved an attempt to use computer technology to kill someone. Dominic Rymer, a twenty-one-year-old male nurse, hacked into the IBM mainframe at Arrowe Park Hospital, Wirral, and modified the prescriptions for two patients.[70] These modifications had certain consequences:

> A nine-year-old boy, suffering from meningitis, was only saved from serious harm by a sharp-eyed ward sister. She spotted that the youngster's prescription had been altered the previous day to include drugs used to treat heart disease and high blood pressure and an investigation was immediately launched.
>
> It was then discovered that . . . Rymer had also secretly used the computer system . . . to prescribe anti-biotics to 70-year-old Kathleen Wilson, a patient on a geriatric ward. She had been given the drug, but had suffered no adverse reaction.
>
> Rymer . . . had also . . . scheduled a patient to have an unnecessary X-ray and recommended that another patient be discharged.[71]

The modifications were traced to Rymer, and the Crown chose to prosecute. He was not charged with attempted murder but with unauthorized access to a computer that resulted in damage to data in the system. At trial, the prosecutor told the court Rymer "used a doctor's pin number to access the computer at the hospital. He had memorized the number five months earlier, after observing a locum doctor having trouble accessing the system. Rymer altered the prescription for the nine-year-old boy suffering from suspected meningitis and prescribed a potentially toxic drug cocktail of Atenol, Temazepam, Bendroflumethiazide, and Coproxomal."[72]

Rymer could not "explain why he had altered the treatment records, but denied having any malicious intent."[73] The judge found him guilty and sentenced him to a year in jail. And the hospital's executive nurse said "tighter computer security" was implemented to ensure this did not happen again.[74]

Rymer could not have been convicted of murder because his manipulations fortunately did not kill anyone. But while he did not actually kill anyone, he could have been prosecuted for attempted murder if the prosecutor could have proved that Rymer manipulated the prescriptions for the purpose of killing these people. Since he was not charged with attempted murder, I assume the evidence did not show that was Rymer's purpose; he may simply have been experimenting, as he seems to have suggested.

The Rymer case illustrates how someone *could* use networked computers to commit murder. A book published several years ago described a creative, and perhaps viable, way to commit cyberhomicide.[75] An uber-hacker known as "Knuth" wants to eliminate someone who helped him orchestrate a huge financial cybercrime; Knuth wants to eliminate a witness and avoid paying the man the money he was promised. Knuth knows the man will be going into a hospital to have surgery, so he tricks a computer science student into hacking the hospital's computer and changing the blood type in the victim's file. Knuth tells the student he is the CEO of the hospital and wants the student to test the security of its wireless network; he says that, if the student can change the record, he can use that as evidence to require better security on the network. Knuth also tells the student the record is a dummy record; it does not involve a real patient. The student makes the change, and the victim goes into the hospital for surgery a month later and dies on the operating table because he is given blood of the wrong type.

That seems a viable cyberhomicide scenario. Personally, I hope it is also an unlikely scenario. I suspect cybermurder is a generally unlikely prospect now and for at least the immediate future. Except for altering medical records, there do not seem to be many ways cyberspace can be used to kill someone.

In 2008, medical researchers at the University of Massachusetts came up with a way to commit what might be the perfect murder: using wireless signals to remotely turn off someone's pacemaker.[76] Computers use wireless signals to program a pacemaker so it can deal with the patient's particular defibrillation requirements; pacemakers therefore receive wireless signals. Unfortunately, their capacity to receive wireless signals is not protected by encryption or any other type of security; pacemakers are unsecured because they were introduced long before we had wireless networking and the opportunities it creates. It is, as a result, *possible* for someone to use wireless signals to shut off a pacemaker and presumably kill the person to whom it belongs.[77]

It is also highly unlikely, at least at this point in time. The technology the researchers used is complex and expensive, which puts this technique outside the reach of most people. And at this point, the attacker would have to be within three to five feet of the victim to shut off the pacemaker; according to some reports, though, researchers are working on a more sophisticated device that could shut down a pacemaker from thirty feet.[78]

Cybermurder will no doubt become a reality. When it does, it should not be legally problematic because the method used to kill the victim is irrelevant as far as the law is concerned. As long as the prosecution can prove the defendant acted with the necessary intent and show a causal nexus between what the defendant did (sent wireless signals to a pacemaker) and the victim's demise, it should be able to win a conviction.

> chapter:5

CYBER CSI:

THE EVIDENTIARY CHALLENGES

OF DIGITAL CRIME SCENES

This chapter examines the challenges cybercrime investigations create for law and law enforcement. These challenges arise because cybercrime investigations target conduct in the virtual world of cyberspace, where evidence is amorphous and ephemeral and the lines between public and private places are uncertain.

This chapter uses a famous—or infamous—hacking prosecution as a case study. The next section outlines the crime, the investigation, and the trial; the next two sections use this case to demonstrate the challenges cybercrime cases pose for prosecutors and investigators.

The Port of Houston Attack

On September 20, 2001, the computer system at the Port of Houston in Houston, Texas, was shut down by a massive distributed denial of service (DDOS) attack.[1] It crashed the system, denying pilots and support companies access to databases they needed to help ships navigate the eighth-busiest harbor in the world. As one observer noted, the attack "could have had catastrophic repercussions" but fortunately did not.[2] But even though the damage was minimal, the attack was unnerving for a country still reel-ing from the 9/11 attacks.

U.S. authorities eventually "followed an electronic trail" to the home in the United Kingdom where eighteen-year-old Aaron Caffrey lived. More precisely, investigators examined the system log files for the Port of Hous-ton computer system and identified the Internet protocol (IP) address of the computer that launched the attack and the IP address of the system he targeted. An Internet protocol address is a numerical formula identify-ing a computer or other device that is connected to a computer network; each IP address is unique. And each IP address identifies the network a computer belongs to and the computer itself. So once the Houston inves-tigators found the IP address that launched the attack and the IP address of the system that was the real target of the attack, they could begin to track down the person responsible.

The investigation revealed that the attacker's target was not the Port of Houston computers but a computer in a different country. The Houston system was shut down when the software the attacker used seized that system—and others—to use as tools in an attack on the real target. The investigators identified the software used in the attack as custom-written software ("coded by Aaron") intended to exploit a known vulnerability in the software the servers were using.[3] And they traced the attack to the home in Fairland, Shaftesbury, Dorset, where Aaron Caffrey lived with his parents.

In January 2002, British officers confiscated Caffrey's computer system and arrested him on "suspicion of unauthorized modification of computer material," a crime under UK law.[4] After officers from the Computer Crime Squad examined the computer, Caffrey was officially charged with hack-ing the Port of Houston system.

The case went to trial in October 2003. The prosecution did not claim Caffrey intended to shut down the Port of Houston computer system. The Crown's theory was that the attack on the Houston system was an inadver-tent but foreseeable consequence of a "revenge" attack Caffrey launched against someone he believed had insulted his American girlfriend. Ac-cording to the prosecution, Caffrey was "deeply in love" with Jessica, an American with whom he had an online relationship, and launched the attack after a South African Internet Relay Chat (IRC) user called Bokkie made anti-American comments in an IRC chat room.[5] Crown investigators not only tracked down Bokkie's comments but also found a comment from "Aaron" that said he wanted to see Bokkie "time-out" because, "if she hates America, she hates Jessica. That is a no-no."[6]

The Crown's evidence not only showed a link between Caffrey's computer and the Port of Houston system but also showed that, after Bokkie made the anti-American comments, Caffrey used what is known as a "who is" search to find her IP address.[7] When Caffrey had Bokkie's IP address, he fed it into the custom-coded DDOS attack software he had on his computer and launched the attack that, incidentally, shut down the Port of Houston system.

That was the Crown's theory, and it was supported by the digital evidence the Crown's forensic examiners had found and analyzed. Because the evidence against Caffrey was so strong, his defense attorney did not challenge most of the elements of the prosecution's case. The defense conceded that Caffrey's computer had launched a DDOS attack that effectively shut down the Port of Houston computers; but instead of arguing that he should not be held liable because his real intention (at least according to the prosecution) was to attack Bokkie, the defense took a very different approach.

The defense's theory was that, while Caffrey's *computer* launched the attack, *Caffrey* did not. According to his attorney, someone installed a Trojan horse program on Caffrey's computer without his knowledge and used it to launch the attack that shut down the Port of Houston system.[8]

Caffrey blamed "Turkish hackers" for trying to frame him, claiming they regularly seized control of chat rooms and other Internet sites.[9] He said his computer's operating system allowed remote access and control and was therefore vulnerable to Trojan horse programs. Caffrey also claimed that the log files investigators relied on were altered to make it appear he was guilty. Finally, when asked about the custom, "coded by Aaron" attack software investigators found on his computer, Caffrey said, "Aaron is a very, very common name."[10]

It was then up to the Crown to rebut Caffrey's claim that someone using a Trojan horse program shut down the Port of Houston system. The prosecution responded with the only argument it had: Crown experts testified that they examined Caffrey's computer very carefully and found no trace of a Trojan horse program on it. Caffrey, who was the defense's only expert witness, told the jury it would have been impossible for the Crown experts to test every file on his computer; he also told them the Trojan might have been self-erasing, so that once it launched the attack it deleted itself from his computer.[11]

The Crown then tried to rebut Caffrey's claim of a self-erasing Trojan horse by pointing out that, when prosecution experts examined his computer, they not only found no trace of a Trojan horse but also found no evidence of log files having been altered and no evidence a "deletion tool" had been used to eliminate a Trojan horse.[12] Prosecution experts claimed that, even if the Trojan horse program Caffrey blamed for the attack had erased itself, the process of erasure would have left traces on his computer, but they found no such traces.

The case went to the jury after two weeks of trial. The five men and six women deliberated for three hours before acquitting Caffrey on all charges.[13] The verdict left prosecutors and police stunned. As an expert who testified for the prosecution noted, "It's very difficult to counter the argument [that] someone else did it and then ran away. We had hoped to show that if someone else did it they would have left footprints and . . . there weren't any."[14]

The Caffrey case illustrates several of the evidentiary challenges prosecutors can face in cybercrime cases. One challenge is proving the defendant's guilt beyond a reasonable doubt. Others concern a prosecutor's ability to have certain types of evidence admitted.

Trojan Horse Defense

The tactic Caffrey used so successfully is an updated version of a venerable defense strategy: the SODDI (Some Other Dude Did It) defense.[15] When criminal defense attorneys try to persuade juries that their clients are not guilty because (1) they did not *commit* the crime with which they are charged (actual innocence) or (2) the prosecution has not *proven* their guilt beyond a reasonable doubt (failure of proof), the attorneys will have to give juries alternate suspects on whom to place the blame: "The typical juror will be less likely to develop reasonable doubts in the abstract, than if the defense is able to sketch out some 'reasonable' alternative theory that will permit jurors to satisfy their natural human curiosity about dramatic events, and also their sense that real events must have some real-life explanation."[16] The SODDI defense has for years been the device on which defense attorneys rely to give jurors a way to find for their client when the defense cannot establish actual innocence, that is, cannot prove who actually committed the crime. It is a way to win an acquittal based on the prosecution's inability to negate the proposition that someone other than the defendant (Some Other Dude) committed the crime. It is usually not successful in prosecutions for real-world crimes, though there have been exceptions (such as the O. J. Simpson murder case).

The major obstacle to successfully presenting a SODDI defense in a prosecution based on conduct in the real world is credibility. Assume that instead of being charged with hacking the Port of Houston computers Caffrey was charged with breaking into the Port of Houston's offices. Assume, further, that the officers investigating the crime found Caffrey's muddy footprints leading up to and into the offices and found his fingerprints on furniture in an office and on the office safe he is accused of robbing. At trial, the officers testify as to what they found and a fingerprint expert explains why the fingerprints in the office are definitely Caffrey's. The case against Caffrey would be even stronger if, in this hypothetical, the officers found his DNA in the office with the safe.

So, assume all of that. Now assume Caffrey tells his attorney he did not commit the crime but has no alibi; the defense's only alternative is to try a SODDI defense. His attorney makes the same arguments to the jury that Caffrey's attorney made in the real case: he says the footprints were made not by Caffrey but by someone trying to frame him. He also argues that the fingerprint and DNA evidence could have been altered to frame Caffrey. The prosecutor responds by pointing out the difficulty of leaving footprints that are indistinguishable from Caffrey's and reminds the jury that neither fingerprint nor DNA evidence can be altered; indeed, none of the evidence against Caffrey can be altered because it is all tangible, physical evidence. Since that is all true and since the evidence is resistant or immune to alteration, the defense has no way of raising reasonable doubt except to claim that some unknown person with some unknowable reason to frame Caffrey fabricated the evidence and did so in a manner that deceived trained officers and experts. In this version of the Caffrey case, the jury will, without any doubt, reject his SODDI defense and convict him.

His defense is simply not credible as a matter of common sense; the jury understands and has confidence in footprints, fingerprints, DNA, and the experts who explain how and why they point to Caffrey.

Caffrey's case, though, arose not in the physical world but in the virtual world of cyberspace, hard drives, and Trojan horse programs. Anyone who uses a computer or knows anything about computers understands that digital data is not as solid, not as immutable, as the physical evidence used in the hypothetical in which Caffrey is charged with burglary. Anyone who follows the news knows there are hackers and knows they can penetrate computer systems. So that part of Caffrey's defense is credible; it gives the jury what the defense arguments in the burglary hypothetical did not—a viable (but unidentified) Other Dude.

In the Caffrey case, the Other Dude was not a person but a group: the Turkish hackers who hijacked websites and computers. This gave the jurors an identifiable human predicate for Caffrey's SODDI defense. Their relative, total ignorance of digital evidence and the intricacies of computer forensics added the missing element by making it possible for them to believe Caffrey and ignore the objectively more credible testimony of the Crown experts. In the burglary hypothetical, the jury has a commonsense understanding of footprints and faith in the validity of DNA and fingerprint evidence, which makes it easy for them to reject the SODDI defense. In the real Caffrey case, the jurors' rather uncertain common sense told them that digital data is malleable and insubstantial; based on their experience (or inexperience), they accepted that data can be altered or erased without leaving any trace, so Caffrey's SODDI defense seemed a "'reasonable' alternative theory" to them. He therefore won.

So have others.[17] Caffrey was charged with a target cybercrime, but the defense he pioneered has been used successfully in cases in which the use of a computer was incidental to the crime. Defendants have used it to avoid being convicted of possessing digital child pornography, and an Alabama accountant used a variation of the defense to persuade a jury to acquit him of tax fraud: he blamed a computer virus for underreporting income on his tax return.[18] Some have used the Trojan horse defense to avoid going to trial by persuading prosecutors to let them plead to lesser charges.[19]

If the Trojan horse defense is routinely used to win acquittals in U.S.

cybercrime cases, the media is not reporting that fact. Since the media tends to report the outcome of cases that go to trial, the lack of media reports of Caffrey-style victories suggests his success may be an aberration.

REBUTTING THE TROJAN HORSE DEFENSE

From the reported cases, it appears prosecutors are deflecting the use of the Trojan horse defense by having computer forensic experts testify either (1) that they found no trace of a Trojan horse program on the defendant's computer or (2) that other circumstances negate the viability of the defense.[20]

In *Chapman v. Commonwealth*,[21] for example, Paul Chapman was charged with ten counts of possessing child pornography and went to trial, where he claimed a virus was responsible for the child pornography found on his computer.[22] The prosecution used the testimony of the computer forensics expert who analyzed Chapman's computer to rebut the defense; the detective testified that he conducted a thorough examination of the computer but did "not detect any viruses" on it and found "no signs" that the child pornography files "carried any viruses."[23] The testimony was presumably effective because Chapman was convicted and the conviction was affirmed on appeal.

Another expert testified differently, but to the same effect, in a Texas case: Larry West was charged with possessing child pornography based on his having loaded images of child pornography onto a computer belonging to his employer.[24] At trial, West apparently claimed that the images "download[ed] themselves from the Internet" onto the computer due to a Trojan horse or other malware.[25] The prosecution used the testimony of Officer Smith, a Houston Police Department computer forensics examiner, to rebut the defense. Smith testified that the structure of the computer files indicated

> someone had gone through the files and named them to place them in order. When asked if it was possible for "pictures to download themselves from the Internet into files like this," Smith answered that he did not think it was possible to do so "in this kind of organized way." Smith also noted that the files were "saved" to the computer and, in his experience, a "Trojan" or "virus" could not "continually download child pornography" into a system like the one at issue.[26]

Smith testimony clearly prevailed: West was convicted, and his conviction was upheld on appeal.[27]

It does not appear that anyone in the United States has had the temerity to raise the improbable "self-erasing Trojan horse program" theory Caffrey used.

There might be a dearth of U.S. cases involving the Trojan horse defense because defense attorneys are not familiar with it. In some reported cases, the defense claimed a virus was responsible for child pornography on the defendant's computer.[28] Prosecutors were able to rebut this "virus defense" by showing that only a Trojan horse program or a worm would be able to download child pornography onto someone's computer without the person knowing it.[29] In other cases, the prosecutor rebutted the attempt to blame a Trojan horse by showing that the defendant not only had child pornography on the hard drive of his computer (which is where a Trojan horse *could* have deposited it) but also had child pornography on DVDs, flash drives, and other media.[30]

After the Caffrey verdict, there was occasional speculation that people might exploit the Trojan horse defense either by installing Trojan horse programs on their hard drives or by simply leaving it unsecured and vulnerable to malware.[31] The theory was that someone charged with, say, possessing child pornography could use the malware that made it onto his computer to disclaim responsibility for the contraband. There is no way to know if this has happened. There is little, if any, reference to a Trojan horse or malware defense in the reported cases; this may not be conclusive, however, because reported cases tend to involve prosecutions that went to trial and resulted in a conviction. It is *possible* that Machiavellian defendants of the type hypothesized by some have exploited adventitiously installed malware to persuade prosecutors to accept a plea to a lesser crime or to forego charging them with a cybercrime. This might be happening, but it seems unlikely; if defendants were exploiting the Trojan horse defense to avoid prosecution or bargain for lesser charges, there should be some mention of this in the media—but there is not.

Before examining the other evidentiary challenges prosecutors confront, it is important to note that the Trojan horse defense can be perfectly valid. It is possible to frame someone by using a Trojan horse program to plant incriminating evidence on someone's computer;[32] the material can be stored in an area of the hard drive where the person will never notice it.

As a former federal prosecutor commented, the "'scary thing'" about the Trojan horse defense is that it "might be right."[33]

Admissibility of Evidence

Every court system has rules governing the admissibility of evidence. They are intended to ensure that the finder of fact in the case—the jurors in a jury trial and the judge in a bench trial—only considers evidence that is authentic and reliable.[34] In the United States, the Federal Rules of Evidence govern the admissibility of evidence in federal trials; each state has similar rules that govern the admissibility of evidence in trials in that state.

Since the rules of evidence tend to be lengthy and complex, this section does not attempt to review all the evidentiary issues that can arise in cybercrime cases. Instead, it focuses on the issues that are most likely to be problematic: whether the evidence is authentic and whether it is inadmissible hearsay.

AUTHENTICITY

One of the things the prosecution (or defense) must do to introduce items into evidence at trial is to "authenticate" them, that is, to show they are what they purport to be. An Ohio Court of Common Pleas case—*State v. Bell*—illustrates the approach one court took to authenticating e-mails.[35]

Jaysen Bell was charged with "one count of rape, three counts each of sexual battery and sexual imposition, and one count of gross sexual imposition stemming from alleged improper sexual conduct involving two foster children, T.T. and T.W., between July 2003 and June 2006."[36] He filed a number of motions seeking to prevent certain evidence from being used at trial, one of which was directed at e-mails and online chats that allegedly occurred between Bell and one of the alleged victims.

The officers who investigated the case obtained a "search warrant for computer equipment located in [Bell's] home. A search of the seized hard drives uncovered stored pornographic images, e-mail messages, and MySpace chat messages," which the prosecution sought to introduce at trial. Bell moved to prevent the state from introducing the e-mails and MySpace chats, claiming the prosecutor could not authenticate them. He argued that "MySpace chats can be readily edited after the fact from a user's homepage" and pointed out that, "while his name may appear on e-mails to T.W., the possibility that someone else used his account to send the messages cannot be foreclosed."[37]

Since Bell was challenging the state's ability to authenticate the e-mails and chats, the court had to decide what the prosecution would have to do to authenticate them. It noted that under rule 901(A) of the Ohio Rules of Evidence, the requirement "of authentication . . . as a condition precedent to admissibility is satisfied by evidence sufficient to support a finding that the matter in question is what its proponent claims."[38] The court explained that the evidence needed to support this finding "is quite low—even lower than the preponderance of the evidence. . . . Other jurisdictions characterize documentary evidence as properly authenticated if 'a reasonable juror could find in favor of authenticity.'"[39]

The Court of Common Pleas found that, under this standard, T.W. could authenticate the e-mails and MySpace chats through testimony that

(1) he has knowledge of defendant's e-mail address and MySpace username, (2) the printouts appear to be accurate records of his electronic conversations with defendant, and (3) the communications contain code words known only to defendant and his alleged victims. In the court's view, this would permit a reasonable juror to conclude that the offered printouts are authentic.[40]

A federal judge reached a very different conclusion in *United States v. Jackson*.[41] Gerald Jackson moved to prevent the government from using a "cut-and-paste" document that allegedly recorded online conversations between himself and postal agent David Margitz, who posed online as a fourteen-year-old girl. Based on online chats he allegedly conducted with what he believed was a fourteen-year-old girl, Jackson was charged using a computer to induce a minor to engage in sexual activity in violation of 18 U.S. Code section 2422(b).[42]

The problem was that the prosecution did not have printed transcripts of the alleged communications between Margitz and Jackson or access to the hard drive on which they were stored. Margitz had wiped the hard drive at some point without making a backup copy of its contents; and he apparently never printed out the conversations he allegedly had with Jackson. Instead, Margitz created a cut-and-paste synopsis of the conversations, which was what the prosecution wanted to introduce at trial.

The prosecution lost. The federal district court held that the synopsis was not admissible because it was not authentic:

> There are numerous examples of missing data, timing sequences that do not make sense, and editorial information.... This document does not accurately represent the entire conversations that took place between [Jackson] and Margitz. [Jackson] argues that his intent when agreeing to the meeting was to introduce his grandniece to the fourteen-year-old girl. [He] is entitled to defend on this basis.... [Jackson] alleges that such information was excluded from the cut-and-paste document.... The court agrees and finds the missing data creates doubt as to the trustworthiness of the document.... Changes, additions, and deletions have clearly been made to this document, and accordingly, the court finds [it] is not authentic as a matter of law.[43]

Since the prosecution lost its primary evidence against Jackson, it could not prove its case beyond a reasonable doubt. And that, aside from anything else, illustrates how important the requirement of authentication can be.

Before moving on to the challenges the hearsay rules create, it is necessary to review a related principle that also ensures the authenticity of evidence offered in court: chain of custody. As a legal encyclopedia explains, "Chain of custody evidence establishes the identity and integrity of physical evidence by tracing its continuous whereabouts. Establishing a chain of custody as to a certain item of evidence provides a means to account for its handling from the time it was seized until it is offered in evidence."[44]

A federal case illustrates the importance of chain of custody. John Wyss was charged with possessing child pornography in violation of federal law.[45] The charge was based on child pornography that investigators found on a computer they claimed belonged to Wyss. He then raised the chain of custody issue, arguing that the government had not documented the seizure, custody, and analysis of the computer in a manner sufficient to satisfy the chain of custody requirement. Since the computer was the only evidence the government relied on at trial, Wyss claimed the lack of authentication of the computer meant he was entitled to be acquitted. In other words, he argued that the government's failure to establish chain of custody for its only piece of evidence meant it could not prove the case against him beyond a reasonable doubt.

The federal judge to whom the case was assigned began his ruling on Wyss's motion for acquittal by noting that the only evidence the government offered to prove that the computer belonged to Wyss was "a bill of sale covering a computer."[46] Although the government did not offer "testimony as to serial numbers or any other definite identification of the computer," the judge assumed, for the purpose of ruling on Wyss's motion, that the bill of sale was for the computer (with child pornography) that the government had seized.[47] In other words, the judge assumed—without deciding—that Wyss had bought this specific computer.

The judge made this assumption because the chain of custody problems lay not in the government's ability to demonstrate that Wyss had *owned* the computer; instead, they lay in its ability to show that Wyss, and *only* Wyss, was the person who put the child pornography on the computer.

Wyss had been renting a house from Stanley Felter's father; when he fell behind in his rent, Stanley Felter entered the house. Felter "made an inspection" and "removed items," including a computer, from the house.[48] Ten days later, Felter contacted a police officer, Deputy John Manley, and had him remove property—"including a computer"—from "a storage unit on Highway 61."[49] Felter apparently persuaded Manley to seize the computer by telling him it had child pornography on it.[50] When the computer was examined, it did have child pornography on it, which led to the charge against Wyss.

The problem the prosecution faced was that there was a complete gap in the chain of custody of the computer. As the federal judge pointed out, assuming the "the computer found in the storage unit is the same computer which was found at the home, there is no evidence regarding what happened to the computer after it was removed from the home and before it came into the custody of Officer Manley, a period of . . . ten days."[51] The judge held that the failure to prove the chain of custody raised a reasonable doubt as to whether Wyss was "responsible for the images on the hard drive, since the images could have been placed there by someone else after the computer was removed from his household and before it came into official custody."[52] He therefore granted Wyss's motion for an acquittal.

The *Wyss* case is an exception. State and federal law enforcement officers are usually meticulous about maintaining and documenting the chain of custody for digital evidence because they know it is uniquely susceptible to claims of tampering or alteration. The *Wyss* case is an unusual instance in which there was a total failure to comply with the chain of custody requirement, presumably because Mr. Felter, a civilian, played such an active role in the investigation.

HEARSAY

The authentication and chain of custody requirements are really concerned with the pedigree of evidence that is to be offered in court. That is, they are concerned with ensuring that the evidence is what it purports to be and is in the state in which it was obtained from the defendant. Essentially, these rules are designed to prevent the use of corrupted evidence; in the *Wyss* case, the computer the prosecution wanted to use *might* have belonged to Wyss, but even if it did, there was no way to know if someone else put the child pornography on it. If the court had relied on that evidence in convicting Wyss of the charge against him, the conviction would have been based on evidence that might have been corrupted, that is, might not have been what it was claimed to be.

The rules governing the admissibility of hearsay evidence are also concerned with ensuring the integrity of the trial process, but they focus on a different issue. To understand what that issue is and why it is important, it is necessary to review the rules governing hearsay.

Hearsay is not admissible unless it falls within certain exceptions to the blanket rule deeming it inadmissible. Rule 801(c) of the Federal Rules of Evidence defines hearsay as "a statement, other than one made by the declarant while testifying at the trial or hearing, offered in evidence to prove the truth of the matter asserted." Every state has a similar provision. Rule 802 of the Federal Rules of Evidence (and comparable state provisions) states that hearsay "is not admissible unless provided by these rules."

Why is hearsay excluded unless it comes within certain exceptions to rules like rule 802? It is a matter of common sense and fairness. If hearsay were not excluded, then John Doe could take the stand and say that Jane Smith told him the defendant—Richard Roe—confessed to the murder he is on trial for. That puts Roe in a very difficult situation: if the jury believes what John says—that is, that Jane heard Roe confess to the murder—they are almost certainly going to convict him (unless he claims he was insane or acted in self-defense). Roe can try to show that John is a liar, is mistaken, is insane, or otherwise cannot be believed, but neither Roe nor his lawyers can do much in terms of challenging the person whose credibility really matters: Jane Smith. Jane is a declarant who is not testifying at trial and whose statement is being offered to prove the truth of the matter asserted, that is, that Richard killed the victim. If Jane were present and testifying, there would be no hearsay issue.

Allowing secondhand evidence—John repeats what Jane allegedly told him—opens the possibility of unfairness and error. Everyone has probably played the rumor game in which something is whispered to one person and passed along by others, only to come out garbled. The hearsay rules are intended to prevent that kind of inadvertent error from infecting a trial; they are also intended to guard against intentional error, that is, fabricated evidence.

Hearsay is increasingly an issue in cases involving digital evidence. To illustrate why it often becomes an issue, the sections below examine cases that involved digital evidence of various types.

Computer-Generated Records

Aaron Colwell appealed his conviction on two counts of making a false report under this Iowa statute:[53] "A person who, knowing the information to be false, conveys or causes to be conveyed to any person any false information concerning the placement of any incendiary or explosive device or material or other destructive substance or device in any place where persons or property would be endangered commits a class 'D' felony."[54] The charges against Colwell arose because, on March 11, 2004, the

> Bloomfield Foundry received two telephone calls warning foundry management of an alleged bomb on the premises. The employees were evacuated and authorities conducted a search of the foundry, which confirmed that the calls were false. Telephone records secured by the police showed that two calls originating from the same phone number were made to the foundry at the time of the bomb-threat calls. During the investigation, it was determined that the originating number was the home number of a foundry employee, Aaron Colwell. Colwell consistently denied making the calls, claiming that he was at a gas station about ten miles from his home around the time the calls were made.[55]

Colwell was charged with two counts of making a false report and convicted by a jury in December 2004. On appeal, he argued that the trial judge erred by admitting "two telephone records documenting calls between" his residence and the foundry because the records were inadmissible hearsay. Like rule 801(c) of the Federal Rules of Evidence, Iowa Rule of Evidence 801(c) defined hearsay as an out-of-court statement offered into evidence to prove the truth of the matter asserted.

The prosecution argued that the records were not hearsay because they were not a "statement" made by a "declarant":

> The computers which generated Exhibits 1 and 2 are programmed to automatically log and compile a record of calls made to or from a certain number.... The State does not dispute that it offered the telephone records to prove the truth of the matter asserted in them—that calls to the foundry at the time the bomb threats were made originated from Colwell's home phone. However, the State [claims] the records are not hearsay because they were produced by a computer that automatically records the trace between numbers when calls are placed.[56]

The Iowa Court of Appeals agreed with the prosecution: "We conclude that the computer-generated records tracing calls . . . in this case are not hearsay, as they lack a human declarant required by our rules of evidence."[57] As a Louisiana court explained a quarter of a century ago, the printout of the results of a computer's "internal operations" is not hearsay because it does not

> represent the output of statements placed into the computer by out of court declarants. Nor can we say that this printout itself is a "statement" constituting hearsay evidence. The underlying rationale of the hearsay rule is that such statements are made without an oath and their truth cannot be tested by cross-examination. Of concern is the possibility that a witness may consciously or unconsciously misrepresent what the declarant told him or that the declarant may consciously or unconsciously misrepresent a fact or occurrence. With a machine . . . there is no possibility of a conscious misrepresentation, and the possibility of inaccurate or misleading data only materializes if the machine is not functioning properly.[58]

Like these courts, other courts have held that because the rule excluding hearsay is concerned with the fallibilities and falsehoods of humans, it does not apply to records generated by computers. So far, anyway, computers cannot lie; and while they can be fallible, the party offering computer-generated records can, as in the *Colwell* case, offer testimony or other evidence to show the computers that generated the records were functioning properly.

E-mails

Computer-generated records may not be hearsay, but computer documents that are generated by a human being are usually considered hearsay. Therefore, when the prosecution or defense wants to introduce such a document, they have to show that it can come in under one of the exceptions to the general rule barring the use of hearsay.

The applicability of such an exception was the issue in a Florida murder case: *Thomas v. State.*[59] Here is how the Florida Court of Appeals summarized the facts and what happened at trial:

> Chaka Baldwin, [Steven] Thomas's girlfriend of four years, was stabbed to death. No physical evidence tied him to the crime, but the State presented circumstantial evidence in support of its contention that [he] was the murderer. One piece of . . . evidence was an e-mail written by Natalie Zepp to Michelle McCord, both employees of the apartment complex where Ms. Baldwin and Mr. Thomas shared an apartment. Defense counsel made hearsay objections, not only to the introduction of the e-mail as a whole, but also to the introduction of statements within the e-mail that Ms. Zepp, the employee who wrote the e-mail, reported Ms. Baldwin made to her.[60]

This is what the Zepp e-mail said: "This resident called and says that *she's had someone (Steven Thomas) living in her ap[artmen]t for the past year that is not on the lease* and . . . wants him out but *he refuses to leave.* What can we do? [H]er number is _____, but I asked that she call you back tomorrow morning as well."[61] The italic portions of the e-mail are the parts the defense particularly objected to, as inadmissible hearsay.

The rest of the e-mail consists of statements describing matters of which Ms. Zepp had firsthand knowledge and could, had the prosecution so desired, have testified about at trial. These portions of the e-mail were admitted under the business records exception to the hearsay rule. The exception is codified in rule 803(6) of the Federal Rules of Evidence and in similar state rules. The rationale "behind the business records exception is that such documents have a high degree of reliability because businesses have incentives to keep accurate records."[62]

> In the *Thomas* case, Michelle McCord, testified at trial that one of her duties as the property manager of Campus Walk Apartments was to keep track of records pertaining to the individual apartments. She inspected the e-mail written by Ms. Zepp, and testified that it was a record kept in the ordinary course of business at Campus Walk Apartments. She testified that the record was made at or near the time the information it contained was provided by a person with knowledge. Finally, she testified it was a regular practice of Campus Walk Apartments to keep records such as the e-mail. . . . After the trial judge determined that "clearly this e-mail is within the firsthand knowledge of Ms. Zepp" and "it's clearly within her duty to try to assist tenants," the trial judge ruled: "Assuming the other requirements for the business record are met, I will admit that part of the record."[63]

The defense attorney argued that "Ms. Baldwin's statement [to Zepp] constituted a separate layer of hearsay—hearsay within hearsay—which could not come in without qualifying under an exception of its own." In making that argument, he relied on a Florida statute that says, "Hearsay within hearsay is not excluded . . . provided each part of the combined statements conforms with an exception to the hearsay rule."[64]

According to the defense, while the rest of the e-mail could come in under the business records exception, the underlined statements could not; the only way they could come in was if another exception to the hearsay rule applied to these statements—and none did, at least not according to the defense attorney. The prosecution argued that all of the information in the e-mail was "within the personal knowledge of Ms. Zepp," so it did not constitute hearsay within hearsay.

The court of appeals agreed with the defense. It held that the trial court erred in admitting the italicized portions of the e-mail because, while "the employee who wrote [it] had firsthand knowledge of Ms. Baldwin's desire to evict—and could . . . have so testified—there was no evidence she had personal knowledge of any of the surrounding circumstances." As the court explained, the e-mail contained two levels of hearsay:

The e-mail is itself hearsay because it is an out-of-court statement being offered for the truth of the matters asserted.... It is Ms. Zepp's account of what Ms. Baldwin told her. Its accuracy depends both on Ms. Zepp's veracity and on Ms. Baldwin's veracity. Within the e-mail—the first tier of hearsay—lies another layer of hearsay: the statement made by Ms. Baldwin to Ms. Zepp, viz., "that she's had someone (Steven Thomas) living in her ap[artmen]t for the past year that is not on the lease and ... refuses to leave." There was no evidence Ms. Zepp had firsthand knowledge of these matters. Rather, her "knowledge" that Ms. Baldwin "had someone (Steven Thomas) living in her ap[artmen]t for the past year... and ... refuses to leave" was hearsay. She was recounting statements she said she heard Ms. Baldwin make. Ms. Baldwin's statements were not ... business records themselves. As recounted by Ms. Zepp, they were not admissible, because they did not qualify for an exception to the hearsay rule in their own right.[65]

The court of appeals also held that the admission of the hearsay was a reversible error, that is, required the reversal of Thomas's murder conviction:

> The hearsay was used ... to prove motive, a critical component of the State's case.... The State used hearsay to show a possible reason for Mr. Thomas's wanting to kill his live-in girlfriend of four years. No other evidence tended to show that Ms. Baldwin had asked him to move out and that he had refused to leave.
>
> Not even Ms. Baldwin's "best friend ... testified ... to any problems in the couple's relationship." ... Because there is a reasonable possibility that admission of Ms. Baldwin's hearsay statement that "[Mr. Thomas] refuses to leave" contributed to Mr. Thomas's conviction, we are constrained to reverse for a new trial.[66]

The *Thomas* case illustrates the complexity—and the importance—of the rules governing the use of hearsay not only in cybercrime cases but also in any case in which one side relies on digital evidence.

Text Messages

In a 2010 Arizona case, Rodolfo Chavez raised the applicability of the hearsay rules in appealing his "conviction and sentence for Possession of Dangerous Drugs" in violation of Arizona law.[67] The case arose when police officers stopped Chavez at

approximately midnight near Southern and Central Avenues in Phoe-
nix because the license plate on the vehicle he was driving was not valid
for highway use. They arrested him when they discovered he was driving on a suspended license. In [searching] the vehicle, police discovered a baggie containing 790 milligrams of methamphetamine between
the driver's seat and central console, a green camouflage bag containing
a trace amount of methamphetamine and baggies (used for packaging
drugs) on the floor in front of the passenger seat, and two cell phones
on the front passenger seat. They also discovered a wallet, containing
nearly $1,300 in various denominations, on the driver's seat.[68]

Officers later "retrieved text messages from the two cell phones found
in the vehicle," and the prosecution decided to use them as evidence at
trial. Chavez moved to suppress the messages, claiming they constituted
inadmissible hearsay because

> "they're statements to prove the fact of the matter asserted, and that
> is that [Chavez] was in possession and was attempting to sell drugs."
> The State argued that the text messages were not hearsay because they
> were statements of co-conspirators in furtherance of a conspiracy to
> sell drugs. The court agreed with the State. . . . At trial, an officer read
> to the jury six of the text messages, and testified that the messages were
> requests to purchase illegal drugs.[69]

The text messages at issue were as follows:

1. "Can you deliver a 'T' to the house?"
2. "Hey, it's Mike. If you're up, can you at least let me get a 30 or 20,
   since you don't want to fix that thing from earlier?"
3. "It's Jessica. Just letting you know that I need a 60."
4. "What up? I was wondering if you can drop a little something off?"
5. "I just need a half."
6. "Can you deliver a 50-shot?"

The officer testified that the numbers in the text messages referred
to a dollar amount of drugs, and "T" was a common term for a "teener,"
or 1.8 grams of illegal drugs.[70]

After being convicted and sentenced to seven years in prison, Chavez
appealed, again claiming the text messages were inadmissible hearsay. In

his brief on appeal, Chavez explained why, in his opinion, the messages were hearsay:

> The text messages were assertions by the out-of-court sender that the recipient had drugs for sale and were offered by the state as evidence that [Chavez] possessed drugs for sale. . . .
>
> A statement is defined as "an oral or written assertion." [Arizona Rules of Evidence 801(a)]. . . . Thus, "the effect of the definition of 'statement' is to exclude from the operation of the hearsay rule all evidence of conduct, verbal or nonverbal, not intended as an assertion."[71]

The prosecution argued, in response, that none of the text messages were intended

> by the declarants as "assertions" of fact and *none* were offered to prove the truth of the words texted. All but three of the text messages were questions which simply do not amount to assertions of fact. . . . Moreover, they were *not* statements "which could be proven as true or false." . . .
>
> [Chavez's] response to "Samantha," "Give me 30 minutes," was not an assertion of fact, [and] was not offered for the truth of the matter asserted. . . . The text "It's Jessica. Just letting you know that I need a 60" and, "I just need a half" were clearly not offered to prove the truth of the matters asserted (that these persons actually "needed" a specific amount of illegal drugs), but as evidence of [Chavez's] intent to sell illegal drugs. . . .
>
> Therefore, the text messages simply do not qualify as "hearsay."[72]

The Arizona Court of Appeals agreed with the prosecution. It found that the text messages were not offered to prove the truth of the matter asserted, that is, that the

> prospective buyers wanted to purchase drugs from Chavez. Rather, they were offered as circumstantial evidence that Chavez had drugs for sale. . . . The fact that multiple persons sent messages asking for drugs further supported an inference that those persons believed that Chavez had drugs for sale. We agree with the courts outside this jurisdiction that have followed this . . . reasoning in rejecting hearsay objections to out-of-court statements from unidentified persons asking to buy drugs from a defendant.[73]

The court therefore upheld Chavez's conviction and sentence.

As these cases illustrate, the hearsay rules are often at issue in cyber-crime prosecutions. The reason hearsay issues arise so often in cybercrime cases is that so much of our interaction online—for example, e-mails, text messages, instant messages, tweets, blog posts, and so forth—involve communications that at least arguably come within the scope of the rules governing the use of hearsay. Courts are, therefore, increasingly having to decide how to apply evidentiary rules that long antedate cyberspace to electronic communications.

Investigative Challenges and Practical Issues

This section reviews some of the practical problems state and federal pros-ecutors confront in dealing with cybercrime investigations.

DIFFICULTIES IN PROSECUTING CYBERCRIMES

Prosecuting cybercrimes requires expertise not generally taught in law schools.[74] One challenge chief prosecutors confront, therefore, is provid-ing at least some of their assistant prosecutors with a grounding in the essentials of digital evidence and computer forensics.

This challenge has its own problematic aspect: given their career paths (and, perhaps, relative maturity), chief prosecutors are likely to have spent their careers dealing with traditional crimes and so may not be particu-larly familiar with cybercrime investigations and digital evidence issues. Chief prosecutors, then, must overcome their unfamiliarity with cyber-crime and digital evidence and realize their need for assistant prosecutors who have the expertise to deal with cybercrime cases.

Chief prosecutors must also find the funding to provide assistant pros-ecutors with training on cybercrime. And they must balance the need to develop and maintain trained cybercrime prosecutors against the persist-ing need to prosecute the traditional crimes that continue to be commit-ted in every U.S. state.

That brings up a related issue: time. Local prosecutors have heavy case loads; it is not unusual for an assistant prosecuting attorney to deal with the disposition of ten to twenty cases in a day. Since cybercrime cases present difficult legal, scientific, and technical issues, the caseload of most assistant prosecutors makes it extraordinarily difficult for them to dedicate the time and energy they need to prosecute crimes involving digital evidence and, often, remote perpetrators.

And that brings up a distinct but related funding issue: the need for funding to pursue cybercrime prosecutions. Assume, for example, that an assistant prosecutor in Goshen County, Indiana, has a case in which a hacker used an Internet service provider (ISP) based in India to attack a computer in that county. The hacker has been charged with violating Indiana's unauthorized access to computers statute. To win the case, the assistant prosecutor must prove that the hacker used the Indian ISP, but to prove that the prosecutor needs the testimony of a representative of the ISP—and it will cost at least ten thousand dollars to bring such a representative from India to testify at trial. That ten thousand dollars will probably constitute a significant share of the funds the prosecutor's office has available for trial expenses for the entire fiscal year, which means the chief prosecutor will no doubt have to decide whether to allocate these funds in the pursuit of this one, nonviolent offense case or decline to do so and effectively sabotage this prosecution.

A final practical issue is retention: the assistant prosecutors who are the most likely to be familiar with computer technology and become cybercrime prosecutors tend to be among the younger members of a chief prosecutor's office. They are also the most likely, of their peers, to move into the private sector after only a few years, as their trial expertise and familiarity with digital evidence make them attractive candidates for private-sector law firms and businesses. Moving from the public to the private sectors is not unique to state prosecutors' offices; something similar occurs in federal prosecutors' offices and among state and federal law enforcement. The private sector, after all, tends to pay much more than state or federal governments.

APPLYING COMPUTER FORENSICS

As most people probably know from movies and CSI-type television shows, forensic science—or "forensics"—involves applying scientific and other expertise to issues that arise in the course of litigation, such as whether particular items are relevant evidence to charges in a criminal case. Forensic science is divided into a number of subdivisions, one of which is computer forensics. Computer forensics involves "the location, examination, identification, collection, preservation and analysis of computer systems and electronically stored information," or digital evidence.[75]

In one sense, the examination of a computer by a computer forensics expert is analogous to a law enforcement officer's conducting a search of a home or office. Both scrutinize a defined context in an effort to identify and recover evidence of a crime. In another sense, though, the two are very different:

> In contrast to physical searches, digital evidence searches generally occur at both a "logical" . . . level and a "physical" level. The distinction between physical searches and logical searches is fundamental in computer forensics: while a logical search is based on the file systems found on the hard drive as presented by the operating system, a physical search identifies and recovers data across the entire physical drive without regard to the file system.[76]

Another difference is that the computer forensic expert will not search the actual computer (or other digital device) that is the focus of the investigation. The expert will, instead, make a "bitstream copy" of the computer's hard drive and use the copy for the analysis.[77] A bitstream copy "duplicates every bit and byte on the target drive . . . in exactly the order they appear on the original."[78] The bitstream copy will be saved as a "read only" file, so that analyzing the copy will not alter the data it contains.[79]

Working from the copy also preserves the original computer's hard drive (or other storage media) intact, available for use at trial, if and when charges are brought against the owner or user of the computer. Experts who work in a state or federal computer forensics laboratory usually analyze the bitstream copies; most police departments do not have the technology or the expertise needed to analyze digital media, or the funds needed to acquire and maintain both.[80]

The process of analyzing a bitstream copy of a hard drive is exacting and time consuming,[81] a state of affairs exacerbated by the ever-increasing size and complexity of computers and other digital devices. Other factors are the limited number of qualified computer forensic analysts and the fact that increased importance of digital evidence means computer forensic laboratories are backlogged, often substantially. Months will elapse from the time law enforcement officers seize a computer to the time when a computer forensics expert examines it.

This has certain implications for the criminal justice system. For one thing, it means a suspect whose computer has been seized pursuant to a search warrant will have to wait months before he or she learns what the forensic analysis has revealed about the contents of the computer and what, if any, charges will be based on the results of that analysis. It also means that, once charged, a suspect will be entitled to have his or her own computer forensic expert examine the digital media at issue, in an effort to refute the conclusions reached by the prosecution's analyst. Both elongate the processes of initiating a criminal case and pursuing it to a conclusion and, in so doing, increase the burden on the justice system, especially the courts.

The need to ensure the defense has an adequate opportunity to examine the digital media at issue in an attempt to refute, or replicate, the results reported by the prosecution expert can also increase the expense involved in a prosecution. The court might need to appoint, and pay, the defense expert.[82] The court might also have to ensure that the defense expert can work with the bitstream copy provided by the government.

In *State v. Dingman*, for example, an appellate court reversed Robert Dingman's conviction for money laundering because the trial judge did not order the prosecution to give the defense expert a copy of Dingman's hard drive in a "software format" the expert could use.[83] Neither Dingman's expert nor his attorney had access to EnCase—the computer forensics software primarily used by law enforcement.[84] The expert, who worked for an agency that provided experts for court-appointed defense attorneys, explained that the office could not afford to purchase EnCase and the training required to use it. She also explained that the software her agency used could not open "many of the files" on the bitstream copy provided by the prosecution, which meant she was not able to conduct an adequate analysis of the copy. The appellate court held that the trial judge erred in only requiring the prosecution to give the defense expert an EnCase-generated copy of the hard drive and therefore reversed the conviction.[85]

The complexity of the evidence-gathering-and-analysis processes, coupled with the funding and personnel constraints under which computer forensic laboratories operate, transforms cybercrime investigations into elaborate, even daunting, undertakings. Forensic analysis—of DNA, ballistics, fingerprints, and other tangible evidence—has long been an established feature of criminal prosecutions. But while physical forensic analysis can be a complex process, it pales in comparison to digital forensic analysis for one very important reason: physical evidence is generally stable; it can be contaminated, but contaminating physical evidence is both more difficult and more likely to be discovered than contaminating digital evidence.

Digital evidence is ephemeral and malleable, an unstable agglomeration of bits and bytes; this aspect makes the forensic analysis of the evidence critical, for both the prosecution and the defense. Because that analysis is so time consuming and requires evolving expertise, law enforcement laboratories are struggling to keep up with the current volume of cases. It is only reasonable to expect that computer technology will be increasingly used in criminal activity, which means digital evidence will become an even more common aspect of criminal cases. It is also reasonable to assume that computer technology will continue to evolve in complexity and sophistication, which means the digital forensics process will become even more involved and time consuming.

If the federal and state governments are able to provide increased funding for computer forensic laboratories and court-appointed experts, this state of affairs should not seriously impede the criminal justice process. If, as seems more likely, such funding will not be available, the process may adapt to the burden digital evidence imposes on the criminal justice system, perhaps in ways that undermine the efficacy of that system.[86] Prosecutors could, for example, triage digital evidence cases, giving priority to those that involve the infliction of particularly serious harms and either assigning the others to a residual category in which the computer forensic analysis will be conducted if and when time permits or simply declining to pursue them. The situation might, on the other hand, be alleviated by the emergence of new, highly automated computer forensic techniques that would alleviate the staffing and training burdens that currently plague computer forensics laboratories.

The use of such techniques could, though, create new problems: defense attorneys could argue that they have no way to ascertain the validity of the results produced by an automated forensic process. They could base their argument on a criminal defendant's right to "confront" witnesses against him or her; the premise is that cross-examination is the best way to test a witness's credibility.[87] A defense attorney could therefore argue that the automated forensic process is, in effect, a "witness" against his client and point out the impossibility of cross-examining a process. While that argument may seem far-fetched, in 2009 the Supreme Court held that a defendant's Sixth Amendment right to confront witnesses against him or her was violated when the trial court admitted "certificates of state laboratory analysts" stating that, based on their analysis, the substance found in the defendant's vehicle was cocaine.[88] The court held that, for the results of the analysis to be admissible as evidence against him, the analysts would have to testify at his new trial, if one were held.[89]

As a law review article points out, the holding in the *Melendez-Diaz* case applies with equal force to computer forensics analysis.[90] If it applies to human analysts, it may also apply to automated analyses,[91] if and when they emerge as a factor in this area.

This chapter examined some of the challenges prosecutors, defense attorneys, and law enforcement officers confront in cybercrime cases. The next chapter continues the review of these issues, focusing on the concerns of privacy in cybercrime investigations.

>chapter:6

CYBERCRIME INVESTIGATIONS
AND PRIVACY

Police are charged with investigating crimes, identifying the perpetrators, and apprehending them. Law enforcement's ability to successfully carry out these tasks depends on the police's ability to collect information about completed or contemplated crimes.

An effective law enforcement reaction is essential to discourage enough prospective offenders from committing crimes that a society will be able to maintain the level of internal order it needs to survive and prosper. Modern law enforcement is, in part, predicated on the premise that potential offenders tend to weigh their chances of being caught when they are deciding whether to commit a crime.[1]

The need for an effective law enforcement reaction also encompasses a related task: preventing crimes from being committed. In addition to investigating completed crimes, therefore, law enforcement officers also work to identify crimes that are in the planning and preparation stage so they can interrupt the would-be criminals before they can inflict actual harm on someone or something.

Citizens want police to collect information and solve or prevent as many crimes as possible. Also, though, citizens want police to stay within certain limits as they collect information; they do not want police to violate individual privacy, at least not unless the officers comply with certain legal requirements.

This chapter examines the constraints U.S. law imposes on officers as they investigate cybercrimes.

Sovereigns, Law, and Law Enforcement

Before analyzing the constraints U.S. law places on criminal investigators, it is useful to review the allocation of sovereignty in the United States and how that allocation impacts the processes of adopting and enforcing criminal laws.

SOVEREIGNS AND LAWS

The United States is a federal system, which means each citizen is bound by the laws adopted by Congress and by those adopted by the legislature of the state in which he or she resides. If the laws adopted by state legislatures could trump the laws adopted by Congress, the United States would descend into legal anarchy. To avoid that, Article VI of the Constitution says the Constitution "and the laws of the United States which shall be made in pursuance thereof" are "the supreme law of the land." The Constitution also makes it clear that the federal government must respect the states and their laws: the Tenth Amendment says the "powers not delegated to the United States by the Constitution, nor prohibited by it to the States, are reserved to the States." And Article IV of the Constitution ensures that the states respect each other's laws, that is, must give "full faith and credit" to the "public acts . . . and judicial proceedings of every other state."

Congress can only adopt laws that are authorized by the explicit language of the Constitution or by powers it delegates to the federal government. States can adopt laws that go beyond the provisions of the Constitution as long as they do not conflict with the Constitution or are otherwise illegal.

LAW ENFORCEMENT

The process of enforcing criminal law in the United States mirrors the allocation of sovereignty under the nation's federal system. In other words, it takes place at both the federal and state levels.

Federal law enforcement is a recent addition. Until 1865, the federal government relied on "private guards" for its "occasional police work."[2] After the Civil War, Congress created the Secret Service to deal with a "crisis of false currency,"[3] and in 1913 made it responsible for protecting the president.[4] The Secret Service was the only federal law enforcement agency until 1908, when the Bureau of Investigation was created as part of the U.S. Department of Justice; its responsibilities expanded along with federal criminal law, and by 1935 it had become the Federal Bureau of Investigation (FBI).[5]

Federal agencies actually play a small role in enforcing criminal law in the United States. Until the twentieth century, there were very few federal crimes.[6] That changed as federal criminal law expanded to meet the challenges of the "culture of mobility" that resulting from the use of automobiles.[7] State criminal statutes "became less and less effective" as criminals exploited state borders to avoid being apprehended. Congress responded by adopting statutes that federalized what had been traditional state crimes, such as bank robbery, car theft, and kidnapping. That began a process that continued for decades and, indeed, continues today.

Congress's expanding federal criminal law did not alter the Constitutional allocation of responsibility for dealing with crime; historically, law enforcement was handled primarily by the states.[8] There is therefore a large network of state and local law enforcement agencies; in 2004, there were 17,876 state and local agencies in the United States, which were staffed by 731,903 full-time officers.[9]

Since state and local enforcement is the default, there are fewer federal officers. In 2004, there were 106,354 federal agents, 40,408 of whom were assigned to criminal investigation and law enforcement duty.[10] FBI agents accounted for 12,414 of these agents and Immigration and Customs Enforcement for 10,691;[11] the other federal agencies are much smaller. The Drug Enforcement Administration (DEA) has 5,235 agents, the Secret Service has 3,200, and the Bureau of Alcohol, Tobacco, and Firearms has 2,400.[12] Each agency is responsible for investigating the crimes that come within its distinct mandate; the DEA, for example, concentrates on drug-related crimes.

Since the crimes federal agencies investigate are for the most part committed within the United States, local, county, and state agencies can have concurrent jurisdiction over them. When that happens, the federal agency will claim priority if the crime involves matters of particular federal concern, such as counterfeiting. "Beyond this sphere, in the areas traditionally policed by the States," the determination of whether a case will be investigated by federal agents or by state officers is usually a matter of negotiation.[13] One of the issues that can factor into such a negotiation is resources; federal agencies can usually devote more time, money, personnel, and expertise to a case than can their state counterparts.[14]

Privacy for U.S. Citizens

The Constitution does not address privacy, as such, but two of its amendments do concern privacy. As the sections below explain, the Fourth Amendment directly addresses police invasions of privacy while the Fifth Amendment addresses privacy indirectly, by creating a privilege not to cooperate with law enforcement under certain circumstances.

There are federal and state statutes that deal with privacy, but this analysis will touch on them only briefly, for two reasons. One is that the statutes either implement the Fourth and Fifth Amendment, so reviewing them would be superfluous, or are state laws that provide more protection than either or both amendments. State statutes that provide more protection than the Fourth or Fifth Amendments only apply to police conduct that occurs in the state that adopted such a law. They are therefore of limited applicability.

The other reason is that statutes are much more fragile than constitutional provisions. It is not particularly difficult for Congress or a state legislature to modify or even repeal a statute. It is, on the other hand, extraordinarily difficult to modify the U.S. Constitution and the amendments that have been added since its adoption.

The Fourth Amendment

The Fourth Amendment states that the "right of the people to be secure in their persons, houses, papers, and effects, against unreasonable searches and seizures, shall not be violated, and no Warrants shall issue, but upon probable cause ... particularly describing the place to be searched, and the persons or things to be seized."

Like much of U.S. law, the Fourth Amendment derives from English common law. Common law criminalized burglary and trespass.[15] These laws were directed at private citizens because law enforcement searches of private property were almost unknown until the printing press arrived in England. Concerned about "dangerous" speech, for example, heresy and political dissent, English courts authorized law enforcement officers to search homes and "any other place where they suspected a violation of the laws . . . to be taking place" and seize the evidence they found.[16] This led to the general warrant, which issued without probable cause and gave officers the authority to "search wherever their suspicions may chance to fall."[17]

Citizens whose homes were subjected to random searches sued the officers for trespass, and won.[18] English courts held that, like a private citizen, a law enforcement officer could be held civilly liable for trespass if he entered someone's property without "lawful authority."[19] The difference was that a law enforcement officer could rely on a warrant, as well as on a property owner's consent, as authorization for an entry.[20]

General warrants were used—and abused—in the American colonies prior to the Revolution. The colonists challenged the warrants in court but lost; the resentment generated from this was a driving factor in the Revolution and in the adoption of the Bill of Rights.[21] The Fourth Amendment was intended to protect citizens' privacy by ensuring officers could not use general warrants. General warrants gave officers unlimited discretion to search wherever they liked, as often as they liked. Fourth Amendment search warrants limit an officer's discretion by requiring "probable cause" for the search. To search a person or place, an officer must cite "specific, articulable facts" that indicate evidence of a crime will be found at that place or on that person.[22]

For over a century, courts had little difficulty applying he provisions of the Fourth Amendment because the conduct officers engaged in was essentially indistinguishable from what officers had been doing for centuries: searching homes, businesses, and people. The first case to raise a more difficult privacy issue was *Ex parte Jackson*, an appeal from a conviction for sending "a circular concerning a lottery" through the mail.[23] In 1876, Congress targeted crooked lotteries by making it a federal crime to use the mail to send "circulars concerning lotteries."[24] Jackson argued that federal agents violated his rights under the Fourth Amendment by searching his mail without a warrant, and the Supreme Court agreed, noting that a distinction existed between "what is intended to be kept free from inspection, such as letters, and sealed packages . . . and what is open to inspection, such as newspapers . . . and other printed matter, purposely left in a condition to be examined. Letters and sealed packages . . . are as fully guarded from . . . inspection, except as to their outward form and weight, *as if they were retained by the parties forwarding them in their own domiciles.*"[25] In *Jackson*, the Supreme Court first articulated the principle that the Fourth Amendment does more than prevent police from breaking into homes and searching them without a warrant. It would not address the issue again for roughly half a century.

TELEPHONES AND THE FOURTH AMENDMENT

Alexander Graham Bell invented the telephone in 1876; the technology spread rapidly, and by the 1920s telephones were a routine feature of life, even in many rural areas.[26] Police had begun tapping telephone conversations—without first obtaining a search warrant—in the 1890s.[27] They claimed there was nothing improper about this because, at the time, people had to use operators to place calls, and operators could (and did) listen in on phone conversations.[28] The police, in other words, regarded phone conversations as analogous to unsealed mail, that is, as outside the scope of the Fourth Amendment.

Olmstead: Wiretapping Not a Search

By the 1920s, automatic switching systems had eliminated the need to rely on an operator to place a call.[29] With automated switching, the phone company's technology connects the call; no human is involved. People therefore began to assume phone calls were private.[30] Many—including some engaged in illicit activities—began using phones more and more, which eventually gave rise to a Fourth Amendment issue that went to the U.S. Supreme Court.

On January 16, 1920, the manufacture, sale, and importation of "intoxicating liquors" became illegal in the United States.[31] Ironically, Prohibition created an increased demand for liquor and a new profession: bootlegger.

When Prohibition went into effect, Roy "Big Boy" Olmstead was a lieutenant in the Seattle Police Department.[32] Attracted by the money bootleggers made, he became the head of an organization that smuggled alcohol into the United States from Canada. Prohibition agents investigating Olmstead's organization put wiretaps on phones used by his gang, including the phone in Olmstead's home. Agents listened to conversations and used what they heard to get a warrant to search Olmstead's home. In 1924, they raided his home and seized records; on January 25, Olmstead and eighty-nine others were indicted on two counts of violating federal Prohibition laws.

Olmstead went to trial and was convicted. He appealed a single issue all the way to the U.S. Supreme Court: whether the agents' eavesdropping on telephone conversations originating in his home violated the Fourth Amendment.[33] Olmstead argued that what the agents did was a "search" because they listened to what would otherwise have been conversations that occurred in private places. He claimed the agents, in effect, "searched" his home without having first obtained a search warrant.

Unfortunately for Olmstead, the justices who comprised the Supreme Court were born and educated in the nineteenth century and therefore did not understand how to analyze technology's impact on traditional conceptions of privacy. A majority of justices held that the use of technology was irrelevant because the Fourth Amendment should be "construed in the light of what was deemed an unreasonable search . . . when it was adopted." They held that, since the agents did not physically enter Olmstead's home, there was no search, noting that the "wires beyond his house, and messages while passing over them, are not within the protection of the Fourth Amendment."

Justice Louis Brandeis dissented. Like his colleagues, Brandeis was a product of the nineteenth century; unlike them, he grasped the significance of technology. He noted that, when the Fourth Amendment was adopted, the only way the government could "secure possession of papers and other articles incident to [one's] private life" was by "breaking and entry" into their home or office. And he explained that, in applying the Constitution, the Court's focus should not be on what has been, but on

"what may be." The progress of science in furnishing the government with means of espionage is not likely to stop with wiretapping. Ways may . . . be developed by which the government, without removing papers from secret drawers, can reproduce them in court, and by which it will be enabled to expose . . . the most intimate occurrences of the home. . . . "That places the liberty of every man in the hands of every petty officer."[34]

Brandeis's views did not prevail, Olmstead went to jail, and for the next almost forty years, telephone conversations were not protected by the Fourth Amendment.

Katz: Wiretapping a Search

In 1965, the FBI was investigating Los Angeles bookie Charles Katz for violating federal gambling law.[35] As agents surveilled Katz, they realized he used three phone booths on Sunset Boulevard to make calls concerning bets; the agents put microphones and recording devices on top of all the booths and recorded Katz's calls.

After being charged with violating federal gambling crimes, Katz moved to suppress the intercepted calls, claiming the interceptions were illegal searches under the Fourth Amendment. The trial court denied the motion, and the Ninth Circuit Court of Appeals affirmed the denial; like the majority of the *Olmstead* justices, these judges found there was no search because the agents put the recording devices on the outside of the phone booths. Since the agents did not trespass into the phone booths when Katz was in them, these judges held there had been no Fourth Amendment searches.

The Supreme Court took the case and disagreed with the lower courts. It noted that those judges' concern with whether there had been a trespass into a physical space focused on the wrong issue because "the Fourth Amendment protects people, not places."[36] The Court explained that "what a person knowingly exposes to the public, even in his own home or office, is not a subject of Fourth Amendment protection . . . but what he seeks to preserve as private, even in an area accessible to the public, may be constitutionally protected." In a concurring opinion, Justice John Harlan explained how courts are to determine whether something is in fact private under the Fourth Amendment:

> There is a twofold requirement, first that a person has exhibited an actual (subjective) expectation of privacy and, second, that the expectation be one that society is prepared to recognize as "reasonable." Thus a man's home is . . . a place where he expects privacy. . . . On the other hand, conversations in the open would not be protected against being

overheard, for the expectation of privacy under the circumstances would be unreasonable.[37]

The *Katz* Court found Charles Katz had a reasonable expectation of privacy in the phone booths: he believed his calls were private because he went into the phone booth and closed the door; the Court also found that we, as a society, would consider that belief to be reasonable. The Court therefore overruled *Olmstead* and intercepting telephone calls became a search under the Fourth Amendment, which means officers must obtain a search warrant before conducting such an interception.

Smith: Third-party Records Not Private

Katz was the first of two subsequent decisions the Supreme Court issued on the Fourth Amendment's applicability to telephone technology. The other came in 1979.[38]

On March 5, 1976, Baltimore resident Patricia McDonough was robbed; after reporting the crime to the police, she began to receive "threatening and obscene" calls from a man who said he was the robber. A few days later, police saw a man matching her description of the robber driving a car that matched her description of the robber's car. They traced the car to Michael Smith and had the telephone company install "a pen register at its central offices to record the numbers dialed from the telephone" at Smith's home. The officers did not get a search warrant authorizing installation of the pen register; they simply asked the phone company to install it, and the phone company complied. The pen register did not—could not—capture the contents of the calls Smith made; all it could do was to record the numbers he dialed from his home phone.

The day after the pen register was installed, Smith called Patricia and it recorded his dialing her number. Police used that and other evidence to get a warrant to search Smith's home, where they found evidence implicating him in the robbery. After he was indicted for robbery, Smith moved to suppress the evidence recorded by the pen register on the grounds that using it to discover the phone numbers he dialed from home was a search under the Fourth Amendment. Like Katz, Smith lost at the lower court level and appealed to the Supreme Court, which took the case.

Here, Smith lost again. The Court applied the standard Justice Harlan outlined in *Katz* and found he did not have a reasonable expectation of privacy in numbers he dialed from his phone. It found Smith could not have believed the numbers were private because he knew he was "giving" them to the phone company: "All telephone users realize that they must 'convey' phone numbers to the telephone company, since it is through telephone company switching equipment that their calls are completed."

The Court also held that, even if Smith believed the numbers were private, this was not a belief society accepted objectively reasonable: "This Court consistently has held that a person has no legitimate expectation of privacy in information he voluntarily turns over to third parties." In making that statement, the Court cited the *Miller* case, in which it held that bank customers have no Fourth Amendment expectation of privacy in information they share with their bank: "The depositor takes the risk, in revealing his affairs to another, that the information will be conveyed by that person to the Government."[39]

The *Katz-Smith* decisions mean that the Fourth Amendment's applicability to telephones (and other technology) is governed by a dichotomy: If the government engages in conduct analogous to what it did in *Katz*, that would be a Fourth Amendment search. If the government uses the modern equivalent of pen registers and trap and trace devices (which record the "originating telephone numbers of incoming" calls[40]) to record the phone numbers John Doe calls and the phone numbers of those who call Doe, that is not a search under *Smith*.

The Supreme Court has so far never revisited its decision in *Smith*. The *Katz-Smith* dichotomy has become increasingly difficult to apply as technology has advanced. Some of the difficulties involve advanced telephone technology, but most involve newer communications technologies, such as e-mail.

Before examining these difficulties, it is necessary to briefly review two federal statutes that codified and, to some extent, expanded upon the holdings in *Katz* and *Smith*. They reveal how Congress responded to both decisions.

Legislation: The Wiretap Act

In 1968, Congress adopted the Omnibus Crime Control and Safe Streets Act, Title III of which was intended to implement "comprehensive, fair and effective reform" in the standards that protect privacy.[41] One provision of Title III—which was codified as 18 U.S. Code section 2511—

made it unlawful to "intercept" a wire or oral communication without complying with requirements set out elsewhere in Title III. Section 2510 of Title 18 of the U.S. Code defined "wire communication" as "all communications carried by a common carrier . . . through our Nation's communications network" and "oral communication" as "any oral communication uttered by a person exhibiting an expectation that such communication is not subject to interception under circumstances justifying such expectation."

Another provision of Title III—18 U.S. Code section 2518—sets out the procedures law enforcement officers must follow to intercept wire or oral communications without violating 18 U.S. Code section 2511. Under section 2518, an officer seeking an order authorizing such an interception follows a procedure similar to, but more demanding than, the procedure officers use to obtain a search warrant. The officer must submit the following to the judge who is asked to issue the authorization: (1) a "full and complete" statement of the facts the officer believes justify the interception, that is, establish probable cause that the intercept will provide evidence of a crime; (2) details as to what federal crime "has been, is being or is about to be committed"; (3) a "particular description of the type of communications" to be intercepted; (4) the identity of the person whose calls are to be intercepted; (5) a "full and complete statement" as to whether other investigative procedures have been tried and failed or why they "appear to be unlikely to succeed if tried" or "too dangerous" to try; and (6) a statement of the period of time for which the interception is to be maintained.[42] The first four requirements track the Fourth Amendment; an officer seeking a warrant to search for physical evidence must submit an application that sufficiently provides this information to the judge from whom the officer seeks the search warrant.[43] The last two exceed what is required to obtain a warrant under the Fourth Amendment and are therefore purely statutory. Congress included them to provide additional protection in this sensitive area.

Title III was only concerned with telephone calls. But by the mid-1980s, it had become apparent that new modes of communication—notably e-mail—could also be intercepted, which created a new threat to privacy. To remedy that, Congress adopted the Electronic Communications Privacy Act (ECPA) in 1986.[44] The relevant provisions appear in two sections of ECPA: Title I protects communications in transit (wiretap act); Title II "contains the Stored Communications Act (SCA), which protects communications held in electronic storage."[45]

Title I expanded the wiretap provisions of Title III of the Omnibus Crime Control and Safe Streets Act by applying them to "electronic communications," as well as to wire or oral communications.[46] Title III, as amended by ECPA, defines electronic communication as "any transfer of signs, signals, writing, images, sounds, data, or intelligence of any nature transmitted ... by a wire, radio, electromagnetic, photoelectronic or photooptical system that affects interstate or foreign commerce."[47] Under the post-ECPA version of Title III, law enforcement officers must follow the Title III procedures outlined above to intercept e-mails and other electronic communications; under Title III, intercepting a communication requires that it be captured while it is "in flight," that is, while it is traveling from one person to another.[48] The requirement that a communication be captured in flight derives from *Katz*; Title III was prompted by the decision in *Katz*, which dealt with intercepting a phone call. Since phone conversations are transient, the only way to capture the content of such a conversation is to record it—intercept it—as it takes place.

That is not true of electronic communications. Like snail mail, e-mails and other electronic communications travel from sender to recipient and then come to rest in the latter's in-box; and like snail mail, e-mails and other electronic communications can be read once they have come to rest, which means their contents can be captured long after a communication has traveled from sender to recipient. In an effort to address this aspect of electronic communications, Title II of ECPA—the SCA—made it a federal crime to unlawfully access an "electronic communication while it is in electronic storage."[49] The crime was codified as 18 U.S. Code section 2701(a), which makes such access illegal unless it is authorized by the Internet service provider, by the owner of the account in which the communication is stored, or by one of the procedures set out in 18 U.S. Code section 2703, another provision of the SCA.

Under section 2703, an officer must obtain a search warrant to access the contents of e-mail that has been stored with an Internet service provider "for one hundred and eighty days or less."[50] An officer can use a search warrant, a subpoena, or a court order to access the contents of e-mail that has been stored "for more than one hundred and eighty days."[51] Subpoenas and court orders are issued without a showing of probable cause, which means they do not comply with the Fourth Amendment.

The distinction between e-mails stored for more or less than 180 days may seem peculiar and arbitrary, and it is, given today's technology. This aspect of the SCA reflects how people used e-mail in the 1980s. Congress found that, at that time,

> "most—if not all—electronic communications systems . . . only keep copies of messages for a few months." [Congress] concluded that beyond this point, the storage is more akin to that of business records maintained by a third party, which are accorded less protection. This is . . . because when the Act was drafted, users generally needed to take affirmative steps to move e-mail messages they wanted to preserve into storage in order for e-mail providers to save them beyond 180 days.[52]

ECPA, then, is based on the assumptions that (1) e-mail stored for 180 days or less is analogous to a letter in the process of traveling through the U.S. mail, while (2) e-mail stored for more than 180 days is analogous to the phone numbers at issue in *Smith*. As is noted below, since this dichotomy does not reflect the realities of modern electronic communication, courts have struggled with whether the Fourth Amendment applies to such communications.

COMPUTER TECHNOLOGY AND THE FOURTH AMENDMENT

Computer technology raises a number of Fourth Amendment issues, but none of them are more intimately entwined with personal privacy than the Fourth Amendment's applicability to online communications: e-mail and other messages; the comments and information posted on websites; and data generated by online transactions. The sections below examine the Fourth Amendment issues each type of communication presents.

E-mail

Since the same issues arise for other types of electronic communications, and since e-mail has been the primary focus of Fourth Amendment litigation, this analysis concentrates on it. Title III (and similar state statutes) draw what has become an arbitrary distinction between e-mail stored for more or less than 180 days. That distinction is purely a statutory creation; it is not part of Fourth Amendment law.

In determining the extent to which the Fourth Amendment protects e-mail, courts have to decide whether e-mail is analogous to a phone call (*Katz*), a letter (*Jackson*), or sharing phone numbers with the phone company (*Smith*). In making that determination, they must deal with the fact that—like letters and phone calls—e-mails involve two types of information: the contents of the message ("content data") and the data that is used to transmit it from the sender to the recipient ("traffic data").

CONTENT DATA. If e-mail is analogized to a sealed letter, the content data is the substance of the communication—the digital equivalent of what is written on the letter and envelope—and the traffic data is the addressing information used to send it—the digital equivalent of the names and addresses written on the envelope. It follows, then, that under the Court's decision in *Jackson*, the Fourth Amendment protects the contents of an e-mail but not the traffic data used to send it. This would mean that officers cannot access the contents of an e-mail as it is being sent unless they first obtain a search warrant. (E-mails that have arrived and are stored in someone's e-mail account are analyzed separately, below.)

There is, though, a problem with the analogy: in *Jackson*, the Supreme Court emphasized that the Fourth Amendment applies to sealed letters because the sender took steps to prevent postal employees from reading them. This premise is consistent with *Katz*: under *Katz*, the Fourth Amendment protects the contents of sealed letters because by sealing the envelope the sender makes an effort to keep the contents of the letter private and therefore assumes it will not be read by postal employees. The *Jackson* Court also held that the Fourth Amendment does not protect items that are not sealed—newspapers and postcards—because the sender has assumed the risk that others will read them as they travel through the mail.

To be strictly analogous to a letter, then, an e-mail should be sealed, that is, the sender should do something to prevent its being read as it travels to its intended recipient. The only way to seal an e-mail is to encrypt it, but almost no one (outside the military and intelligence communities) encrypts e-mails for two reasons: encrypting e-mail tends to be a complex, cumbersome process; and most Americans assume e-mail is private so there is no need to encrypt it. Most Americans, in other words, assume an e-mail is like a sealed letter; it will not be read by anyone except its intended recipient.

That, however, is not true. Internet service providers (ISPs) can, and do, scan the contents of at least some of the e-mails sent via their systems;[53] the same is true of noncommercial providers, such as universities.[54] E-mail providers screen e-mails in an effort to prevent their systems from being used for illegal purposes, but they are not the only ones who can read e-mails as they travel through a system; the employees of an ISP or other provider can read unencrypted e-mails, just as a postal employee can read a postcard.[55] Some, therefore, claim the Fourth Amendment does not protect unencrypted e-mail. In a recent case, the Justice Department argued that e-mail "resembles less a sealed letter than a postcard amenable to warrantless inspection, because 'its contents are plainly visible to the [ISP], who can access it via its servers at any time.'"[56]

Most Americans may not agree with this view, but it is difficult to distinguish unencrypted e-mail from a postcard. One who sends an unencrypted e-mail has not, as the *Jackson* Court put it, sealed the message to keep it from prying eyes; the sender therefore has, as the *Katz* Court said, assumed the risk that employees of the ISP will read the e-mails. If the Fourth Amendment does not protect the contents of unencrypted e-mail, then ISPs who scan e-mail and find evidence of a crime can turn the e-mails over to law enforcement without the latter's having to obtain a warrant. And if the Fourth Amendment does not apply to unencrypted e-mails, officers could presumably ask an ISP to scan someone's e-mail and report what it finds without getting a search warrant.

The analysis above assumes that the contents of an e-mail are accessed while the e-mail is in transit. Like a phone call or a letter traveling through the mail, the e-mail has been intercepted before it could reach the recipient. As a practical matter, though, officers rarely access the contents of e-mail as it is being transmitted from sender to recipient. The usual practice is to use a search warrant or a Title III subpoena or court order to require the ISP to give the officers access to e-mail stored on the ISP's servers. This creates an issue that does not arise for letters or phone calls: whether the Fourth Amendment protects the contents of e-mails once they arrive at their destination and are stored on the ISP's servers.

This issue does not arise for telephone calls because the only way officers can acquire the contents of a phone call is to capture the conversation as it occurs; the creation and transmission of the content occur simultaneously, and the content exists only momentarily. E-mails, on the other hand, are stored on an ISP's server after they arrive and until they are read, and many people keep read e-mails stored in their account for months or even years. This means the government has an additional way to obtain e-mail content: law enforcement officers can ask an ISP to copy the archived e-mails and give the copies to them. If the Fourth Amendment protects archived e-mails, the officers will have to get a warrant to obtain copies of them; if they are not protected by the Fourth Amendment, the officers can simply ask for copies and the ISP can, if it is so inclined, create them and turn them over. If the ISP refuses, the officers can use a Title III subpoena or court order to obtain the copies.

This was the issue in a case that spent years being litigated in the federal judicial system. It began in 2005, when federal agents investigating Steven Warshak for "mail and wire fraud . . . and related federal offenses" used the SCA to obtain copies of e-mails Warshak left in his Yahoo! account.[57] The agents obtained a court order—under 18 U.S. Code section 2703(d)—that directed the ISP to provide them with copies of the e-mails. Unlike a magistrate issuing a search warrant, the judge who issues such an order does not have to find probable cause to believe the e-mails are evidence of a crime. The section 2703(d) procedure therefore does not comply with the requirements of the Fourth Amendment.

When Warshak learned what the agents had done, he sued the Department of Justice for violating his rights by obtaining his e-mails without a warrant. He argued that, since the phone company's ability to listen in on phone calls does not deprive calls of Fourth Amendment protection, an ISP's ability to read stored e-mails should not deprive e-mails of Fourth Amendment protection. A federal district court agreed with him and so did a three-judge panel of the U.S. Court of Appeals for the Sixth Circuit. The Justice Department appealed the three-judge panel's decision to the entire Court of Appeals for the Sixth Circuit in what is called an "en banc" procedure, and that court blinked.

The en banc court ducked the issue by using a technical rule to hold that the case was not "ripe" for review by the courts.[58] It said the lower courts should not have entertained Warshak's claims because there was no live controversy; Warshak had already been indicted, and there was no indication the government would seek further copies of his e-mails from Yahoo! The en banc court therefore vacated the opinions of the lower courts, which means they ceased to have any legal effect.

That, however, was not the end of the story. In December 2010, a three-judge panel of the U.S. Court of Appeals heard Warshak's appeal of his conviction for running a "massive scheme to defraud" customers of a business he operated.[59] Warshak raised the Fourth Amendment issue, and this time it *was* ripe for review. Like the earlier three-judge panel, this court held that an ISP subscriber has a reasonable expectation of privacy in e-mails

> "that are stored with, or sent or received through, a commercial ISP."
> . . . The government may not compel a[n] . . . ISP to turn over the contents of a subscriber's e-mails without first obtaining a warrant based on probable cause. . . . Because they did not obtain a warrant, the government agents violated the Fourth Amendment. . . . Moreover, to the extent that the SCA purports to permit the government to obtain such e-mails warrantlessly, the SCA is unconstitutional.[60]

The court found that "the mere *ability* of a third-party intermediary to access the contents of a communication cannot be sufficient to extinguish a reasonable expectation of privacy." And it noted that, in *Katz*, "the Supreme Court found it reasonable to expect privacy during a telephone call despite the ability of an operator to listen in."

On March 7, 2011, the Sixth Circuit denied the government's motion asking that the Sixth Circuit rehear the case. This means the Department of Justice must either accept this court's ruling or appeal it to the Supreme Court. If the Justice Department appeals, that could produce the twenty-first century's version of *Katz*, that is, a Supreme Court decision that addresses the Fourth Amendment's applicability to modern electronic communications.

TRAFFIC DATA. Courts assume that the information used to transmit e-mails—the "to" and "from" fields in an e-mail plus the data it generates as it moves through a series of mail servers to its final destination—is not protected by the Fourth Amendment. The *Jackson* Court did not specifically address this issue, but modern courts have found that addressing information is not private under either of two theories. One is *Katz*: courts have held that, by writing the name and address of the person to whom a letter is sent on the outside of the envelope, one "knowingly exposes" that information to public view and, in so doing, forfeits any Fourth Amendment expectation of privacy in it.[61] The other theory is based on *Smith* and holds that e-mail traffic data is logically indistinguishable from the numbers individuals dial to place phone calls; in both instances, people surrender Fourth Amendment privacy by sharing that information with a third party.[62]

Web Postings

Under *Katz*, the Fourth Amendment does not protect any content posted on a publicly accessible website; as the *Katz* Court said, what one knowingly exposes to public view is not private. Since anyone can access the site and see what is posted, law enforcement officers can do the same without obtaining a search warrant. Officers can, and do, use postings on MySpace and other websites in investigating criminal activity.[63]

What if the site is password protected? That was the issue in *United States v. D'Andrea*,[64] a federal prosecution for sexually abusing a child. On December 2, 2004, an anonymous woman called a child abuse hotline and said the eight-year-old daughter of Kendra D'Andrea "was being sexually abused by her mother and the mother's live-in boyfriend." She said they had posted photographs of the abuse on a password-protected website and provided the log-in name and password needed to access the site. A child abuse investigator used the information to log into the site, where he found photos of a child being sexually abused; he downloaded the images and called the police, who used the images and the information from the caller to get a warrant to search D'Andrea's apartment. When they executed the search warrant, they found information that further incriminated D'Andrea and her boyfriend.

After being charged with sexually abusing a child, D'Andrea moved to suppress the images the investigator downloaded from the password-protected site. She said the investigator violated the Fourth Amendment by accessing the site and downloading the images without getting a search warrant. D'Andrea claimed the site was protected by the Fourth Amendment because only those who knew the log-in name and password could access it. She argued that, by using a password and log-in name, she ensured the privacy of the website, just as Charles Katz ensured the privacy of his phone calls by using a phone booth.

In ruling on this issue, the judge noted that an expert on Fourth Amendment law believes "that a person who avails herself of a website's password protection should be able to claim a reasonable expectation of privacy in the site's contents." But while the judge found this view persuasive, he found that he did not have to decide this issue because the investigator did not break into the site, that is, did not bypass the measures D'Andrea used to secure it. Instead, the investigator used the log-in information the anonymous caller provided to access the site. Since she was not a law enforcement officer (she was a former girlfriend of D'Andrea's boyfriend), the Fourth Amendment did not apply to her; she, like any private citizen, was free to share information with the police. By sharing the log-in information with this person, D'Andrea assumed the risk she would give it to the police.

As the Supreme Court said in *United States v. Jacobsen*, "When an individual reveals private information to another, he assumes the risk that his confidant will reveal that information to the authorities, and if that occurs the Fourth Amendment does not prohibit governmental use of that information."[65] So although D'Andrea almost certainly created a Fourth Amendment expectation of privacy in the site by password protecting it, she lost that right by giving the log-in information to someone who gave it to the police.

The judge's ruling is clearly correct as a matter of Fourth Amendment law. This means the only way that someone can sustain Fourth Amendment protection for a password-protected site is by not sharing log-in information for the site with anyone else.

Web Surfing

When people surf the web, shop online, or engage in any other online activity, they leave a record of where they were and what they did. Someone may be alone in a private, locked room while doing any or all of these things, and may therefore assume the actions are private, but that is not true. The activities of individuals are often more visible online than in the real, physical world.

If law enforcement wants to track someone's activities in the real world, it will have to assign officers to monitor the person's movements in public and to interview witnesses who can describe what the person does in private places. Law enforcement agencies can install and use certain technologies—like GPS tracking devices—to monitor where people go in their vehicles, but beyond that they will have to use officers to monitor someone's movements. Since that is a time-consuming, resource-intensive process, it means law enforcement can only track a relatively few people at any one time.

Monitoring what people do online is much easier: technology tracks every site someone visits and what that person does on each site. It also keeps a record of each activity, which is stored with the ISP or with the operators of the sites. This information can be very useful for law enforcement; federal agents investigating the possibility that a suspect is planning a terrorist bombing could, for example, use the records of the suspect's Internet activity to find out if that person is trying to buy explosives or is researching how to build a bomb. If the suspect is using the Internet, there will be records showing what sites the person visited and what he or she did on those sites.

Does the Fourth Amendment protect that information? If it does, the agents will have to obtain a search warrant to gain access to it; to obtain a warrant, they will have to convince a magistrate they have probable cause to believe this person is planning a terrorist bombing. That is not an impossible task, but it means the agents will not be able to obtain the online records early on in their investigation, as a matter of course. They will have to wait until they develop the necessary probable cause from other sources.

If the Fourth Amendment does not protect the information, the agents can obtain it without getting a warrant; they could simply ask the suspect's ISP and the websites to provide it. If the ISP or websites refuse, the agents can use a subpoena—a judicial order that commands the recipient to take certain action or be sanctioned—to require the ISP and websites to comply. Unlike a search warrant, a subpoena issues without a showing of probable cause to believe evidence of a crime is in a particular place.[66]

A few courts have considered whether the Fourth Amendment protects the data people generate when online. In *United States v. Forrester,* federal agents installed a "mirror port"—the twenty-first-century equivalent of a pen register—on Louis Alba's account with an ISP. The agents suspected Alba and Mark Forrester were involved in manufacturing Ecstasy, a controlled substance.[67]

They used the mirror port to monitor "the IP addresses of the websites that Alba visited." An IP—or Internet protocol—address is a "unique 32-bit number" that is assigned to websites and other devices on a computer network.[68] Google has many different IP addresses, one of which is, or was, 216.239.51.99.[69] To access Google or any other site, regular users do not use the numerical IP address; instead, they use a domain name, a pattern of text their computer translates as a request to access an IP address and implements.[70] In the *Forrester* case, the agents used the mirror port installed on Alba's account with his ISP to track the sites he visited, just as the officers in *Smith* used a pen register to capture the numbers Smith dialed from his home phone.

The evidence the mirror port compiled was used to charge Alba with violating federal drug laws and convict him on those charges. He appealed, claiming the use of the mirror port violated the Fourth Amendment. The U.S. Court of Appeals for the Ninth Circuit disagreed because it found the technique used here was constitutionally

> indistinguishable from the use of a pen register that the Court approved in *Smith*. . . . Internet users, like the telephone users in *Smith*, rely on third-party equipment to engage in communication. . . . "Internet users have no expectation of privacy in the . . . IP addresses of the websites they visit because they should know this information is provided to and used by Internet service providers for the specific purpose of directing the routing of information. Like telephone numbers," . . . IP addresses are not merely passively conveyed through third party equipment, but rather are voluntarily turned over in order to direct the third party's servers.[71]

The U.S. Court of Appeals for the Third Circuit reached the same conclusion in *United States v. Christie*.[72] As long as *Smith* is a valid precedent, courts cannot reach any other conclusion.

As long as *Smith* survives, therefore, Fourth Amendment privacy and the use of modern communications technologies are irreconcilable. Many agree with Justice Thurgood Marshall, who, in dissenting in *Smith*, argued that the result created a technological Hobson's choice: if I use technology, I lose privacy; to have privacy, I must avoid technology.

There is a way to invoke Fourth Amendment protection for online activities. The Fourth Amendment presumably protects encrypted e-mails because the sender of the e-mail has, in effect, sealed the envelope. Encryption can also be used to protect other online activities and to secure hard drives and other data storage devices,[73] thereby making it difficult or even impossible for law enforcement to access the data contain. As the next section explains, law enforcement can try to compel people to give up the key needed to access encrypted data or devices, but the Fifth Amendment may give them the ability to successfully resist such efforts.

The Fifth Amendment

The Fifth Amendment contains several clauses, each of which establishes a distinct right. One, for example, creates the prohibition against double jeopardy, that is, against trying someone twice for the same crime.

The clause that is relevant to this discussion says that "no person . . . shall be compelled in any criminal case to be a witness against himself." Like the Fourth Amendment, this clause has its roots in English law and history: in the sixteenth and seventeenth century, the English Court of Star Chamber used a procedure called the oath ex officio to bring people to court and force them to answer questions that could implicate them in crimes "of which they were neither formally accused nor suspected."[74] If someone refused to take the oath or, having taken it, refused to answer, that person would be punished. In 1641, parliament outlawed the oath ex officio, prompted by complaints from citizens who said individuals should be forced to testify against themselves; the theory was that the government should collect its own evidence instead of forcibly extracting what it needed from a suspect. English colonists brought that notion to what became the United States, and it was eventually incorporated into the Fifth Amendment.

The clause quoted above is known as the privilege against self-incrimination because it operates like an evidentiary privilege, in that it gives someone the privilege to refuse to testify. The privilege does not, as the Supreme Court has explained, bar the government from *asking* someone questions; it merely gives the person the ability to refuse to *answer* those questions.[75]

Also, the privilege is not absolute. To invoke the Fifth Amendment privilege, individuals must show they are being (1) *compelled* to (2) give *testimony* that (3) *incriminates* them (i.e., implicates them in a crime).[76] If someone is willing to testify voluntarily, there is no need for compulsion, and the Fifth Amendment does not apply. It usually comes into play when the government wants someone to testify at a trial or a grand jury proceeding but they refuse; the government can use a subpoena to force the person to appear and testify. If individuals who were served with subpoenas show up at the trial or grand jury proceeding and refuse to answer questions, they will be held in civil contempt and incarcerated until they agree to testify, unless they can invoke the privilege.[77]

The subpoena satisfies the first requirement because it compels the person to testify or face sanctions (absent a claim of the privilege). The second requirement limits the application of the Fifth Amendment privilege to testimony, that is, to communicating facts or opinions. The Supreme Court has held that the Fifth Amendment does not apply to physical evidence,[78] which means someone can invoke the privilege and refuse to answer questions posed by a prosecutor but cannot invoke it to refuse to allow the government to take samples of handwriting, blood, or hair.

If individuals subpoenaed are being asked questions, they will be able invoke the Fifth Amendment privilege if answering the questions will incriminate them, that is, will implicate them in criminal activity.[79] The Fifth Amendment is not a privilege to refuse to speak; it is a privilege to refuse to be a witness against yourself, that is, to give testimony that can be used to prosecute you for a crime. So if a grand jury subpoenas John Doe to testify and, once he has been brought before the grand jury room and put under oath, asks "what is the date of your birth?" Doe almost certainly cannot claim the privilege and refuse to answer. To invoke the privilege, Doe would have to show—without actually incriminating himself—that answering that question would provide evidence that could be used to convict him of a crime. Conversely, if, under the same circumstances, the prosecutor asked Doe, "where were you on March 3, 2011, when Sam Smith was murdered?" Doe might very well be able to claim the privilege; to do so, he would have to be able to articulate, in general terms, why his answer to that question might incriminate him.

The Fifth Amendment *might* help people secure the privacy of data they store online or on their computers. The privilege's applicability—or inapplicability—to individuals' attempts to refuse to provide the password or encryption key they have used to secure computer data has arisen in a very few cases, one of which arose in Vermont.

THE FIFTH AMENDMENT AND COMPUTERS

On December 27, 2006, Sebastien Boucher and his father crossed the Canadian border into the United States at Derby Line, Vermont.[80] Like everyone entering the United States, they were subjected to an initial inspection of their passports; unlike most who enter the United States, the Bouchers were selected for secondary inspection. If the federal agent who conducts the initial inspection thinks the traveler is carrying contraband, the agent will refer the person for a secondary inspection, which involves searching the person's luggage.

As Officer Chris Pike conducted the secondary inspection, he saw a laptop in the car, booted it up, and looked through the files it contained. Pike found forty thousand image files, "some of which appeared to be pornographic" based on the filenames. He asked Sebastien if there was child pornography on the laptop; Sebastien said he was not sure. He said he downloaded pornography and sometimes his downloads included child pornography; Sebastien said he deleted those images when he found them.

At that point, Pike called Agent Mark Curtis for assistance. Curtis asked Sebastien to show him where the downloaded files were. Sebastien was given access to the laptop and "navigated to a part of the hard drive designated as drive Z." Curtis began looking through the Z drive and saw what he believed was child pornography. After searching some more, Curtis arrested Sebastien, shut down the laptop, and seized it as evidence. Two days later, another officer began a forensic examination of the laptop; when he tried to access the Z drive, he could not because it was encrypted "through the use of the software Pretty Good Privacy . . . which requires a password." Curtis and a Secret Service agent tried repeatedly to access the Z drive but failed; according to the Secret Service agent, the only way to access it without the password "is to use an automated system which repeatedly guesses passwords." He noted that unlocking "drive Z could take years."

Since the only way to access the Z drive was with the password and

Sebastien would not voluntarily provide it, the government resorted to a subpoena. A federal grand jury served Sebastien with a subpoena that ordered him to enter the password into the laptop or be held in contempt. Boucher took the Fifth, that is, he claimed that providing the password would be compelled testimony that incriminated him. The Department of Justice argued that the password was physical evidence, not testimony, and so claimed Sebastien was not entitled to take the Fifth Amendment as the basis for refusing to enter the password.

In responding to this argument, Sebastien relied on a Supreme Court case: *Fisher v. United States.*[81] In *Fisher,* the Court held that, while someone cannot claim the Fifth Amendment privilege as the basis for refusing to provide physical evidence like hair samples because physical evidence is not testimony, someone subpoenaed by a grand jury can invoke the Fifth Amendment if the act of producing the evidence would itself be testimonial. The *Fisher* Court said the act of producing evidence is testimony within the Fifth Amendment if it concedes that the evidence exists, that the subpoenaed person has it, and that the evidence produced is what the grand jury asked for, that is, producing it authenticates it. The *Fisher* Court also said that the act of producing evidence will not be testimonial if all of these are a "foregone conclusion," that is, if the government already knows the person has the evidence.

When I teach *Fisher,* I use this example to illustrate when the act of producing evidence will be testimonial and when it will not: if a grand jury issues a subpoena to a murder suspect that demands the suspect "produce to the grand jury the gun you used to kill Martin Balco," the suspect can take the Fifth Amendment and refuse to comply. By handing over the gun, the suspect is implicitly saying it exists, that she or he has it, and that this is the gun the suspect used to kill Balco. If, on the other hand, the grand jury knows the suspect has the gun that was used to kill Balco (they have videotape of the suspect buying it or a friend saw it and heard her say, "This is what I used to kill Balco"), then handing it over does not tell the government anything it does not already know. If the act does not communicate anything, it is not testimonial and the suspect cannot take the Fifth Amendment.

In the *Boucher* case, the federal magistrate judge who was initially assigned to decide the issue held that giving up the password was a testimonial, incriminating act:

Compelling Boucher to enter the password forces him to produce evidence that could . . . incriminate him. . . .

Entering a password into the computer implicitly communicates facts. By entering the password Boucher would be disclosing . . . that he knows the password and has control over . . . drive Z. The procedure is equivalent to asking Boucher, "Do you know the password to the laptop?"[82]

The magistrate judge therefore quashed the grand jury subpoena, that is, voided it.

This meant the only way the government could obtain the password was to give Sebastien immunity. The Supreme Court has held that, if prosecutors give individuals immunity from prosecution in exchange for their testimony, this deprives them of the ability to claim the Fifth Amendment privilege.[83] The rationale is that the privilege is not a privilege to refuse to cooperate with the government; it is a privilege to refuse to be compelled to implicate oneself in a crime. According to the Court, if the government promises it will not use what someone says to prosecute that person, they have no need for the privilege. But immunity was not an option in this case: giving Sebastien immunity would defeat the purpose because it would mean that none of the files on the laptop could be used to prosecute him for child pornography (or any other crime).

The Department of Justice instead chose to appeal the magistrate judge's decision to the federal district judge who presides over the U.S. District Court for the District of Vermont. It also decided to change tactics somewhat: in its appeal to the district judge, the Justice Department said it was not asking Sebastien to provide "the password for the encrypted hard drive, but . . . to produce the contents of his encrypted hard drive in an unencrypted format by opening the drive before the grand jury."[84] The Department of Justice also argued that Sebastien could not take the Fifth Amendment as to the contents of the laptop because they were a foregone conclusion as under *Fisher.*

The Department of Justice won. The magistrate judge decided the foregone conclusion principle did not apply in this case "because the government has not viewed most of the files on the Z drive, and therefore does not know whether most of [them] . . . contain incriminating material." The district court judge disagreed; he found that for the foregone conclusion principle to apply the government does not have to be "aware of the incriminatory *contents* of the files"; all it needs to know is that they exist in a particular location. The judge pointed out that the government knew this because Agent Curtis had looked through parts of the Z drive and seen files, some of which appeared to be child pornography, on it. The district court judge also held that Sebastien's producing an unencrypted version of the hard drive would not authenticate it or the files on it because "he has already admitted to possession of the computer, and provided the Government with access to the Z drive." The judge therefore reversed the magistrate judge's ruling quashing the subpoena, reinstated the subpoena, and ordered Sebastien to provide an unencrypted version of the hard drive.

Sebastien apparently persisted in refusing to provide the password (which may have meant he was incarcerated while doing so), despite the district court judge's ruling. On September 25, 2009, he pled guilty to possessing child pornography and "agreed to surrender the password, on condition that what investigators found" could not be used against him at his sentencing.[85] When investigators accessed the Z drive, they found "2,000 still images and 118 video files depicting prepubescent children being sexually assaulted by adults," but none of that evidence was used at his sentencing.[86] Sebastien was sentenced to three years in prison, which is probably much less than he would have gotten if the investigators had been able to access the material on his laptop without the password. Aside from anything else, this case illustrates the role encryption can play in securing the privacy of data.

Encryption is of little use if people can be compelled to surrender their passwords or encryption keys to the government. Under the magistrate judge's ruling, people can use encryption to put their digital data beyond the government's reach; under the district court judge's ruling, they can use encryption to protect their data from private citizens but not from the government. Some believe the magistrate judge reached the correct result in this case.

>chapter:7

TRANSNATIONAL INVESTIGATION
OF CYBERCRIME

As earlier chapters noted, cybercrime creates many new challenges for law enforcement. Those chapters dealt with challenges that arise under U.S. law and the structure of U.S. law enforcement; they therefore focused primarily on cases in which the commission of the cybercrime occurred within the United States. This chapter examines a separate set of challenges: those that arise when the commission of a cybercrime involves perpetrators in one country and a victim in another country.

Cybercriminals can easily target victims in other countries. That complicates law enforcement's task because police agencies are territorially based; every law enforcement agency is located in, and derives its authority from, a particular nation-state.[1] A law enforcement agency from one country—for example, the United States' Federal Bureau of Investigation or France's National Police—therefore has no legal authority to conduct an investigation in another country's territory. This makes it difficult (or even impossible) for national police to investigate transnational cybercrimes and apprehend cybercriminals who are located in another country.

Consider the Bullitt County cyber bank heist. The victim—the county government—was in Shepherdsville, Kentucky. The means the default responsibility for investigating the crime would fall to local law enforcement, probably the Bullitt County Sheriff's Office. The Bullitt County Sheriff's Office is no doubt perfectly qualified to investigate bank thefts when they occur in the real, physical world; such investigations focus on finding witnesses who can describe the robber or the vehicle the robber used to flee the scene of the crime, locating fingerprints and other trace evidence, and examining surveillance cameras for images of the thief. The investigation may also focus on finding informants who may be able to identity the thief and on other, traditional investigative methods.

None of those methods were viable options in the Bullitt County cyber bank theft. The investigation of that crime focused primarily on digital evidence: trained computer investigators would analyze the processes the perpetrators used to access the county's account and initiate the wire transfer to determine (1) the methodology used to carry out the crime and (2) the location from which the perpetrators operated. The investigators should be able to gather most of the evidence they need to determine the methodology used in the crime by analyzing digital evidence left in the bank's computers and the county treasurer's computer.

They might also be able to determine the country from which the perpetrators operated. Assume, for the purposes of analysis, that the Sheriff's Office investigators were able to determine, with a fair level of confidence, that the perpetrators used an Internet service provider (ISP) in Kiev, Ukraine. That creates two logical possibilities: one is that the perpetrators were (and presumably still are) in Kiev; the other is that they used the Kiev ISP as their direct route into the Bullitt County bank but were physically located elsewhere. To determine which scenario is correct, investigators need to be able to get information from the Kiev ISP. Local law enforcement officers in the United States use search warrants or subpoenas to obtain information about subscribers from U.S.-based ISPs. The Sheriff's Office investigators in this scenario could use a search warrant or a subpoena issued by a Bullitt County judge to obtain subscriber information from a U.S.-based ISP, but neither has any legal effect in Ukraine (or any other country). A Bullitt County warrant or subpoena would, at best, be enforceable in the state of Kentucky; it would not be enforceable in any other U.S. state because each U.S. state is itself a distinct sovereign entity.

In an effort to overcome this difficulty, the local investigators might (as they apparently did) contact the FBI and ask for assistance; the FBI could (assuming the evidence establishes probable cause) obtain a search war-

rant from a federal magistrate or a subpoena from a federal grand jury, either or both of which would demand that the Kiev ISP provide subscriber
information that would let investigators identify the person or persons
who used the ISP's account to target the Bullitt County bank. The problem, of course, is that federal warrants and subpoenas are also only enforceable in the territory of the sovereign that issues them, that is, in the
United States. In either instance, then, the Kiev ISP could (and no doubt
would) simply ignore the warrant or subpoena.

These scenarios are simplified versions of how such an investigation
would proceed, but they illustrate the procedural problems U.S. law enforcement faces in investigating transnational cybercrimes. The next
two sections examine two cases in which U.S. officers used very different
strategies to pursue cybercriminals who operated from outside the United
States.

Case 1: Invita

The Invita case began when the FBI was called in to investigate a series
of intrusions from Russia "into the computer systems of businesses in
the United States."[2] The intrusions targeted Internet service providers,
e-commerce sites, and banks:

> The hackers used their unauthorized access to the victims' computers
> to steal credit card . . . and other . . . financial information, and . . . tried
> to extort money from the victims with threats to expose the sensitive
> data to the public or damage the victims' computers. The hackers also
> defrauded PayPal through a scheme in which stolen credit cards were
> used to generate cash and to pay for computer parts purchased from
> vendors in the United States.[3]

According to some sources, the attackers "broke into the computers of
at least" forty U.S. companies, including the Nara Bank of Los Angeles
and the Central National Bank in Waco, Texas.[4] They sometimes broke
into systems and then tried to coerce the owners of the systems into hiring
them as "security consultants"; the coercion came in the form of threats
to release data they had obtained from the system unless they were hired
as "consultants." One company hired the cybercriminals as "consultants,"
only to have them use its computer system as the vector for attacking

systems belonging to other companies.[5] When one company did not pay the five-hundred-thousand-dollar "consulting" fee the attackers demanded, they launched a distributed denial of service (DDOS) attack that took its website off line.[6]

The president of that particular company went to the FBI soon after the attackers contacted him; FBI agents suggested he drag out the negotiations and use the process to gather as much information as possible about them.[7] He agreed and spent months negotiating with the hackers, who used e-mail and a stolen satellite phone to contact him. After negotiations dragged on for some time, one of the hackers e-mailed the president and told him to forget about the extortion fee; the hacker said he would forego the fee if he could get a visa to come to the United States and a job once he arrived. He said he wanted to bring his wife and child with him. The president put the hacker—now known as "Victor"—in touch with an FBI agent, to see if they could work out a deal by which the hacker would be given immunity from prosecution in exchange for assisting federal law enforcement with this and other investigations.

The deal fell through, but in the meantime over "a dozen U.S. Attorneys and FBI agents" from four states were holding "brainstorming conferences" on how to stop the hackers, who were seen as a serious threat to U.S. businesses. Federal authorities had already tried and failed to apprehend one of them through traditional channels: the hacker not only identified himself as "Alexey Ivanov" to his extortion victims but also sent a number of them his résumé and photograph, apparently as part of a search for legitimate employment in the United States. Since Ivanov's résumé and certain aspects of the attacks indicated that he was in Russia, the U.S. Justice Department sent a request through diplomatic channels to Russian authorities, asking them to detain Ivanov and question him about the attacks. The Russians did not respond to the initial contact or to a repeated request. Because the United States does not have an extradition treaty with Russia, they were not obliged to turn Ivanov over to the United States for prosecution, had the United States made such a request. Since U.S. law enforcement had no legal authority to arrest Ivanov in Russia, the federal prosecutors and agents decided to use a "sting" operation to get him to come to the United States.

It took the form of a job interview: FBI agents created a fake company called "Invita" and sent Ivanov a letter "telling him they had heard good things about him and were considering him" for a position with their company. The letter said he would have to come to Invita offices in Seattle to interview for the job; Ivanov agreed to come and asked if he could bring his "business partner" Vasiliy Gorshkov with him. The agents posing as Invita employees said Gorshkov could come but Invita would only pay for Ivanov's travel expenses; Gorshkov would have to pay his own way.[8]

Gorshkov agreed, and in November 2000 the men flew from Chelyabinsk, Russia, to Seattle. An undercover FBI agent picked them up at the airport and brought them to the Invita office, where they chatted with FBI agents posing as Invita employees. The agents then asked the Russians to demonstrate their hacking skills, using two Invita computers; the Russians did not know the FBI had installed keyloggers—programs that record what is typed on a keyboard—on the computers. As the Russians hacked, the loggers recorded what they typed; the information recorded included the usernames and passwords they used to access the tech.net.ru server—their unofficial company's server in Russia.[9] It held tools they needed to demonstrate their skills. After the demonstration was over, the two were told they would be taken to the apartment that had been rented for them; on the way, FBI agents stopped the car and arrested both of them.[10]

Without getting a search warrant, Invita FBI agents retrieved the usernames and passwords the loggers recorded and used them to access the tech.net.ru server and download 250 gigabytes of data.[11] The agents did not tell Russian authorities what they were doing, in violation of a 1997 agreement to which both the United States and Russia were parties.[12] Gorshkov and Ivanov were indicted for violating federal cybercrime law, and prosecutors prepared to use evidence from the tech.net.ru server at their trials.

Gorshkov moved to suppress all of the evidence, arguing that it was obtained in violation of the U.S. Fourth Amendment because the FBI agents did not obtain a search warrant before accessing the Russian server. He lost: the federal judge to whom his case was assigned held that the Fourth Amendment did not apply to the agents' actions; as the court noted, the U.S. Supreme Court has held that it only applies to searches and seizures "of a non-resident alien's property outside the United States."[13] Both Gorshkov and Ivanov were Russian citizens and, as such, nonresident aliens of the United States; and the federal judge found that the search of the Russian computer took place entirely "in" Russia, not in the United States. Given that, the Fourth Amendment did not apply to the agents' accessing the tech.net.ru server and downloading its contents.

Gorshkov also claimed the evidence should be suppressed because the agents' actions violated Russian law. Article 272 of the Criminal Code of the Russian Federation makes it a crime to access a computer without authorization and copy information stored on it. The FBI agents who accessed the tech.net.ru server were not authorized to do so. They were able to access it only because their loggers captured the log-in information necessary to do so; and once they accessed the server, they copied information stored on it. Notwithstanding all of that, Gorshkov lost again; the federal judge held that Russian law did not apply to the FBI agents' "actions in this case."

Ivanov wound up pleading guilty to "multiple counts of conspiracy, computer hacking, computer fraud," and other federal crimes and was sentenced to four years in prison.[14] Gorshkov went to trial and was convicted on twenty counts of committing the same crimes; he was sentenced to three years in prison.[15]

In 2002, almost two years after the FBI agents accessed the tech.net.ru server, Russia's Federal Security Service—a police agency—charged one of the Invita agents with hacking in violation of Russian law.[16] The charge was apparently symbolic—a way of asserting Russian sovereignty over persons and things in the territory Russia controls. In announcing the charge, a spokesperson explained that "if the Russian hackers are sentenced on the basis of information obtained by the Americans through hacking, that will imply the future ability of U.S. secret services to use illegal methods in the collection of information in Russia and other countries."[17] The Federal Security Service sent the criminal complaint to the U.S. Department of Justice and asked that the FBI agent be surrendered for prosecution in Russia; the United States has apparently never responded.

Case 2: Rome Labs

This case began when system administrators at the Rome Air Development Center (Rome Labs) at Griffiss Air Force Base in New York discovered that hackers had installed sniffer programs on the Rome Labs networks.[18] Password sniffer programs collect the passwords of people who log into a computer system, so discovering such a program suggested that the hackers had the ability to access Rome Labs' sensitive databases. As a Senate report later noted, Rome Labs was the "Air Force's premier command and control research facility. Its projects include artificial intelligence system, radar guidance systems, and target detection and tracking systems."[19]

The Rome Labs administrators contacted the Defense Information Systems Agency, which notified the Air Force Office of Special Investigations (AFOSI). AFOSI agents and computer security experts went to Rome Labs and began investigating the intrusion. They found that, in addition to installing the sniffer programs, two unknown individuals had hacked seven Rome Labs systems and "gained complete access to all" the information on the systems. AFOSI agents also discovered that one of them was using the "access code of a high-ranking Pentagon employee" to access the Pentagon's computer systems; the code gave the hacker the ability to "delete files, copy information and even crash the system."

The investigation lasted for weeks: AFOSI agents determined that the hackers, who called themselves "Datastream Cowboy" and "Kuji," were using the Rome Labs' systems to attack targets in the United States and other countries. But while the agents could monitor some of their activity, the hackers were untraceable because they wove "a path through computer systems in South Africa, Mexico and Europe before launching their attacks." The agents eventually used online informants to identify Datastream Cowboy as a sixteen-year-old who lived in the United Kingdom; Datastream Cowboy was naive enough to give an informant his home telephone number.

Armed with that information, agents contacted New Scotland Yard's computer crime unit and asked them to trace the number to a home address. The British agents rather quickly traced it to a "house in a cul-de-sac, part of the anonymous north London suburbs." AFOSI agents flew to London and staked out the address with British police officers; they wanted to be sure Datastream Cowboy was online when they entered the home to arrest him and execute a search warrant. On May 12, 1994, the officers on the stakeout got a call telling them he was online; they went to the home, knocked on the door, swept inside after a man answered, and went upstairs to a "loft-room" where they found Datastream Cowboy "tapping frantically away on the keyboard" of his computer. New Scotland Yard officers arrested sixteen-year-old Richard Pryce, a music student, who admitted breaking into the Rome Labs systems and other U.S. military systems.

It took two more years before a New Scotland Yard agent was able to track down Kuji. In June 1996, British agents decided to "sift through . . . the mass of information" on Pryce's hard drive once again; this time they found the name Kuji next to a telephone number.[20] The number led them to twenty-one-year-old Mathew Bevan, "a soft-spoken computer worker" who was the son of a police officer.[21]

Bevan and Pryce were both charged with multiple counts of violating the United Kingdom's Computer Misuse Act and with a single count of conspiracy. The conspiracy charges were later dropped and, in March 1997, Pryce pled guilty to twelve counts of violating the Computer Misuse Act. All of the charges against Bevan were dropped in November 1997, "after the Crown Prosecution service decided it was not in the public interest to pursue the case."[22]

Formal and Informal Options with Transnational Cybercrimes

When cybercrimes involve victims in one country and perpetrators in another, law enforcement officers cannot rely on the usual procedures they employ to find evidence and apprehend domestic perpetrators. The problem of collecting evidence and apprehending perpetrators in another country is not unique to cybercrime; criminals have historically fled the jurisdiction where they committed their crimes in an effort to avoid being prosecuted and punished.

What is different about cybercrime is the frequency with which this scenario occurs; it used to be an aberration but has increasingly become the norm. And unfortunately, law has not kept up with this trend.

Transnational crimes—including transnational cybercrimes—create two kinds of challenges for law enforcement officers: collecting evidence from abroad and obtaining custody of a suspect who is abroad. To understand the challenges, it is necessary to review the options that are available to officers in each instance.

Cybercrime investigators have two alternatives they can use to obtain evidence from abroad: rely upon the formal devices that have historically been used to gather evidence in transnational criminal cases or use informal cooperation. Cybercrime investigators also have two alternatives they can use to gain custody of a suspect who is in another country: rely on extradition, the formal device that is used to transfer a suspect from one country to another, or use informal, unilateral action by the country seeking the suspect.

COLLECTING EVIDENCE

As the U.S. Department of Justice notes, the formal devices officers can use to obtain evidence from abroad include letters rogatory, treaty requests, and requests for assistance under executive agreements.[23]

A letter rogatory is a request from a court in one country to a court in another country; it asks the foreign court to perform a judicial act, such as authorizing local authorities to collect evidence located in that country.[24] The investigator seeking the evidence has to draft the letter rogatory, making sure that what he or she is requesting will be clear to the judge in the foreign country; since different countries want different things in a letter rogatory, officers usually consult the Department of Justice's Office of International Affairs (OIA) to find out what they need to include. A letter rogatory usually includes the name and affiliation of the investigating officer; enough facts for a foreign judge to understand that a crime has been committed and that the evidence sought relates to that crime; the nature of the assistance sought; the text of the statutes violated; and a promise of reciprocal assistance.[25] The promise consists of the United States' agreeing to provide similar assistance to officers conducting an investigation on behalf of the foreign country.[26] The promise is essential because letters rogatory are based on comity, that is, congenial relations between the two countries.[27]

After he drafts the letter rogatory, the officer will have to get a U.S. judge to sign it and then have it authenticated by whatever device is appropriate under international law; here, again, the officer will need to consult with the OIA to find out what method of authentication is needed and how he or she goes about obtaining it. The next step is having the letter rogatory translated (unless it is going to an English-speaking country). The final step is for the officer to deliver the letter rogatory (translated, if necessary) to the OIA, which will send it to the Department of State or to the American embassy in the country whose assistance is being sought. The usual process is for the U.S. diplomatic representative to deliver the letter rogatory to the foreign ministry of the country to which it is directed; the foreign ministry will send it to the ministry of justice, and the ministry of justice will refer it to the appropriate judge, who will execute it. Once the evidence has been collected, it will be returned to the officer via the same process. If a letter rogatory is found to be deficient at any point prior to being implemented, it will be returned to the officer, who will be responsible for revising it to eliminate the defects.

As is probably evident from this description of the process, letters rogatory are a time-consuming method of obtaining evidence from abroad. The Department of Justice tells its prosecutors to assume "the process will take a year or more."[28] And a year is an optimistic estimate; in reality, it can take years for a letter rogatory to be implemented, if it is implemented at all. Officers often wait years, only to find that their letter rogatory has not and will not be implemented.[29]

Requests under a mutual legal assistance treaty (MLAT) are "generally faster and more reliable than letters rogatory."[30] In 2009, the United States had MLATs in force with fifty-three countries.[31] As one author noted, the MLAT process "is designed to work more quickly than letters rogatory since the MLATs impose an international legal obligation on the requested state to respond, whereas letters rogatory can only request a response."[32]

An officer seeking evidence from abroad must first consult the Department of Justice's OIA to find out if the United States has an MLAT with the country in which the evidence is located. If the United States has an MLAT with the country, the officer will need to find out what investigations it covers because MLATs deal with specific crimes (e.g., drugs). If the MLAT covers the crime the officer is investigating, the officer will draft a request for assistance from the other country; the OIA has models "tailored to the treaty under which assistance is being requested."[33] An MLAT request contains essentially the same information as a letter rogatory, except the promise of reciprocity will be omitted and certain information (such as the name, address, and citizenship of all those affected by the request) will be added.[34] After the officer drafts the MLAT request, he or she submits it to OIA for review; OIA will either use it to prepare the final request or send the draft back to the officer to be revised. Since U.S. MLATs designate the Department of Justice as the entity authorized to make an MLAT request, an OIA representative will sign the request, have it translated (if necessary), and send it to the entity in the foreign country that has the authority to execute it.[35]

MLAT requests may have a quicker turnaround time than letters rogatory, but they are still a slow, cumbersome process. As a federal prosecutor noted, MLATs "take months or even years to produce the required" evidence.[36] While such delays can be aggravating or problematic in traditional criminal investigations, they are likely to be devastating in cybercrime investigations. Letters rogatory and MLATs were developed to obtain physical evidence, which tends to be stable and enduring; the digital evidence involved in cybercrime investigations is fragile and tenuous. When officers have to rely on letters rogatory or MLAT requests to obtain evidence in cybercrime cases, they run the risk that the digital evidence they seek will be deleted before their requests ever reach the appropriate foreign authorities.[37]

The last formal device is a request under an executive agreement. An executive agreement is a compact a U.S. president makes with representatives of another country; unlike treaties, it does not have to be approved by Congress.[38] Executive agreements can be an effective means of obtaining evidence from abroad but are not likely to be a useful resource for an officer conducting a cybercrime investigation. As the Justice Department notes, most executive agreements "apply to investigations arising from illegal narcotics trafficking."[39] So far, none seem to apply to cybercrime investigations.

Since the formal methods are not likely to be effective in obtaining evidence in cybercrime cases, law enforcement officers rely on informal methods, when they are available. This was done in the Rome Labs case: The AFOSI investigators contacted New Scotland Yard officers, who cooperated with the U.S. investigation of the Rome Labs intrusions. British officers helped the air force agents track down Datastream Cowboy, and they were the ones who eventually identified Kuji. Since the suspects were prosecuted in the United Kingdom, the evidence the U.S.-UK officers collected was not turned over to U.S. prosecutors and used at trial. However, that does not detract from the fact that officers from both countries worked closely together in a spirit of cooperation to track down the suspects and collect evidence of their crimes.

Currently, informal cooperation of the kind that existed in the Rome Labs case is the most efficient means by which law enforcement officers in country A can obtain assistance from officers and other authorities in country C. In 2001, the Council of Europe promulgated a cybercrime treaty intended to improve formal cooperation among law enforcement in countries that sign and ratify the treaty; so far, only a few have done so. Unless and until most, if not all, of the nations of the world ratify the treaty or enter into alternate arrangements that improve formal cooperation, informal cooperation among law enforcement will continue to be the most effective way of obtaining evidence from abroad in cybercrime investigations.

ARRESTING SUSPECTS

Officers have two ways to gain custody of suspects who are in another country: extradition, the formal device that has historically been used to transfer suspects from one country to another, and extralegal unilateral action by the country seeking the suspect.

Extradition requires a treaty between the countries. Without such a treaty, "extradition is not considered a binding obligation to most countries."[40] The United States has extradition treaties with over one hundred countries, but that leaves many countries with which it does not have such a treaty.[41] As we saw earlier, the United States does not have an extradition treaty with the Russian Federation.

Even when the United States has an extradition treaty with a country, extradition is often "difficult to obtain, legally and practically."[42] Here, as with using a letter rogatory or MLAT to obtain evidence, the legal process is complicated and can be cumbersome. As the Department of Justice explains, extradition "involves four basic steps": contacting the Department of Justice's OIA; determining extraditability; deciding whether to ask for provisional arrest; and submitting the documents required to support the formal request for extradition.[43]

The officer seeking custody of a suspect in another country works with the OIA to determine if the United States has an extradition treaty with that country and, if it does, to initiate the process of extradition. The first step in initiating extradition is determining the "extraditability" of the suspect, a process that involves analyzing eight factors.[44] While all the factors play a role in determining whether a suspect can be extradited, citizenship is clearly the most important. As the Justice Department notes, "Many countries will not extradite their own citizens."[45] If the OIA decides the suspect is extraditable, it will work with the officer to assemble the complex documentation needed to support the request for extradition.[46]

Even if the suspect is clearly extraditable and the OIA's request and supporting documentation are impeccable, the request may not be granted, especially if the country is being asked to extradite its own citizen. Countries have historically been reluctant to turn their own citizens over for prosecution by a foreign state. Indeed, the constitutions of some countries bar them from extraditing their own citizens for prosecution abroad.[47]

Historically, international law dealt with a country's refusal to extradite its citizen by applying the principle of "aut dedere aut judicare," which says a country that is asked to extradite its citizen must either extradite or prosecute the person itself.[48] Britain prosecuted Aaron Caffrey for his role in the attacks on the Port of Houston; the United States was presumably willing to allow him to be prosecuted in his own country. That, though, tends to be unusual: when a country's citizen has been the victim of a crime, the citizens and officials of that country often feel justice will not be done unless the perpetrator is prosecuted, convicted, and punished by the state whose laws he or she violated. The need to prosecute locally is a function of a traditional aspect of criminal law: publicly denouncing those who violate the sovereign's law. It is also to some extent a product of concern that the offender's own country will "go too easy" on him or her.

Cases in which perpetrators' countries are willing to prosecute them for the crimes they committed abroad are a source of tension between countries, but the tension will be alleviated if perpetrators' countries carry through on their promise and the victim countries see the perpetrators are going to be punished. The truly difficult cases are the ones in which perpetrators' countries will not or cannot extradite them and refuse to prosecute them for the crimes they committed abroad.

This in effect occurred in the Invita case: the FBI identified two Russians as the hackers who were attacking targets in the United States, but the United States could not seek their extradition because there is no extradition treaty in effect between the United States and the Russian Federation. The formal device used to obtain a suspect from abroad was, therefore, not available, and as a result, the "extradite or prosecute" principle did not apply. That is, since Russia was under no obligation to extradite the hackers, it was under no obligation to prosecute them. In this and similar scenarios, the victim country has no official recourse; its only options are to give up on prosecuting the offenders or resort to extralegal unilateral action to obtain custody of them. In other words, a victim country in this situation has no option but to go outside the law.

In a sense, U.S. authorities chose that second option: they tricked Alexey Ivanov and Vasiliy Gorshkov into coming to the United States, where they could be, and were, arrested. When individuals are inside a country's territory, its law enforcement officers can arrest them; his presence in the country's territory gives it the authority to make the arrest.[49] So the Russian hackers effectively guaranteed their arrest by coming to the United States.

What, if anything, could the FBI have done if the hackers refused to come to the United States to interview with Invita? Informal cooperation was not an option; absent an extradition treaty, Russian authorities cannot turn their citizens over to another state for prosecution. The United States did, though, have another, albeit problematic, option: kidnap the hackers from Russia and bring them to the United States to stand trial. The U.S. Supreme Court has long approved the use of kidnapping to bring foreign suspects to the United States for trial.[50] As the Supreme Court explained in a relatively recent case, it has so far never departed from the rule it announced in 1886 that

> the power of a court to try a person for crime is not impaired by the fact that he had been brought within the court's jurisdiction by reason of a "forcible abduction."... Due process of law is satisfied when one present in court is convicted of crime after having been fairly apprized of the charges against him and after a fair trial in accordance with constitutional ... safeguards.[51]

While abduction is an option under U.S. law, it is rarely used. A Department of Justice manual tells prosecutors that "due to the sensitivity of abducting defendants from a foreign country," they may not "secure custody over persons outside the United States (by government agents or the use of . . . bounty hunters or private investigators) . . . without advance approval" from the department.[52] Since the U.S. policy of abducting suspects is controversial under international law, the Department of Justice presumably applies a stringent test in deciding whether to approve abduction. So far, anyway, there appear to be no cases in which cybercrime suspects have been abducted and brought to the United States for prosecution.

While abduction was a legal option in the Invita, case, it was not a practical one. The FBI would have had to send agents to Chelyabinsk, where the suspects lived; once in Chelyabinsk, the agents would have had to find both suspects, take them into custody without being noticed by the local authorities, and then smuggle them out of Russia. It would be an essentially impossible task, with a potentially serious downside: if the FBI agents were caught, they could have faced kidnapping and other charges in Russia.

Global Initiatives for Transnational Cybercrime

A number of organizations are—and have been—trying to develop solutions for transnational cybercrime. The efforts began in Europe in 1983. The Organisation for Economic Co-operation and Development (OECD) organized a group of experts, who met to discuss the legal issues posed by transnational cybercrime; based on the results of that meeting, the OECD commissioned a two-year study focusing on the possibility of harmonizing and internationalizing national cybercrime laws.[53]

In 1986, the OECD issued a report that summarized the results of the study. It surveyed existing cybercrime laws and recommended a set of offenses all countries should criminalize.[54] The OECD followed this report with a series of other efforts, all of which were designed to support this approach.

In 1985, the Council of Europe convened its own panel of experts, who spent four years studying the legal issues raised by cybercrime.[55] In 1989, they issued a recommendation that emphasized the need to ensure that countries criminalized a basic set of offenses; the set of offenses the Council of Europe experts identified was similar to the offenses the OECD experts identified in their report. In 1995, the Council of Europe issue a recommendation to its member states that focused on the legal issues involved in investigating cybercrime. In 1997, the Council of Europe convened another group of experts and assigned them the task of drafting a cybercrime treaty that would harmonize national laws dealing with cybercrime offenses and investigations. In 2001, this effort produced a treaty known as the Convention on Cybercrime.[56]

Those who drafted the convention believed gaps and conflicts in national laws impede law enforcement's ability to respond to cybercrime. The convention is therefore intended to remedy this by ensuring that countries outlaw the various cybercrimes and give law enforcement the authority it needs to investigate cybercrimes. The convention is implicitly predicated on the assumption that all countries will eventually ratify it, which would mean every country would have comprehensive, consistent cybercrime laws.

To be a party to the convention and be bound by its provisions, a country has to sign the convention and formally ratify it. The convention was opened for signature on November 23, 2001. Ten years later, it had been signed by forty-seven countries and ratified by thirty. Most of the countries that have signed the convention are European countries that are legally entitled to sign because they belong to the Council of Europe.

Four non-European countries—Canada, Japan, South Africa, and the United States—were allowed to sign it because they were involved in drafting the convention. Ten years after the convention was opened for signatures and ratification, the United States was the only one of the four that had ratified the convention, which meant it was the only one of them that was bound by it. Other non-European countries are being invited to sign and ratify the convention, but none had done so by 2011. Since there are roughly 195 countries, the convention has so far done little to improve global law enforcement's effectiveness against cybercrime.

In 1990, the United Nations adopted a resolution inviting governments to be guided by policies developed at a UN conference held earlier that year. The resolution called for UN member states to ensure that their criminal laws were adequate to deal with cybercrime. The United Nations followed this resolution with a cybercrime manual issued in 1995; it examined the general phenomenon of cybercrime, the law needed to control it, and the need for international cooperation in combating it.

More recently, the United Nations delegated the task of dealing with cybercrime to one of its agencies: the International Telecommunications Union (ITU).[57] The ITU is responsible for dealing with information and communication technology issues. Like the OECD and the Council of Europe, the ITU focuses on the need for countries to have adequate, consistent cybercrime laws.

The theory underlying these and similar efforts is that, if countries all adopt adequate, consistent cybercrime laws, it will become easier to investigate transnational cybercrimes and to have cybercriminals extradited for prosecution. There is currently no initiative that seeks to create a global cybercrime law enforcement agency. The assumption is that cybercrime is best handled by individual countries, each of which has adopted laws that let it prosecute cybercriminals and cooperate with other countries in investigating cybercrimes and apprehending those who perpetrate them. In other words, the nations of the world tacitly assume the best approach for dealing with cybercrime is the approach they use for crime, with some legislative improvements.

Interpol, the international police organization, has its own cybercrime initiative, but it, too, focuses on supporting law enforcement at the national level. Interpol's mission is to facilitate "cross-border police cooperation," and to that end it "supports and assists all organizations . . . whose mission is to . . . combat international crime."[58] Interpol acts as a resource for officers investigating cybercrimes by helping them obtain evidence and other information from abroad.[59] It also has regional cybercrime working groups that train officers from different countries in the processes of investigating cybercrime. But while it makes useful contributions in this and other regards, Interpol does not have the resources to become a global cybercrime policing force.

Since the global efforts to deal with transnational cybercrime focus entirely on harmonizing national laws to facilitate cooperation among national police agencies, there is little, if any, likelihood that a world cybercrime police agency will be created in the foreseeable future. Creating such an agency would be analogous to the tactic the U.S. government employed to deal with mobile criminals like Bonnie and Clyde. Congress addressed the Bonnie and Clyde problem by federalizing what had been exclusively state crimes: by adopting statutes that made bank robbery, kidnapping, and other crimes federal offenses, Congress made it possible for federal authorities to pursue criminals across state lines.

The strategy the United States used to deal with the Bonnie and Clyde phenomenon is a logical way to deal with transnational cybercrime, but it founders on a critical difference between sovereign countries and the states in a federal system like the United States. While each U.S. state is a sovereign in its own right, it is also a subordinate entity in a larger federal system; as long as the federal government does not exceed constitutional limits on its authority, it can exercise authority over what have traditionally been matters of purely state concern. The Bonnie and Clyde strategy works because the states and the federal government are all part of one system. The strategy does not work at the global level because each nation-state is an independent sovereign; there is no larger, comprehensive system, and one is not likely to emerge in the foreseeable future.

Nation-states are protective of their sovereignty and are therefore unlikely to surrender any quantum of their authority to maintain order in their territory by agreeing to the creation of a world cybercrime police; since such an agency would take jurisdiction over cybercrimes committed by and against the citizens of the various nation-states, it would deprive the nation-states of a portion of their sovereignty. The countries of the world are not prepared to do this, and most people are probably not prepared for it either. Despite the tactical advantages of the global policing approach, most individuals would have serious concerns about becoming subject to the authority of not only local and federal police but also a police agency that is not part of their country.

Since global policing is simply not a viable option now and for the foreseeable future, the national policing model is the only approach to cybercrime. This means cybercrime investigations will continue to be undertaken by the thousands, perhaps millions, of law enforcement agencies operating under the authority of the 195 countries of the world. It also means that cybercrime investigations will continue to be plagued by the jurisdictional and other parochial issues that constitute the twenty-first century's version of the Bonnie and Clyde phenomenon. Although many believe otherwise, the efforts to encourage countries to adopt consistent cybercrime laws are unlikely to resolve these problems.

>chapter 8

MUTATING CYBERTHREATS:
CRIME, TERRORISM, AND WAR

Cybercrime is only one of several threats that exist in cyberspace. This chapter analyzes what constitutes a "threat" and how the nature of the traditional threats to social order mutates once they move into cyberspace.

Traditional Threat Categories

Crime, terrorism, and war and the distinctions between each are reasonably well defined and reasonably stable in the physical world.[1] The definitional clarity and empirical stability of the real-world threat categories is a function of two factors: One is that the categories evolved as pragmatic responses to the challenges territorially based sovereign entities (e.g., city-states and nation-states) must overcome if they are to survive. The other is that these threats emerged in a physical environment far less malleable and therefore far less ambiguous than the conceptual environment of cyberspace.

Probably the greatest challenge societies confront is the need to maintain order, both internally and externally. Order is essential if the citizens of a society are to carry out the functions (e.g., procure food and shelter, and reproduce) essential to ensure their survival and that of the society. As failed states demonstrate, a society cannot survive if its members are free to prey on each other in ways that undermine the level of order needed to maintain a functioning society. To maintain internal order, a society must ensure that its citizens are organized and socialized in a fashion that lets them carry out essential functions and that this order is not undermined by the disruptive activity of some citizens. To maintain order externally, a society must fend off encroachments and attacks by other societies. To do this, a society must have trained personnel who are equipped with the weaponry they need to repel external attacks.

Societies use two sets of rules to maintain internal order. One consists of civil rules that define the basic structure of the society. These rules deal with status (e.g., when people become adults and which adults have which rights), property (e.g., who can own property and how one acquires property), familial bonds (e.g., kinship and marriage), and other critical matters. Many civil rules are informal norms; most citizens internalize these norms, which keeps their behavior within socially acceptable bounds. Other civil rules take the form of laws, the enforcement of which falls to civil courts and civil litigation (suits between individuals).

Unlike other social species, humans are intelligent and can therefore deviate, that is, can deliberately decide not to follow a rule. Most of the individuals in a society will not intentionally disobey the society's civil rules, but some will. Societies use a second set of rules—criminal rules—to control conduct that deliberately violates a society's rules and challenges its ability to maintain order. These rules are intended to discourage rule violation by letting the state sanction those who commit "crimes."

A crime consists of violating a rule—a law—that prohibits certain conduct or causing certain "harm." The crime of murder, for example, prohibits causing the death of another person; the crime of theft prohibits someone's taking another person's property without that owner's permission and with the intention to deprive the owner of it. As these examples indicate, criminal rules often relate to matters governed by civil rules; the prohibition against theft reinforces civil rules that establish and define the parameters of property ownership.

Criminal rules discourage rule violations by prohibiting certain activity and by prescribing and inflicting sanctions (e.g., incarceration and execution) on those who engage in that activity. So if Jane Doe murders John

Doe, the society she belongs to will convict her of murder and impose a sanction. The primary goal is to deter Jane from breaking more criminal rules (and the civil rules they reinforce); a secondary goal is to deter others from following her example. The punishment imposed on Jane underscores the unacceptability of engaging in such conduct and presumably deters future rule violation.

This system assumes that individuals commit crimes. This assumption also applies to terrorism, which consists of committing what would otherwise be a crime for ideological reasons. Criminals commit crimes for financial reasons (e.g., fraud or theft) or passion (e.g., anger or sex). The motive for most crimes is personal: I steal to benefit myself; I murder out of revenge. Terrorists commit crimes (e.g., killing people and damaging property) but do so to promote an ideology. Since terrorists commit crimes (albeit for distinct motives), societies have historically regarded terrorism as a type of crime. Timothy McVeigh, for example, was prosecuted and executed for his terrorist attack on the Oklahoma City federal building, and members of al-Qaeda were prosecuted and punished for the 1998 bombing of U.S. embassies in Africa.[2]

Historically, crime and terrorism were both internal phenomena, that is, were committed within the territory of sovereign entity. The internal character of crime and terrorism was a function of necessity: in the real world, it is physically impossible for a person to steal property from someone in another country; the constraints of geography and historic limitations of travel meant crime and terrorism were domestic threats that could be addressed with local law and by local law enforcement agencies.

War differs from crime and terrorism in two respects: One is that it is a struggle between sovereign entities. While individuals carry out war, warriors are merely implements; the players are sovereigns engaged in a political struggle. War has historically been reserved for sovereign entities because only they could summon the resources (manpower and weapons) needed to wage war. Historically, individuals engaged in crime and terrorism, and nation-states engaged in war; each category was distinct: individuals did not "commit" war, and sovereign entities did not commit crime or terrorism. The other respect in which war differs from crime and terrorism is that war threatens a society's ability to maintain external order and maintain the stable geographical and political environment that is also essential for its survival. War has historically been an outside threat; crime and terrorism have historically been an inside threat.

Since societies have dealt with crime and war (and, to a lesser extent, terrorism) for millennia, they have developed rules—laws—that define each threat category and distinguish it from the others. Societies also eventually developed rules that define war and set certain parameters on how it is to be conducted, for example, civilians are not legitimate targets.

Threats via Cyberspace

Cyberspace erodes the distinctions between the three threat categories by undermining the validity of certain assumptions that underlie how societies define and respond to the real-world threats.

Cyberspace eliminates the constraints of the physical world and makes geography irrelevant: cybercriminals can attack victims in other countries as easily as they can attack someone in their neighborhood. And while there may not, as yet, have been a verified incident of cyberterrorism, the same is likely to be true of it, as well. This aspect of cybercrime and cyberterrorism means they are no longer purely internal threats; rather, they can be internal threats, external threats, or a combination of both.

Cyberspace also vitiates identity: cybercriminals and cyberterrorists can be anonymous or assume false identities with an efficacy that is impossible in the physical world. The elimination of physical constraints and the alteration or elimination of identity combine to erode the efficacy of the traditional law enforcement model, which nation-states use to enforce their criminal laws.

Since it evolved to deal with crime, which is subject to the physical constraints of the real world, the model assumes local crime, local perpetrators, and a physical crime scene. Police use these characteristics of crime to identify and apprehend perpetrators; as everyone probably knows, it is exceedingly difficult to commit a physical crime without leaving trace evidence at the scene (and perhaps being observed by witnesses). Officers investigating a crime can also focus on links between the victim and perpetrator because it is equally difficult to mask one's movements and relationships in the physical world. These investigative procedures, and the assumptions that underlie them, become problematic when criminal activity is mediated through the cyberworld.

The model's efficacy is further eroded by a third characteristic of cybercrime and cyberterrorism: since crime and terrorism can be automated, perpetrators can cause harm on a scale that surpasses what is possible in the real world. The increase in the scale of the harm inflicted challenges the model because of the sheer number of new crimes and because the new crimes constitute a new quantum of criminal activity that is added to the real-world crime with which law enforcement must continue to deal.

Cyberspace also has a negative effect on how societies deal with external threats. War is unambiguous in the physical world; when the Japanese attacked Pearl Harbor, there was no doubt this was war. The attackers wore uniforms and used airplanes and ships, all of which displayed Japan's national insignia; this was one indicator of war (attack by a nation-state, not individuals). Another indicator was the weaponry itself, which was far beyond the capacity of individuals to acquire and utilize.

There may—or may not—have been instances of cyberwar. Clearly, though, it will not require the use of sophisticated, expensive weapons that can only be utilized by nation-states. Like cybercrime and cyberterrorism, cyberwarfare will involve the use of digital signals—bits and bytes—which are available to anyone with a computer, Internet access, and the requisite computer expertise.

All these factors erode the assumptions on which the three threat categories are based. A cyberattack that comes (seems to come) from outside a nation-state's territory and is directed at what would be considered military targets *might* be cyberwar, but it might be cybercrime or cyberterrorism. In cyberspace, states lose their monopoly on war and individuals lose their monopoly on crime and terrorism.

This creates serious problems for countries like the United States, which rigidly bifurcate response authority into civilian (crime and terrorism) and military (war). The bifurcation is predicated on the assumption that response personnel can easily distinguish crime and terrorism from war. That premise is valid in the physical world but is increasingly problematic for conduct vectored through cyberspace. The distinction between crime, terrorism, and war in cyberspace becomes problematic due to assigning attribution.

Attribution is an explicit element of the laws of war and is implicit in the laws governing crime and terrorism.[3] It encompasses two issues: attacker attribution (who carried out an attack) and attack attribution (what kind of an attack was it).

Attacker Attribution

Attacker attribution has historically been less problematic for war than for crime or terrorism. The laws of war require warring states to identify themselves; even if a nation-state breaches that obligation, it is generally not difficult to identify the nation responsible for an act of war in the real world. The clothing military attackers wear and the equipment they use display insignia indicating their national affiliation. The language they speak and the location from which an attack is launched can also indicate the country from which it originated; in the real world, it is relatively easy to determine the physical location from which an attack was launched.

Identifying those responsible for a crime is usually more difficult. Criminals have a strong incentive to avoid identification because it is generally the first step toward being apprehended, convicted, and sanctioned for their misdeeds. Since crime control is essential for maintaining internal order, nation-states have developed a standardized, generally effective approach for identifying those who commit crimes in their territory.

This criminal investigation approach assumes activity in the real world because until recently physical reality was the only arena of crime commission. This approach focuses on finding physical evidence at a crime scene and locating witnesses who saw the perpetrator. It assumes the perpetrator was, and perhaps still is, in the local geographical area. If attacker attribution fails for one crime, officers will assume the attacker remains in the area and will consequently be alert for the possibility that he or she will reoffend and then be identified.

Attacker attribution for terrorism is more complicated than attack attribution for war but less complicated than attack attribution for crime. While those who carry out a terrorist attack may not identify themselves personally, they often identify themselves as acting on behalf of a terrorist group. And if the sponsoring group does not claim credit for an attack, the structure and style of the attack may inferentially identify the organization responsible. That may lead investigators to the individuals who carried out an attack. Since the current strategy treats terrorism as a type of crime, the criminal investigation approach is often used to identify and apprehend individual terrorists.

In analyzing how cyberspace complicates attacker attribution, it is helpful to employ an example: In October 2006, a "sensitive Commerce Department bureau"—the Bureau of Industry and Security (BIS)—suffered a "debilitating attack" on its computer system.[4] BIS was forced to disconnect its computers from the Internet and eventually discarded the infected computers and replaced them with new ones. The attack was traced to sites hosted by Chinese Internet service providers (ISPs), but the attackers were never identified.[5]

The real-world attacker-attribution calculi rely on the place where an attack occurred or originated from in determining attacker identity. With virtual attacks, "place" tends to be at once more ambiguous and less conclusive than in real-world analyses.

POINT OF ATTACK ORIGIN

The place from which a virtual attack originated is ambiguous because, while attacks might be routed through Internet servers in China, they might not originate in China. It is common for online attackers to use "stepping stones"—computers owned by innocent parties—in their assaults.[6] The stepping stone computers can be anywhere in the physical world because real space is irrelevant to activity in cyberspace. So while use of the Chinese servers might mean the attacks came from China, the attacker might be in Russia or Peoria, Illinois.

What if BIS-style attacks were repeated, with each coming from Chinese servers and targeting computers used by U.S. agencies? Could attacker attribution be based on inferences drawn from the repetitive use of what seems the same point of origin? It would be risky to rely on mere repetition; aside from anything else, a virtual Machiavelli might be framing China by routing structurally similar attacks through its real space.

Repetition coupled with other circumstances might support using point of attack origin inferences to establish attacker attribution. Assume BIS-style attacks are launched against another U.S. agency's computers. Investigators trace these attacks to servers in Guangdong, China. For two years, sporadic attacks targeting U.S. civilian and government computers have been traced to Guangdong; some say Chinese military hackers conducted the attacks, and others say Guangdong University students were responsible. Can attacker-attribution inferences be predicated on the discontinuous repetition of similar target attacks coming from the same real-world locus in China? Does the (reasonably reliable) identification of a single point of origin support the inference that the recent BIS-style attacks came from Guangdong?

For the purposes of analysis, assume the facts outlined above support the inference that "someone" in Guangdong launched the hypothesized BIS-style attacks. That raises the next question: how, if at all, does the inference that the attacks came from Guangdong advance the process of identifying the someone who is responsible for them?

Point of Attack Origin in War

Point of attack origin historically played an important role in attacker attribution for acts of war because the targets of such attacks usually inferred that an attack originating in another nation-state is attributable to that nation-state. If this logic is applied to the scenario above, the United States could rationally infer that the BIS-style attacks on U.S. government agency computers were acts of war launched by China. It could, in effect, construe the attacks as the virtual equivalent of Japan's real-world attack on Pearl Harbor. The problem with this derivative inference of responsibility lies in equating an attack inferentially launched from Chinese territory with an attack launched by China.

Historically, it was reasonable to equate transnational attacks with acts of war because only a state could launch such an attack. That is still true in the real world, but cyberspace gives each nation-state an incremental, highly permeable set of virtual national borders. Anyone with Internet access and certain skills can launch a cross-border virtual attack, not on the territory, but on the machinery of an external nation-state. A virtual attack is not territorially invasive, but it produces effects in the victim state's territory that are damaging in various ways and in varying degrees.

Point of attack origin therefore plays a more problematic role in analyzing online warfare. Is it similarly problematic in the crime-terrorism calculus? The next section examines this issue.

Point of Attack Origin with Crime and Terrorism

While crime and terrorism are conceptually distinct threats, it is logical to consider them jointly because both represent threats to internal order and both are the product of individual actions. Point of attack origin historically played a much more limited role in crime and terrorism attacker attribution than in war attribution. While point of attack origin can inferentially indicate who may have been responsible for a crime or an act of terrorism, the link between origin and attribution is much more attenuated than in war analysis.

The primary reason for this is that, in the real world, point of attack origin and point of attack occurrence are often so closely related as to be indistinguishable for crime, as well as for terrorism. A crack dealer sells crack in his neighborhood; the points of origin and occurrence of his drug crimes are functionally identical. A terrorist group operating from city A bombs a restaurant in nearby city B; since the points of attack origin and occurrence were separated by only a short distance, one can argue they are functionally identical here as well. If there is little or no differentiation between the point of attack origin and the point of attack occurrence, identifying the point of origin is unlikely to markedly advance the process of identifying the attacker.

Point of attack origin therefore tends to be one, perhaps minor, factor in the processes law enforcement officers use to identify those responsible for crime and terrorism. It has played a lesser role in crime-terrorism attacker attribution because these threats to internal order have come primarily, if not exclusively, from domestic actors. Domestic actors are presumptively in the nation-state where the attack occurred, and investigators tend to assume that they remain in the area where it occurred.

As crime and terrorism migrate online, point of attack origin can assume more importance in attacker attribution. Cyberspace eliminates the need for physical proximity between attacker and victim and creates the potential for increased differentiation between point of attack origin and point of occurrence. In other words, it erodes law enforcement's ability to assume an attacker is parochial. The viability of that default assumption still holds for real-world crime, and can hold for real-world terrorism, but its applicability to online crime and terrorism is increasingly problematic.

The parochial-attacker assumption is most likely to hold for "personal" attacks: cybercrimes and acts of cyberterrorism in which the perpetrator's motives are idiosyncratically emotional. In these cases—for instance, John uses cyberspace to stalk his former girlfriend, or Jane uses it to attack her employer—the perpetrator and victim are in the same area, but instead of using physical activity in that real space to conduct the attack, the perpetrator vectors it through cyberspace.

This creates an epistemological issue: when attacker and attacked are in the same real-space area throughout an attack conducted online, did the attack originate in the real space occupied by attacker and victim, online, or in both? For the purposes of attacker attribution, the answer should be both.

In personal attack cases, the connections between attacker and victim mean the parochial-attacker assumption is likely to be useful in identifying the attacker. So far, cybervendettas seem to primarily originate in real-world contacts between attacker and victim. Investigators can therefore rely on the approach used for real-world crime and terrorism, that is, focus on inferences derived from a real-world context. The attack, then, should be construed as originating in the real space occupied by attacker and victim.

What about attacks in which the attacker is not, by any definition, in the same real space as the victim? In the BIS attacks, the target was in Washington, D.C., while the attackers were (presumably) in China. An identified point of attack origin serves a very different function in cases like this, for several reasons.

First, it serves an initial, essentially negative function in attacker attribution. It tells investigators that the parochial-attacker assumption and derivative investigative approach they use for real-world crime and terrorism will probably be of little use in identifying the attackers. When an attack presents functionally coterminous points of attack origin and occurrence, a localized crime scene becomes the focal point of the investigation. Evidence, inferences, observations of witnesses, and connections between victim and attacker all radiate from and revolve around this unitary crime scene. It creates a comprehensible focus for the investigation and, in so doing, makes the investigation a manageable task.

Cyberspace fractures the crime scene into shards, the number of which depends on the particular circumstances of an attack. One constant shard is the alpha point of attack origin—the place where the attacker is physically located and from which she or he launches the attack. Other, variable shards are the intermediary points of transmission used in the attack; each represents the occurrence of a constituent, spatially diverse event that contributed to the success of the ultimate attack. The other constant shard, the omega shard, is the place of attack occurrence.

Fracturing the crime scene into shards makes identifying the point of attack origin and linking it to the attacker much more difficult. Aside from anything else, a fractured crime scene can result in false positives—in investigators assuming an intermediary point of transmission of an attack is the originating point for the attack.

Another issue that can complicate the process of backtracking through a series of incremental attack stages is the legal process involved. Incremental attack stages will almost certainly involve the use of computers in different countries. To gain access to the information needed to trace an attack through those computers, law enforcement will have to obtain assistance from government and civilian entities in the countries in which the computers were used. This process can be difficult, time consuming, and even futile. The formal methods used to obtain assistance can take months or even years; since digital evidence is fragile, it may have disappeared by the time investigators obtain the assistance they need.

Even if investigators obtain the assistance they need and can trace an attack to its point of origin, this may not markedly advance their effort to identify the attacker. Investigators in the BIS case ascertained that the attacks came from servers in China, but this information could neither directly nor inferentially establish who was responsible for the attacks or, indeed, what kind of attacks they were.

In sum, while point of attack origin can play a role in identifying the attackers in a cybercrime or cyberterrorism event, its function tends to be limited and will probably become more so as cyberattackers become more sophisticated about hiding their tracks.

POINT OF ATTACK OCCURRENCE

For real-world warfare, point of attack occurrence is the essential complement to point of attack origin: point of attack origin indicates which country initiated war; point of attack occurrence indicates which country is the victim of war.

As with point of attack origin, the point of attack occurrence calculus becomes ambiguous when war migrates online. Consider the BIS attacks: They occurred in the United States. What, if anything, does that indicate about who is responsible for them?

Assume the attacks originated in Guangdong, China. Is it reasonable to infer that cyberattacks originating in China and occurring in the United States represent acts of war attributable to the Chinese government? Unlike real-world acts of war, enemy personnel and armament are not present on U.S. soil. There is only the virtual presence of signals, which traveled through cyberspace by routine means, the same means used by civilian and government traffic every second of every day. The signals bear neither state insignia nor other markers of nation-state allegiance. The only bases for concluding they constitute components of an attack by China are their point of origin, their geographic destination, and the nature of the harm they inflicted (damage to U.S. government computers).

The ambiguity involved in determining point of attack origin is clear. Here, however, the point of attack occurrence is not ambiguous; it clearly occurred in the United States. The ambiguity lies in the implications of this point of occurrence. In the real world, the occurrence of an act of war on nation-state A's territory is equivalent to a declaration of war by the state responsible for the attack because war has historically been about territory. The violation of one nation-state's territorial integrity by agents of another nation-state is a challenge to its ability to maintain external order.

In the real world, the singular inference to be drawn from an attack originating in the territory of one nation-state and occurring inside the territory of another is war. Real-world transborder attacks have been equated with war because only nation-states could launch such attacks.

Cyberspace changes that: the mere fact that the attacks targeted computers on U.S. soil cannot support the inference that they are the equivalent of Hitler invading Poland. In utilizing point of attack occurrence in attacker attribution, it is necessary to modify the assumption equating transborder attacks with war so that it incorporates a basic reality of the online environment: U.S. government and civilian computers are attacked because they are attractive targets for criminals, terrorists, and ultimately, perhaps nation-states bent on war. Since U.S. computers are attractive targets for all three categories of attackers, any of whom can launch transborder attacks, an externally launched attack occurring "in" the United States does not necessarily indicate an act of war on the part of the state from whose territory it originated.

What about crime and terrorism? Point of attack occurrence is an integral component of attacker attribution for both. Investigations concentrate on the place where the attack occurred. This investigative model is based on the assumption that the players in the attack dynamic occupied shared real space, since physical proximity is an essential prerequisite for the commission of real-world crime or terrorism.

Thus, point of attack occurrence plays a central role in investigating these real-world events. It is the most likely source of physical evidence and eyewitness testimony that can be used to identify an attacker and link him or her to the crime or act of terrorism. The larger spatial context in which the crime scene resides provides a potential source of further testimony and data that can become the basis of inferential linkages between victim and attacker. And sometimes the place where the attack occurs is itself a source of inference as to the identity of an attacker. If someone is murdered in a home with an armed alarm system, this suggests the attacker knew the victim.

Here, again, the importance of point of attack occurrence diminishes as attacks move online. A real-space attacker's gaining entry to a home with an alarm system suggests the attacker knew the victim, but a cyberspace attacker's gaining entry to a computer hooked to a cable modem does not. The physical constraints that govern action in the real world make it eminently reasonable to draw certain inferences from the place where an attack occurred; the absence of those constraints makes it problematic to predicate similar inferences on the place where a virtual attack occurred. Cyberspace nullifies the influence of the three spatial dimensions that constrain action in the real world and, in so doing, erodes the significance of place in attacker attribution.

Point of attack occurrence can still play some role in attacker attribution for online crimes and terrorism because it is part of a larger crime scene and will therefore contain evidence that can be used in an attempt to track the perpetrators. Unlike a real-world crime scene, it is not self-contained; the evidence it contains is part of a sequence of digital evidence that is strewn around cyberspace. Since the point of attack occurrence accounts for only part of the evidence, its role in the process of identifying the attacker is accordingly reduced.

Attack Attribution

Attacker attribution has historically been problematic in the real world, at least for crime and terrorism, but attack attribution has not. This is due to the distinction societies have drawn between threats to internal and external order.

The distinction arose from the realities of the physical world. Until relatively recently, the limitations of travel and state monopolization of military-grade weaponry made it functionally impossible for nonstate actors to challenge a nation-state's ability to maintain its territorial integrity. External order was a purely sovereign concern; nation-states challenged each other in the international arena and resolved matters with military combat. Nonstate actors were limited to challenging a state's ability to maintain internal order; criminals' pursuit of self-gratification and the more doctrinaire activities of terrorists threatened to erode social order in varying ways and to varying degrees. However, as activities move online, threats increase and change, and attack attribution must be determined in not only the real world but also cyberspace.

ATTACK ATTRIBUTION IN THE REAL WORLD

Crime is easily identified because it involves the civilian-on-civilian infliction of familiar categories of harm, such as theft, murder, and arson. And it tends to be limited in scale because of the constraints physical reality imposes on action in the real world. Crime usually involves one-on-one victimization, that is, one perpetrator and one victim (at a time).

Real-world terrorism is usually easy to identify, though it often involves activity that would otherwise constitute crime. Real-world terrorism can usually be distinguished from crime because (1) it seems irrational in that it has no obvious mundane motive, such as self-enrichment or revenge and (2) the scale on which it is committed often exceeds what we encounter with crime.

Real-world war is even easier to identify: when the Japanese bombed Pearl Harbor, no one who saw the attack could have had the slightest doubt this was war—not crime, nor terrorism. The attackers wore military uniforms complete with Japan's national insignia, flew the Japanese flag, and used airplanes and other weapons that were not available to civilians. They also attacked military targets.

ATTACK ATTRIBUTION IN CYBERSPACE

The BIS attacks are a useful conceptual vehicle for this analysis, but the focus is now on identifying the nature of the attack. The first step is parsing what is known of the attacks. They were clearly deliberate, orchestrated attacks, not computer malfunctions; they targeted computers used by a U.S. government agency; they originated in China; and it is reasonable to assume they came from Guangdong, which some claim is associated with China's cyberwarfare efforts.

The attacker-attribution analysis examined the ambiguity of the attack, and the same issues arise here. The circumstances suggest it was a sortie into cyberwar—an attack launched by the Chinese government. Historically, an attack originating from the territory of one nation-state and terminating on the territory of another presumptively constituted an act of war; that presumption suggests the BIS attacks were war. The validity of that conclusion is reinforced since the attacks targeted government computers; the nature of the target inferentially supports the premise that the attacks were a foray into cyberwarfare.

While it is not clear what the BIS attacks were meant to accomplish, one could logically conclude they were a reconnaissance by China's military, testing the security of U.S. government computer systems. But it is impossible to arrive at this conclusion with the requisite level of confidence because the markers involved in the analysis take on an ambiguity lacking in the real world. The fact the attacks originated from the territory of another nation-state is a circumstance that can be considered, but it carries much less weight than in the real world; in cyberspace, anyone with an Internet connection and a base level of computer skills can attack a computer in another country. The transnational aspect of the attack might, or might not, be significant; the same is true of the attacks' originating in Guangdong and targeting computers used by the U.S. government. For years, Guangdong has been producing hackers, and for years civilian hackers of various nationalities have been exploring U.S. government computers. It is as possible that the attacks came from student hackers in Guangdong as it is that they came from the Chinese government.

What if a BIS-style attack targeted a corporate computer system? The nature of the target inferentially suggests it was cybercrime, as we assume criminals attack other civilians. That conclusion would be reinforced if the attackers' actions conformed to what one expects of cybercriminals, if, say, they extracted funds from corporate accounts or personal information from databases. Since civilians are presumptively the targets of crime, not war, an attack such as this would almost certainly be construed as cybercrime.

Relying too heavily on this assumption could be a mistake. The attack on the corporate entity could be cyberwar, not cybercrime. China's focus on cyberwar includes attacks on civilian entities. If the default approach to attack attribution continues to rely on the attacks-on-civilians-are-crimes assumption, there will no doubt be situations in which an act of cyberwar is construed as cybercrime.

An analogous, but perhaps less serious, problem arises if the attack on the corporate entity is cyberterrorism. Cyberterrorist attacks are unlikely to be isolated incidents; a cyberterrorist event is more likely to be part of a sequence of attacks that may be separated spatially or temporally and that have different points of origin. The attack appears to be cybercrime, and except for serial killers and the odd career robber or serial arsonist, law enforcement is not accustomed to approaching a crime as part of a sequence. This means the response to the components of a sequenced cyberterrorism attack would probably be discrete and isolated; officers in different locations would respond to incidents without realizing they were part of a larger attack.

This problem arises because of the United States' (and other countries') partitioned responsibility for responding to crime and terrorism versus warfare and because of the tendency to assume crime is a localized phenomenon. A subsidiary factor contributing to the problem is that the markers used to differentiate crime and terrorism from war in the real world are absent or unreliable when it comes to virtual attacks. In the real world, three markers are used to determine the nature of an attack: (1) point of attack origin, (2) point of attack occurrence, and (2) motive for an attack.

The utility of the first two markers erodes as attacks migrate online. The same is also true, but in a different way and for different reasons, for the third factor. Technology enhances the ability to inflict harm but does not alter the human psyche; unless and until technology transforms people into cyborgs or some other variety of posthuman life, it is reasonable to assume the motives that have historically driven individuals to inflict harm will continue to account for their doing so, on- or off line. Motive is and will continue to be a valid differentiating factor for cyberattacks: profit drives most crime; ideology drives terrorism; and nation-state rivalries have historically driven warfare. The difficulty arises not with the ability to rely on established motivations as a "marker" that inferentially indicates the nature of an attack. It arises instead with the ability to ascertain the motive behind a specific attack.

It is clear what the BIS attackers did but not why they did it. This is likely to be true for many future attacks as well: while the motive behind what are almost certainly routine cybercrime incidents is usually apparent (e.g., greed or revenge), that may not always be true. Terrorists, for example, are increasingly using cybercrime to finance their real-world efforts, which give us a mixed-motive scenario: the motive for committing cybercrimes is profit, a criminal motive; but the motive for obtaining the profit is to engage in acts of terrorism, a noncriminal motive. It is also increasingly possible that nonstate actors could commit cybercrimes to obtain the money needed to launch cyberattacks on a nation-state.

Examples of Mutating Cyberthreats

Over the past few years, there have been a number of incidents that illustrate how traditional threats mutate in cyberspace. This section examines two of these incidents: the 2007 attacks on Estonia and the 2010 WikiLeaks episode.

ATTACKS ON ESTONIA

In April 2007, Estonian authorities moved "a bronze statue of a World War II–era Soviet soldier" from a park in Tallinn to a military cemetery in one of the city's suburbs.[7] They expected "violent street protests" from Estonia's "large Russian-speaking minority" but did not anticipate what else was about to happen, at least not initially.[8]

Since Estonia is a very "wired" country, it is not surprising that the plans being made online came to the government's attention: individuals were using Russian-language chat rooms and other online fora to organize distributed denial of service (DDOS) attacks on websites operated by the Estonian government and by private-sector entities.

The attacks began on April 26; by April 29, a torrent of data had shut down the Estonian parliament's e-mail server. The director of Estonia's Computer Emergency Response Team (CERT-EE) assembled experts from the country's Internet service providers, banks, government agencies, and police forces; he also reached out to government agencies in other countries for assistance in tracking sources of the attack. By the end of the first week, the Estonian forces were having some success in limiting the effects of the attack, but they knew the worst was yet to come. The attacks seemed to come from Russia, and May 9 was an important Russian holiday, the anniversary of its defeating Nazi Germany and the day on which the country honors its fallen soldiers. The CERT-EE director urged his team to try to keep their sites and services operating; he was under orders to keep an important government site online but was told that other government sites, including the Estonian president's website, could be sacrificed, if necessary.

On May 9, traffic to Estonian servers increased to thousands of times its normal flow; sites that usually received one thousand hits a day were getting two thousand hits a second.[9] The traffic increased on May 10, shutting down Estonia's largest bank. After shutting down the president's website and other government sites, the attacks shifted to civilian targets: newspapers, television stations, phone systems, schools, businesses, and other financial institutions. To maintain some internal Internet service, Estonian authorities had to block access to Estonian sites by people outside the country; this meant Estonians traveling abroad could not access their e-mail, bank accounts, or other resources.

The DDoS attacks began to wane on May 10 but continued sporadically for weeks. Estonia's largest bank was still dealing with intermittent assaults three weeks later; other victims had similar experiences.[10] The last major wave of after-attacks finally ended on May 18.

The Estonian government believed the attacks were Russian-sponsored cyberwarfare. They cited several reasons they thought Russia was responsible: Comments posted in Russian-language chat rooms indicated the attacks were retaliation for Estonia's removing the statue of the Soviet soldier from a city park to a more remote location. These chat rooms were used to organize the attacks, which inferentially indicated that Russia was behind them; and Estonian authorities claimed that a member of the Russian security service was "one of the masterminds" behind the attacks.[11] Estonian investigators also said they traced Internet addresses used in the attacks to Russian agencies, including President Vladimir Putin's office.[12]

As time passed and experts analyzed the attacks, the Estonian government backed off on its claim that they were cyberwar. Analysts discovered that the attacks were launched with a rented botnet and began to decline when the rent ran out.[13] Some described the Estonian attacks as being "more like a riot than a military assault."[14] Many, then, concluded that the attacks were "mere" cybercrime, protests by individuals unhappy with the relocation of the statue of the Soviet soldier.

The actual nature of the attacks was called into question, at least to some extent, in 2009, when Konstantin Goloskokov, a "commissar" of Nashi, a "political youth movement in Russia,"[15] announced that he and some associates were responsible for the 2007 Estonian attacks.[16] Goloskokov described the attacks as "cyber-defense" and said, "We taught the Estonian regime the lesson that if they act illegally, we will respond in an adequate way."[17]

Thus, it is not clear whether the Estonian attacks were cybercrime, cyberterrorism, or cyberwarfare. If they were launched by individuals who were acting on their own, that is, without state sponsorship, then the attacks were cybercrime or cyberterrorism. (The distinction between them lies in the motive: if the attacks were part of an extortion scheme, they would be cybercrime; if the attacks were launched for political motives, they would be cyberterrorism.) Under existing law, individuals can commit cybercrime or cyberterrorism but not cyberwarfare. If, on the other hand, the attacks were launched by Russian military hackers, they would qualify as cyberwarfare, and the 2007 cyberattacks would be the functional equivalent of Russia's dropping bombs on locations in Estonia.

The most intriguing scenario is that in which Goloskokov and other Nashi associates launched the attacks on their own, without the involvement of other, non-Nashi-affiliated civilians or of Russian military hackers. If Nashi members carried out the attacks, it becomes necessary to determine whether they were acting on their own or at the behest of, and perhaps with the support of, the Russian government. If they acted on their own, then the attacks would be either cybercrime or cyberterrorism.

If, on the other hand, Nashi members acted at the behest and with the support of the Russian government, the attacks could be cyberwarfare —or something relatively new: state-sponsored cybercrime. State-sponsored cybercrime consists of individuals committing crimes at the behest of, with the support of, and with the intent of benefitting a nation-state. It is not recognized as a separate threat category, for at least two reasons, one of which is that it has emerged relatively recently. The other reason is that state-sponsored cybercrime does not fit into the legislative and enforcement structures that currently exist: if the Estonian attacks were state-sponsored cybercrime, the only recourse the Estonian government would have under existing law is to prosecute the Nashi members for cybercrime. There is no formal legal system for holding a nation-state accountable for sponsoring cybercrime; Estonia's only recourse would presumably be some sort of diplomatic sanctions.

CYBERATTACK ON WIKILEAKS

WikiLeaks is an organization that uses its website to publish "private, secret, and classified media" submitted by anonymous sources.[18] On November 28, 2010, it began publishing leaked "confidential," but not top secret, cables from U.S. embassies.[19] WikiLeaks' actions rather quickly elicited a response.

On December 2, EveryDNS.net, which provided hosting services to the WikiLeaks domain, terminated WikiLeaks as a client because it had become "the target of multiple" DDOS attacks that threatened "the stability of the Every DNS.net infrastructure."[20] Some believed the U.S. government was behind the DDOS attacks, while others disagreed.

Also on December 2, Amazon removed WikiLeaks "from its infrastructure-as-a-service platform" after inquiries from an aide to Senator Joseph Lieberman.[21] The next day, PayPal blocked the account of a foundation that collected donations for WikiLeaks, and on December 6, MasterCard took similar action.[22] On December 7, Visa followed suit, suspending payments to WikiLeaks.[23] Their actions were apparently prompted by concern that processing payments for WikiLeaks somehow facilitated illegal activity.[24]

These and similar responses to WikiLeaks' publishing the leaked cables elicited a counter-response: "Anonymous," a "loosely affiliated group of activist computer hackers," launched DDOS attacks against Amazon, PayPal,

MasterCard, Visa, and other businesses that had withdrawn support from WikiLeaks.[25] Some media sources described the attacks as "cyberwar,"[26] while others referred to them as a "cyber sit-in."[27] Dutch police arrested a teenager for participating in the attacks on Visa and MasterCard, but there has been no indication what, if anything, he was charged with.[28] Apparently in retaliation, Anonymous attacked the Dutch National Police Service's website.[29]

Did the WikiLeaks episode involve cyberwar? I think not, but I can understand why some might have reached that conclusion based on two aspects of the episode: the DDOS attacks on EveryDNS.net and the DDOS attacks on MasterCard, Visa, PayPal, and other companies that withdrew their support of WikiLeaks.

There is no evidence the U.S. government was responsible for the EveryDNS.net attacks, and many believe that scenario is implausible for various reasons. For the purposes of analysis, though, assume the U.S. government was behind those attacks. Would that constitute cyberwarfare?

This hypothetical includes one essential element of cyberwar—a digital attack launched by a nation-state—but lacks the other, that is, the attack targets another nation-state, as such. EveryDNS.net is owned by Dyn Inc., which has its corporate headquarters in Manchester, New Hampshire.[30] If assuming, for the purposes of analysis, the U.S. government was responsible for the DDOS attacks on EveryDNS.net, the attacks cannot constitute cyberwarfare because (1) they targeted a company not a nation-state and (2) the company in question is located in and operates under the laws of the United States. There is no conceivable scenario in which a nation-state can engage in cyberwarfare by attacking what is, in effect, one of its own citizens.

Interpreting the attacks on EveryDNS.net as an attack on servers that host WikiLeaks produces the same conclusion. According to one source, those servers are in Sweden;[31] even if one assumes, for the purposes of analysis, that the DDOS attacks on EveryDNS.net targeted the Swedish WikiLeaks servers, the attacks still would not rise to the level of cyberwarfare. In this scenario, they target computer servers located on Swedish territory, but the servers are owned and used by a private entity, not by the Swedish government.

The other scenario some sources characterized as cyberwarfare involves the DDOS attacks Anonymous launched on MasterCard, Visa, and PayPal. Anonymous is a group of hactivists, the members of which reside in various countries. Assume, for the purposes of analysis, that the computer servers targeted by the DDOS attacks were all located on U.S. territory. The attacks, then, presumably involved some activity by individuals who are not citizens of the United States and who were located outside the United States when they participated in attacks on corporations that qualify as U.S. citizens.

None of this is sufficient to transform the attacks into cyberwarfare. There is no nation-state involvement and no basis on which to hypothesize nation-state involvement in the MasterCard, Visa, and PayPal DDOS attacks. The attacks, therefore, are either cybercrime or cyberterrorism. DDOS attacks are a crime, and terrorism is a crime committed for ideological purposes; if, as seems to have been the case, the MasterCard, Visa, and PayPal DDOS attacks were launched to punish those companies for not supporting WikiLeaks, this at least arguably establishes the empirical basis needed to charge the perpetrators with cyberterrorism.

Clearly, then, this episode involves conduct that does not qualify as cyberwarfare and therefore must, by default, be a matter to be dealt with by law enforcement. The problem that arises in this scenario is one of implementation: the activity involved in the commission of what seem to be crimes occurred in various countries and was carried out by individuals whom it may be difficult, even impossible, to identify. Identifying even a few of the perpetrators is likely to be a time- and resource-consuming endeavor, which creates questions about the extent to which digital attacks such as these are a legitimate law enforcement priority. Jurisdictional issues could further complicate the process of bringing the perpetrators to justice, as victim countries seek to extradite suspects in the face of opposition from their home countries.

Implications of Jurisdictional Constraints

Nation-states control internal threats by adopting laws that proscribe certain behaviors ("crimes") and imposing sanctions on those who engage in such behaviors. They use a similar strategy to control external threats: nation-states arm themselves in an effort to discourage other nation-states from attacking them, and they use their military might to repel attacks, if and when they are launched.

The efficacy of both strategies depends on a nation-state's ability to respond effectively to a threat. Responding to a threat requires that a nation-state (1) identify the nature of the threat and (2) implement measures designed to resolve the threat as efficiently and effectively as possible. Nation-states use a bifurcated response system: law enforcement responds to internal threats (crime and terrorism); the military responds to external threats (war). The bifurcation is a function both of pragmatism (e.g., military weaponry is unsuited for civilian law enforcement purposes) and policy (e.g., a bifurcated system is considered to be a mainstay of democracy).[32]

Bifurcated response processes become problematic as threats move into cyberspace because they assume law enforcement officers and military personnel can easily determine whether a threat is internal or external. That assumption breaks down as threat activity moves into cyberspace because the threat categories (and attendant threat identification processes) assume conduct in the physical world.

As state and nonstate threat entities increasingly utilize cyberspace in their attacks, it becomes increasingly difficult to differentiate crime, terrorism, and warfare. If potential responders cannot reliably ascertain the nature of a threat, they may not respond or may respond when they should not. In other words, the ambiguity of online threat activity erodes the ability not only to identify threats but also to respond to them.

Assume FBI agents discover an ongoing, BIS-style attack on the computer system used by the U.S. air traffic control system. The agents determine the attacks are coming from a location in China that is associated both with China's preparation for cyberwarfare and with university student hackers. If the attacks are cybercrime or cyberterrorism, the FBI can and must respond to them. If they are cyberwarfare, then the military must respond.

Given the nature of the attacks and the potential harm involved if they continue, the FBI has little time in which to decide whether they are crime, terrorism, or war. In its effort to make that decision, the FBI considers the place from which the attacks originate, the place where they occur, and the motive for the attacks. The FBI is fairly certain the attacks originate in China but cannot rule out the possibility they originate elsewhere and are merely being routed through China. The FBI is certain that the attacks target a U.S. government agency and, in so doing, threaten serious harm to U.S. civilians.

FBI agents cannot ascertain the motive for the attack with any certainty; they have not received an extortion demand, which inferentially suggests the attacks are not cybercrime. The FBI cannot link the circumstances of the attacks and apparent sources of the attacks either to known terrorist groups or to the Chinese government. The FBI therefore has neither direct nor inferential evidence indicating that the attacks are either cyberterrorism or cyberwarfare. Unless and until the FBI can determine that they are neither, FBI agents cannot involve U.S. military personnel, because of the bifurcation noted earlier, that is, under U.S. law, military personnel cannot participate in law enforcement.

The FBI could presumably alert the military to the occurrence of the attacks and let the military conduct its own assessment of the nature of the attacks and need for and propriety of the military's responding to them. To avoid the need to consider whether such action would violate any aspect of U.S. law, assume the military is already aware of the attacks and has been conducting its own attempt to ascertain whether they are cybercrime, cyberterrorism, or cyberwarfare. Also assume the military has only the information that is available to the FBI, which means its analysis of the nature of the attacks will essentially mirror that of the FBI. Since the nature of the attacks is inconclusive, the military will need to weigh the risk of responding (perhaps erroneously) against the risk of not responding. Because war threatens a nation-state's existence, the military may decide the risk of not responding outweighs the risk of doing nothing. If the military responds, the response will constitute an act of cyberwar; the question is whether the response will constitute offensive or defense cyberwarfare. The U.S. military will say the response constitutes defensive cyberwarfare because they were responding to acts of cyberwar initiated by the Chinese government; depending on the circumstances, the Chinese government may argue (perhaps quite accurately) that it was not responsible for the attacks. If China was not responsible for the attacks, the U.S. military's response will constitute offensive cyberwarfare; since offensive warfare is unlawful under the laws of warfare, the U.S. military has committed an illegal act.

These may not be the only scenarios the facts outlined above can support. They should, though, illustrate that a nation-state's ability to respond effectively to a threat depends on its ability to ascertain what type of threat is at issue. This becomes more and more difficult as activities increasingly migrate into cyberspace. If nation-states cannot reliably ascertain the nature of the threats they confront, their ability to respond is impaired, which reduces the disincentives to engage in threat activity. That, in turn, erodes a nation-state's (or nation-states') ability to deter and thereby control various cyberthreats.

It is highly unlikely that the threat identification and response issues outlined here are a transient phenomenon; it is likely they will not only persist but also increase in incidence and complexity as the use of computer technology becomes more sophisticated and more pervasive. If that speculation is accurate, states have two choices: They can continue to rely on our current threat identification and response processes for real-world threats and consign cyberspace to the status of outlaw territory, that is, an area in which no state attempts to maintain order. That option is appealing if one assumes it is possible to segregate cyberspace from real space, but activity in cyberspace has consequences in the physical world. Abandoning cyberspace to lawlessness would therefore only increase the threat activity originating in that domain.

The other choice is to modify the threat identification and response processes. The obvious modification is to abandon the bifurcated threat response strategy and replace it with a unitary response strategy that could respond to nation-state-sponsored cyberthreats as well as to cyberthreats the architects of which are individuals or organized groups of individuals. If the United States for example, abandoned the bifurcated response strategy, it would also discard the three threat categories on which it currently relies; there would be no need to differentiate between cybercrime, cyberterrorism, and cyberwarfare if a single institution was responsible for identifying and responding to both.

That approach has an appealing simplicity and an undeniable logic. Notwithstanding that, it may not be a viable option, if only because of concerns that fusing the military and law enforcement institutions can threaten the stability of democratic government.

However, there must be other, less drastic ways to modify our current threat identification and response processes so they can more effectively address cyberthreats. The first step toward exploring the possibility of such alternatives is to accept that the system we currently rely upon is fatally flawed with regard to cyberthreats.

Cyberspace as an Evolving Threat Vector

Facilitating remote attacks is an important factor in the evolution (or devolution) of traditional threats, but it is not cyberspace's only contribution to this phenomenon. Cyberspace also weakens the distinctions between crime, terrorism, and warfare by altering the nature of the effects of the attacks and by bringing new players into the mix.

The Estonian attacks illustrate this: The scale of the attacks and the magnitude of the harm they inflicted are *analogous* to the effects of a traditional military attack. But they differ from traditional military attacks in that the effects were economic and psychological, for instance, the attacks interfered with people's ability to travel, communicate, or access bank accounts.

No one's physical property was damaged or destroyed, which may suggest that the effects of such attacks are not, and cannot be, equivalent to the effects of the London Blitz or other sustained military assaults. If one construes the effects of attacks as limited to the type of physical destruction and carnage that has traditionally been associated with warfare, it is, of course, not possible to equate the Estonian cyberattacks to the London Blitz or similar physical attacks. But if one looks beyond the superficial dissimilarities between traditional warfare and cyberattacks, it is possible to identify functional similarities between the two.

The Blitz—the German bombing of British cities in 1940 and 1941 —was intended to demoralize the population by destroying buildings and killing and injuring as many people as possible.[33] The purpose of demoralizing the population was to pressure British leaders into surrendering. The goal, then, was psychological; the physical damage and injury the bombing inflicted was simply a tool used to achieve that goal. More accurately, it was *the* tool that was then available to achieve that goal, just as in ages past, sieges, carnage, and other uses of physical coercion were the implements used to demoralize or destroy a population and defeat an opposing sovereign.

Carnage and physical coercion are no longer the only tools sovereigns can use in an effort to undermine or even eradicate the viability of other sovereigns. Cyberattacks like those Estonia endured in 2007 can, I believe, also be used to achieve that goal, although perhaps in different ways. Sovereign A might, for example, use cyberattacks to erode, but not eradicate, the economic viability of sovereign B. In this scenario, sovereign A does not want to conquer sovereign B; it merely wants to make sovereign B less effective as an economic (or political) competitor.

This scenario still assumes cyberwarfare involves a struggle between two nation-states, which would probably be true today but may not be true in the future. Indeed, it may not be true today: many believe the Estonian attacks were launched by hackers—not by Russia or any other nation-state. Assuming, for the purposes of analysis, that this is true, the attacks were an instance in which private citizens perpetrated the equivalent of cyberwarfare against a nation-state. Warfare has been, and so far remains, the exclusive province of nation-states, which means individuals cannot wage war and, by extrapolation, cannot wage cyberwar.

Historically, individuals could not wage war against a nation-state, partially because they did not have access to the weapons and manpower needed to do so. Based on the Estonian attacks and other, more recent incidents, it appears individuals can—or at least will eventually be able to—use cyberspace to launch attacks on nation-states.

Where does all this leave us? It is impossible to know at this point, because this is an era in which the traditional threat categories and the tools used to implement them are in flux. The three traditional threat categories—crime, terrorism, and warfare—may fuse into a single category that focuses on a particular activity's ability to undermine the stability of a nation-state (or successor sovereign entities).

The traditional threat categories may, on the other hand, survive but in the context of a larger governance system, that is, a system that transcends the territorial parochialism of the nation-state and unites the constituencies that currently comprise discrete sovereign entities. Or the future might be very different: one in which territorially based, hierarchically organized nation-states disappear, to be replaced by decentralized entities that outsource the tasks of maintaining order and security to private entities. That approach would be consistent with the view that cyberspace favors nonhierarchical, flexible organizational structures.

Or traditional nation-states may survive, evolved to adapt to the decreasing importance of territorial boundaries in a world of pervasive technology. For that scenario to prevail, those responsible for nation-state governance will have to recognize the impact cyberspace has on the doctrines and assumptions that shape nation-state governance and modify that governance structure in ways that allow it to accommodate nontraditional threats.

EPILOGUE

The criminals are absolutely ripping us to shreds.
We're not even slowing them down.[1]

A professional who works in online finance made the above comment at
a meeting of Infragard,[2] an FBI initiative that brings civilian professionals
and FBI agents together to collaborate in the battle against cybercrime.
His comment reflects the frustration many—if not most—of those who
are engaged in the battle against cybercrime feel as they see their hard
work having little, if any, effect on the progress of online crime.

Chapters 6 and 7 outlined the factors that make cybercrime such a challenge for law enforcement, in the United States and elsewhere. Perhaps the
most important factor is the current structure of global governance: The
world is divided into a patchwork of territorially based sovereignties, each
with its own laws, its own interests, and its own set of enforcement priorities. This creates a twenty-first-century version of the Bonnie and Clyde
problem U.S. law enforcement officers grappled with eighty years ago.

The challenges cybercrime presents for twenty-first-century law enforcement officers are analogous to the challenges Bonnie and Clyde
and their peers presented for their Depression-era U.S. peers in that both
scenarios involve perpetrators who exploit sovereign boundaries to elude
capture and prosecution. The U.S. Congress addressed the domestic
Bonnie and Clyde problem by making bank robbery and a host of other
crimes, such as kidnapping and car theft, federal crimes; since the federal

government has jurisdiction throughout the territorial United States, this deprived would-be Bonnies and Clydes of their ability to use state boundaries to frustrate the efforts of law enforcement.

A similar strategy might be the solution to the ever-expanding proliferation of cybercrime we see in the early twenty-first century: if the world were a seamless web of consistent, effective cybercrime laws, it would be impossible—or at least much more difficult—for online criminals to evade justice. Yet, it is exceedingly unlikely that such a strategy can, or will be, implemented in the foreseeable future. Perhaps the greatest impediment is that countries have idiosyncratic laws to which they are, and are likely to continue to be, quite attached.

The United States, for example, has its First Amendment, which means U.S.-based websites may broadcast content that is considered offensive, criminal, and perhaps even a type of information warfare in various countries around the world. Those of us in the United States see this as a perfectly normal, worthwhile state of affairs; we generally do not see communicating information as a threatening or otherwise unlawful endeavor. Other countries, however, do not agree. Every year since 1998, Russia has introduced a resolution at the United Nations calling for an international agreement to combat what it calls "information terrorism."[3] Russia, and other countries that support the proposed resolution, see the United States' essentially unrestricted dissemination of information as a type of terrorism, and possibly as a type of online warfare.[4]

This is but one example of the disconnects that exist among the laws of the various nations of the world—disconnects that are likely to persist for decades or even centuries. It is clear that harmonizing cybercrime laws across the almost two hundred countries that currently exist is not a viable solution to the challenges cybercrime presents for lawmakers and law enforcement officers.

Thus, the governments of the world—or, more properly, the governments of the world whose citizens are targets of cybercrime—are left with two choices: learn to live with cybercrime or devise new and innovative solutions for combatting it. The first choice is simply not a viable option. Surrendering to the depredations of cybercriminals is at least in certain respects analogous to the Romans' bribing barbarians in an effort to discourage them from sacking Rome: like this tactic, tolerating cybercrime would only encourage cybercriminals to increase their depredations and, in so doing, could ultimately undermine the viability of the nation-states they targeted.

It is clear that the countries of the world face an unprecedented challenge, one that involves not only the threat of cybercrime but also the prospects of cyberterrorism and cyberwarfare. As Michael Hayden, former director of the National Security Agency and the Central Intelligence Agency, noted recently, the "cyberworld is so new that the old structures, you know—state, non-state, public, private—they all break down. . . . The last time we had such a powerful discontinuity is probably the European discovery of the Western Hemisphere."[5]

If we want to survive this discontinuity without sinking into a twenty-first-century version of the Dark Ages, we need to do something our ancestors did not: we need to recognize that the world is changing and attempt to devise solutions that can effectively address the challenges these changes present and, in so doing, ensure that the future brings progress, rather than decline.

Introduction

1. Similar scenarios have actually occurred. *See, e.g.,* Commonwealth v. Smith, 58 Mass. App. Ct. 381, 790 N.E.2d 708 (Massachusetts Court of Appeals 2003) (defendant indicted for assault with intent to murder for biting an officer and declaring that he was "HIV positive" and "I hope I kill you").

2. *See id.*

3. For more on this, *see* Susan W. Brenner, *Is There Such a Thing as "Virtual Crime?"* 4 California Criminal Law Review 1 (2001), http://www.boalt.org/CCLR/v4/v4brenner.htm.

4. For more on this, *see* Susan W. Brenner, *Toward a Criminal Law for Cyberspace: Distributed Security,* 10 Boston University Journal of Science and Technology Law 1, 5–49 (2004).

5. The account of the crime is taken from these sources: *Hacker Robs Bullitt County of $415,000,* WLKY.com (July 1, 2009), http://www.wlky.com/news/19922512/detail.html; *$415,989 Taken from Bullitt Bank Account,* Courier-Journal, July 1, 2009, 2009 WLNR 15630449; Kelly House, *$415,989 Taken from Bullitt Bank Account,* Courier-Journal, July 2, 2009, at A1, 2009 WLNR 15629810; Brian Krebs, *PC Invader Costs Ky. County $415,000,* Security Fix, Washington Post, July 2, 2009, http://voices.washingtonpost.com.

6. Krebs, *supra* note 5.

7. Krebs, *supra* note 5.

8. *See Hacker Robs Bullitt County, supra* note 5; Daniel Wolfe, *Security Watch,* American Banker, July 8, 2009, at 5, 2009 WLNR 12942404.

9. *See $415,989 Taken, supra* note 5.

10. *See, e.g.,* John Leyden, *Online Crimes Not Just "Speccy Geeks,"* Researchers *Warn*, Register (July 1, 2010), http://www.theregister.co.uk.

11. The description of the security measures the county and the bank used to protect their accounts and of how the cybercriminals were able to bypass those measures is taken primarily from Krebs, *supra* note 5.

12. Krebs, *supra* note 5.

13. *Id.*

14. *Id.*

15. *Id.*

16. *Id.*

17. *Id.*

18. Cybercriminals usually keep transfers below ten thousand dollars because banks are required to file a currency transaction report (CTR) with the Internal Revenue Service for any transaction of ten thousand or more.

19. Krebs, *supra* note 5.

20. *See* Emily Hagedorn, *Bullitt County Sues Bank over Loss from Online Theft*, Courier-Journal, August 6, 2009, 2009 WLNR 15639322.

21. *See Auditor: Bullitt Lacked Proper Controls in Online Theft*, Courier-Journal, September 16, 2009, 2009 WLNR 18493935.

22. *See Theft Used Stealthy Computer Code*, Courier-Journal, July 27, 2009, 2009 WLNR 15691911.

23. *See, e.g.,* Elinor Mills, *Zeus Trojan Steals $1 Million from U.K. Bank Accounts*, CNET News (August 10, 2010), http://news.cnet.com.

24. Marie Leone, *Come Together over Cybercrime*, CFO (June 29, 2010), http://www.cfo.com.

25. *See* 18 U.S. Code § 3181, http://www.state.gov/s/l/treaty/faqs/70138.htm.

26. *See* David Ronfeldt & John Arquilla, *What Next for Networks and Netwars?* in Networks and Netwars: The Future of Terror, Crime and Militancy 311, 313 (John Arquilla & David Ronfeldt eds., 2001), http://www.rand.org/pubs/monograph_reports/MR1382/MR1382.ch10.pdf.

27. Arthur C. Millspaugh, Crime Control by the National Government 56 (1937).

28. E. R. Milner, The Lives and Times of Bonnie and Clyde 135 (1996).

29. The cybercrime framework seems to have been developed by attorneys for the U.S. Department of Justice. *See, e.g.,* Scott Charney & Kent Alexander, *Computer Crime*, 45 Emory L.J. 931, 934 (1996) (discussing the Department of Justice's Computer Crime Initiative); Scott Charney, *The Justice Department Responds to the Growing Threat of Computer Crime*, 8 Computer Security J. 1–12 (Fall 1992) (describing an example of how the cybercrime framework seems to have been developed by attorneys for the U.S. Department of Justice).

30. *See, e.g.,* Susan W. Brenner, *Nanocrime?* 2011 University of Illinois Journal of Law, Technology and Policy 39, 58–59 (2011).

31. Arizona Revised Statutes § 13-2301(E)(1). As noted above, other statutes include similar definitions. *See, e.g.,* Florida Statutes § 815.03(1); and Nevada Revised Statutes § 205.4732. These statutes also usually define a "computer." Arizona's definition is representative of that found in other statutes: "'Computer' means an electronic device that performs logic, arithmetic or memory functions by the manipulations of electronic or magnetic impulses and includes all input, output, processing, storage, software or communication facilities that are connected or related to such a device in a system or network." Arizona Revised Statutes § 13-2301(E)(3).

32. "Malware" is a portmanteau, that is, a word created by combining the words "malicious" and "software." *See, e.g.,* Chad A. Kirby, *Defining Abusive Software to Protect Computer Users from the Threat of Spyware,* 10 Computer Law Review and Technology Journal 287, 291 (2006).

33. *See, e.g., How a 'Denial of Service Attack' works,* CNET News (February 9, 2000), http://news.cnet.com.

Chapter 1. Hacking

1. *See* Steven Levy, Hackers: Heroes of the Computer Revolution 18–69 (1984). The account of the MIT hackers that follows in the text is taken from this source.

2. Frequently Asked Questions, MIT Hack Gallery (accessed February 21, 2012), http://hacks.mit.edu/Hacks/misc/faq.html.

3. *See* Mary Thornton, *"Hackers" Ignore Consequents of Their High-Tech Joy Rides,* Washington Post (1984), at A1.

4. *See* Levy, *supra* note 1, at 26–36.

5. *See* Katie Hafner & Matthew Lyon, Where Wizards Stay Up Late: The Origins of the Internet (1996).

6. Eric S. Raymond, A Brief History of Hackerdom (2000), http://www.catb .org/~esr/writings/cathedral-bazaar/hacker-history/ar01s02.html.

7. *See* Eric S. Raymond, The Jargon File (October 1, 2004), http://www.catb .org/jargon.

8. Raymond, The Jargon File, *supra* note 7, at chap. 1, http://www.catb.org/ jargon/html/introduction.html.

9. *See* Vinton Cerf, The Birth of the ARPANET (1993), http://www.netvalley .com/archives/mirrors/cerf-how-inet.txt.

10. *See* Susan W. Brenner, Law in an Era of Smart Technology 105–110 (2007).

11. Martin Campbell-Kelly & William Aspray, Computer: A History of the Information Machine 247 (1996).

12. *See WarGames*, Wikipedia (last updated February 5, 2012), http://en .wikipedia.org/wiki/WarGames.

13. Joseph B. Treaster, *Hundreds of Youths Trading Data on Computer Break-ins*, Special, New York Times, September 5, 1983, at 1.

14. *See* Christos J. P. Moschovitis et al., History of the Internet (1999), http:// www.historyoftheinternet.com/chap3.html.

15. *See* Barton Gellman, *Young Computer Bandits Byte Off More than They Could Chew*, Washington Post, August 30, 1983, at A2.

16. *See* John Gallant, *Film Provided Model for NASA Security Breach, Teen Says*, Computerworld 18 (August 27, 1984).

17. *See* Hafner & Lyon, *supra* note 5, at 164–92.

18. *See id.* at 224–49.

19. *See* Michael Weinstein, *Electronic Funds Transfer Review: A Look at Security*, American Banker 11 (April 2, 1984).

20. *See* Scott Brown, *WarGames*: A Look Back at the Film that Turned Geaks and Phreaks into Stars, 16 Wired Magazine 140 (July 21, 2008).

21. *See* Tom Shea, *The FBI Goes After Hackers*, InfoWorld 38 (March 26, 1984).

22. *See id.*

23. *See* William Gibson, Neuromancer 51 (reissue ed. 1995).

24. *See, e.g.,* Robert Trigaux, *The Underbelly of Cyberspace*, St. Petersburg Times, June 14, 1998, at 1H.

25. *See* Douglas Thomas, Hacker Culture 81 (2002).

26. The account of Kevin Poulsen's career as a hacker is taken from these sources: Jonathan Littman, The Watchman: The Twisted Life and Crimes of Serial Hacker Kevin Poulsen (1997); and Jonathan Littman, *The Last Hacker*, Los Angeles Times Magazine 18 (September 12, 1993).

27. *See Hacker Gets 51 Months in Radio Contest Scam*, Los Angeles Times, April 11, 1995, at 2 ($36,925 to radio station KIIS, $20,000 to KPWR, and $1,000 to KRTH).

28. Leslie Berger, *Computer Hacker Who Jumped Bail Gets 41 Months*, Los Angeles Times, November 28, 1995, at 5 (article about the sentencing of "Agent Steal").

29. Leslie Berger, *Spying Charge against Hacker Is Dropped*, Los Angeles Times, November 10, 1995, at 1.

30. *See* Littman, *The Last Hacker, supra* note 26.

31. *See, e.g.,* Mark Guidera, *Hackers Targeting Credit Cards*, (Albany) Times Union, August 14, 1994, at A8.

32. *See, e.g.,* Brian Akre, *Cybercrime Epidemic at Major Corporations*, Times-Picayune, October 25, 1995, at C1.

33. *See Reno Urges Cybercrime Crackdown in Americas*, Deseret News, November 26, 1998, at A03.

34. *See, e.g.*, John Montgomery, *Computer Crime*, 24 American Criminal Law Review 429, 430 (1987).

35. *See, e.g.*, Federal Computer Systems Protection Act: Hearings on S.1766 Before the Subcommittee on Criminal Laws and Procedure of the Senate Committee on the Judiciary, 95th Cong., 2d sess. 6 (1978).

36. Federal Computer Systems Protection Act, S. 1766, 95th Cong., 1st sess., 123 Cong. Rec. 21,025 (1977), subsequently revised and introduced as S. 240, 96th Cong.

37. *See* 125 Cong. Rec. 1191 (1979) (statement of Senator Ribicoff).

38. *See, e.g.*, Joseph M. Olivenbaum, *CTRL-ALT-DELETE: Rethinking Federal Computer Crime Legislation*, 27 Seton Hall Law Review 574, 584 note 32 (1997).

39. *See* Robert Trigaux, *Computer Crime Will Test Banks' Detection, Prosecution Capability*, American Banker 9 (March 11, 1981).

40. Robin K. Kutz, *Computer Crime in Virginia: A Critical Examination of the Criminal Offenses in the Virginia Computer Crimes Act*, 27 William and Mary Law Review 783, 789–90 (1986).

41. *Id.* at 790. Alabama later also took this approach. *See id.* 790 note 34.

42. *See, e.g.*, Douglas H. Hancock, *To What Extent Should Computer Related Crimes Be the Subject of Specific Legislative Attention?* 12 Albany Law Journal of Science and Technology 97, 117 (2001).

43. *Trespass*, in Black's Law Dictionary (8th ed. 2008).

44. *See* Model Penal Code, American Law Institute (1961–1962), http://www.ali.org/index.cfm?fuseaction=publications.ppage&node_id=92.

45. Model Penal Code § 221.2(1).

46. *See* Model Penal Code § 221.1(1).

47. *See, e.g.*, David Stout, *Youth Sentenced in Government Hacking Case*, New York Times, September 23, 2000, http://www.nytimes.com.

48. *See, e.g.*, Catherine Wilson, *Teen Given Six Months for Hacking into NASA*, ABC News (September 22, 2000), http://abcnews.go.com.

49. *See Interview: Anonymous*, PBS *Frontline* (2001), http://www.pbs.org/wgbh/pages/frontline/shows/hackers/interviews/anon.html.

50. *New York Computer "Hackers" Indicted*, Los Angeles Times, July 9, 1992, at 3, 1192 WLNR 4039184.

51. *See, e.g.*, Jo-Ann M. Adams, *Controlling Cyberspace: Applying the Computer Fraud and Abuse Act to the Internet*, 12 Santa Clara Computer and High Technology Law Journal 403, 410 (1996).

52. Jeff Nemerofsky, *The Crime of "Interruption of Computer Services to Au-*

thorized Users"—Have You Ever Heard of It? 6 Richmond Journal of Law and Technology 23, 36 (2000).

53. Dodd S. Griffith, *The Computer Fraud and Abuse Act of 1986: A Measured Response to a Growing Problem,* 43 Vanderbilt Law Review 453, 459 note 32 (1990).

54. Richard C. Hollinger & Lonn Lanza-Kaduce, *The Process of Criminalization: The Case of Computer Crime Laws,* 26 Criminology 101, 110 (February 1988).

55. *See, e.g.,* Griffith, *supra* note 53, at 458.

56. *Id.*

57. *See id.* at 459–60.

58. *See, e.g., Definiteness of Vagueness of Laws, Regulations, and Orders,* in Constitutional Law § 972, American Jurisprudence (2nd ed. 2010).

59. U.S. Code § 1030(e) (1984 act).

60. Griffith, *supra* note 53, at 466.

61. *Id.*

62. *Id.* at 466–67.

63. *See id.* at 470.

64. *See id.* at 468.

65. *See id.* at 468.

66. *See id.* at 468.

67. *See* Carol R. Williams, *A Proposal for Protecting Privacy during the Information Age,* 11 Alaska Law Review 119, 128 note 54 (1994).

68. S. Rep. No. 432 at page 3, 99th Cong., 2d sess. 1986, 1986 U.S.C.C.A.N. 2479, 1986 WL 31918.

69. *See* Computer Abuse Amendments Act of 1994, Pub. L. No. 103-322, 108 Stat. 1796, 2097 at § 290001(b).

70. *See* 18 U.S. Code § 1030(e)(2).

71. *See* S. Rep. No. 432 at 6, 99th Cong., 2d Sess. 1986, 1986 U.S.C.C.A.N. 2479, 1986 WL 31918.

72. Pub. L. 104-294, Title II, § 201.

73. *See* Pub. L. 107-56, Title VII, § 814(d)(1), amending 18 U.S. Code § 1030(e) (2)(B).

74. Arthur J. Carter IV & Audrey Perry, *Computer Crimes,* 41 American Criminal Law Review 313, 320 note 37 (2004).

75. Senate Report No. 99-432, Computer Fraud and Abuse Act of 1986, 1986 U.S. Code Congressional and Administrative News, 2479, 2488.

76. Senate Report No. 99-432, *supra* note 75, at 2488–90.

77. *See* Pub. L. 107-56, Title V, § 506(a), Title VIII, § 814, 115 Stat. 366, 382.

78. *See* U.S. Department of Justice, Prosecuting Computer Crimes (2007).

79. U.S. Department of Justice, Prosecuting Computer Crimes (2007).

80. Statement of Senator Leahy at Markup of Hatch-Leahy-Schumer Substitute Amendment to S. 2448 (2000), U.S. senator Patrick Leahy, http://leahy.senate.gov/press/200010/001005.html.

81. Brian M. Hoffstadt, *The Voyeuristic Hacker*, 11 Journal of Internet Law 11, 14 note 33 (2007).

82. Statement of Andrew Lourie, Acting Principal Deputy Assistant Attorney General and Chief of Staff—Criminal Division, U.S. Department of Justice Before the U.S. House of Representatives Committee on the Judiciary—Subcommittee on Crime, Terrorism and Homeland Security Concerning the "Privacy and Cybercrime Enforcement Act of 2007" (December 18, 2007).

83. *Id.*

84. *See, e.g.,* Susan W. Brenner, *State Cybercrime Legislation in the United States of America: A Survey*, 7 Richmond Journal of Law and Technology 28 (2001).

85. *See id.*

86. *See* Hawaii Revised Statutes §§ 708-895.5, 708-895.6 & 708.895.7.

87. Alaska Statutes § 11.46.484(a)(3).

88. *See* New York Penal Law § 156.10(1).

89. Florida Statutes § 815.03(1).

90. State v. Allen, 260 Kan. 107, 917 P.2d 848 (Kansas 1996).

91. *Id.*

92. *Id.*

93. *Id.*

Chapter 2. Malware and DDoS Attacks

1. *See* Tom Gillis, Securing the Borderless Network 61–80 (2010).

2. Malware includes viruses, worms, Trojan horse programs, rootkits, spyware, adware, botnet programs, and keystroke loggers and dialers. *See id.*

3. *See, e.g.,* Marshall Brain & Wesley Fenlon, *How Computer Viruses Work*, HowStuffWorks (accessed February 22, 2012), http://www.howstuffworks.com/virus.htm.

4. *See* Brain & Fenlon, *supra* note 3.

5. *See* Robert Lemos, *The Computer Virus—No Cures to Be Found*, ZD Net (November 25, 2003), http://news.zdnet.com.

6. *See, e.g.,* Jeremy Pacquette, *A History of Viruses*, Symantec (July 16, 2000), http://www.symantec.com/connect/articles/history-viruses.

7. *See* Lemos, *supra* note 5. *See also Elk Cloner,* Wikipedia (last updated February 20, 2012), http://en.wikipedia.org/wiki/Elk_Cloner (quoting the Elk Cloner poem).

8. *See* Lemos, *supra* note 5.

9. *See, e.g.,* Pacquette, *supra* note 6.

10. *See Virus: Boot/Brain,* F-Secure (accessed February 22, 2012), http://www.f-secure.com/v-descs/brain.shtml.

11. *See* Lemos, *supra* note 5.

12. *See Computer Viruses Hit One Million,* BBC News (April 10, 2008), http://news.bbc.co.uk/2/hi/technology/7340315.stm (specifically, the number of viruses had reached 1,122,311).

13. *See, e.g.,* Heidi Blake, *Eastern European Cyber Criminals "Draining British Bank Accounts,"* Telegraph, August 11, 2010, http://www.telegraph.co.uk.

14. *See, e.g., What Is a Computer Worm?* Antivirus World (accessed February 22, 2012), http://www.antivirusworld.com/articles/computer-worm.php.

15. *See id.*

16. *See id.*

17. John Brunner, The Shockwave Rider (1975).

18. *The Shockwave Rider,* Wikipedia (last updated February 1, 2012), http://en.wikipedia.org/wiki/The_Shockwave_Rider.

19. *Id.*

20. *Id.*

21. *See* Andy Sudduth, The What, Why, and How of the 1988 Internet Worm: The History of Worm Like Programs (last updated July 2001), http://snowplow.org/tom/worm/worm.html.

22. The account of the Morris worm is primarily drawn from United States v. Morris, 928 F.2d 504 (2d cir. 1991).

23. *Compare* United States v. Morris, 928 F.2d 505 (2d cir. 1991) *with Morris Worm,* Wikipedia (February 2, 2012), http://en.wikipedia.org/wiki/Morris_worm.

24. *See* United States v. Morris, 928 F.2d 505 (2d cir. 1991).

25. *Id.* at 506.

26. *See* Sudduth, *supra* note 21.

27. *See, e.g.,* Mark R. Colombell, *The Legislative Response to the Evolution of Computer Viruses,* 8 Richmond Journal of Law and Technology 18 (2002).

28. United States v. Morris, 928 F.2d 506 (2d cir. 1991).

29. *Id.*

30. *See* Matthew Spina, *The Worm Had Venom,* Syracuse Post-Standard, February 12, 1989, at A1.

31. *See* Lauren DiDio, *Virus Victims Are Stoic in Face of Multinet Attack*, Network World 6 (November 14, 1988).

32. Michael Alexander, *Morris Felony Charge Expected by End of July*, Computerworld 4 (July 17, 1989).

33. *See Designer of Computer "Virus" Indicted*, Tulsa World, July 27, 1989, A5. *See also* Brief for Appellant, United States v. Morris, 1990 WL 10029997 *2 (2d cir. 1990).

34. *See* John Markoff, *Computer Intruder Is Found Guilty*, New York Times, January 23, 1990, A21.

35. *See* John Markoff, *Computer Intruder Is Put on Probation and Fined $10,000*, New York Times, May 5, 1990, 11.

36. *See Robert Tappan Morris*, Wikipedia (last updated February 8, 2012), http://en.wikipedia.org/wiki/Robert_Tappan_Morris.

37. *See, e.g.,* John C. Dolak, *The Code Red Worm*, The SANS Institute InfoSec Reading Room (2001), http://www.sans.org.

38. *See, e.g.,* George Hulme, *Internet Goes Red*, Information Week (July 20, 2001), http://www.informationweek.com; *White House Dodges Web Virus*, BBC (July 20, 2001), http://news.bbc.co.uk/2/hi/science/nature/1448431.stm.

39. *See, e.g.,* Robert Lemos, *"Nimda" Worm Strikes Net, E-mail*, CNET News (September 18, 2001), http://news.cnet.com.

40. *Slammed!* Wired (July 2003), http://www.wired.com.

41. *See* Mark Bowden, *The Enemy Within*, Atlantic (June 2010), http://www.theatlantic.com.

42. *See* Sumner Lemon, *Conficker Worm Hasn't Gone Away*, NetworkWorld (January 15, 2010), http://www.networkworld.com/news/2010/011510-conficker-worm-hasnt-gone-away.html.

43. *See, e.g., Conficker Worm to Become a Bigger Threat in 2010*, Help Net Security (August 12, 2009), http://www.net-security.org/malware_news.php?id=1154.

44. *See* Gregg Keizer, *Is Stuxnet the "Best" Malware Ever?* ComputerWorld (September 16, 2010), http://www.computerworld.com.

45. *See id.*

46. Josh Halliday, *Stuxnet Worm Is the "Work of a National Government Agency,"* Guardian, September 24, 2010, http://www.guardian.co.uk.

47. *See* William J. Broad, John Markoff & David E. Sanger, *Israeli Test on Worm Called Crucial in Iran Nuclear Delay*, New York Times, January 15, 2011, http://www.nytimes.com.

48. *Id.*

49. *See* John Leyden, *Stuxnet "A Game Changer for Malware Defence,"* Register (October 9, 2010), http://www.theregister.co.uk.

50. *See* Patrick J. Leahy, *New Laws for New Technologies: Current Issues Facing the Subcommittee on Technology and the Law,* 5 Harvard Journal of Law and Technology 1 (1992).

51. *Id.*

52. *Id.* at 22.

53. *See* Susan C. Lyman, *Civil Remedies for the Victims of Computer Viruses,* 11 Computer/Law Journal 611 (1992) (citing H.R. 55, 101st Cong., 1st sess. [1989]).

54. *Id.*

55. Pub. L. No. 103-322, 108 Stat. 2097.

56. *See, e.g.,* Haeji Hong, *Hacking through the Computer Fraud and Abuse Act,* 31 U.C. Davis Law Review 283, 286 (1997).

57. California Penal Code § 502(a)(10).

58. *See, e.g.,* Arizona Revised Statutes § 13-2316(A)(3).

59. *See, e.g.,* Georgia Code § 16-9-151(5).

60. *See id.*

61. Stuart Fox, *"Viruses Are Winning": Malware Threat Outpaces Antivirus Software,* Tech News Daily (August 2, 2010), http://www.technewsdaily.com.

62. Trend Micro Research Team, *ZeuS: A Persistent Criminal Enterprise,* Trend Micro 4 (March 2010), http://us.trendmicro.com/imperia/md/content/us/trendwatch/researchandanalysis/zeusapersistentcriminalenterprise.pdf.

63. *See id.* at 15–16.

64. *Understanding Denial-of-Service Attacks,* United States Computer Emergency Readiness Team (November 4, 2009), http://www.us-cert.gov/cas/tips/ST04-015.html.

65. *Id.*

66. *See, e.g.,* Clinton Wilder & Bob Violino, *Online Theft,* Information Week 30 (August 28, 1995).

67. Dave Dittrich, *DDoS Attack Tool Timeline,* University of Washington (July 2000), http://staff.washington.edu/dittrich/talks/sec2000/timeline.html.

68. Raymond Gozzi Jr., *Zombie Computers,* ETC: A Review of General Semantics (December 31, 2000), 2000 WLNR 4638991.

69. *See id.*

70. *Id.*

71. *Id.*

72. *Id.*

73. *See* Mary Kirwin, *Punishments Rarely Fit the Cybercrime*, Globe and Mail, September 23, 2004, at B15.

74. Brian Blomquist & Mary Huhn, *Prez Holds Summit to Stop Cyberhacks*, New York Post, February 16, 2000, at 2B, 2000 WLNR 8163868.

75. *Id.*

76. Tu Thanh Ha & Barrie McKenna, *The Hacker Who Talked Too Much*, Globe and Mail, April 20, 2000, at A1.

77. David L. Wilson, *Boy, 15, Charged in Web Attacks*, San Jose Mercury News, April 20 2000, 2000 WLNR 1581343.

78. David A. Vise & Ariana Eunjung Cha, *"Mafiaboy," 15, Held in Strike*, CNN.com (April 20, 2000), 2000 WLNR 3307263.

79. Wilson, *supra* note 77.

80. *See id.*

81. *See, e.g., "Mafiaboy" Suspect Ordered to Keep Off the Net*, Newsbytes (April 19, 2000), 2000 WLNR 9879497.

82. *"Mafiaboy" Pleads Guilty in DDoS Attacks*, Infoworld (January 22, 2001), 2001 WLNR 12061632.

83. *See, e.g.,* Tony Long, *February 7, 2000: Mafiaboy's Big Moment*, Wired (February 7, 2007), http://www.wired.com.

84. *See, e.g., "Mafiaboy" Pleads Guilty to Hacking*, USA Today, January 22, 2001, 2001 WLNR 3781916.

85. *See, e.g.,* David Colker, *"Mafiaboy" Hacker to Serve 8 Months*, Atlanta Journal and Constitution, September 16, 2001, 2001 WLNR 3933610.

86. *See, e.g.,* Stephen Labaton, *Internet Criminals Employ Army of Unwitting Allies*, International Herald Tribune, June 25, 2005, 2005 WLNR 10077090; Siona LaFrance, *Firewall Alarm*, New Orleans Times Picayne, March 12, 2002, at 1, 2002 WLNR 1387421.

87. *See, e.g.,* Deb Radcliff, *Remote Control Wars*, SC Magazine (June 6, 2006), http://www.scmagazineus.com.

88. Gideon J. Lensky, *Inside the Mature Service Industry of Botnets*, Internet Evolution (September 10, 2008), http://www.internetevolution.com/author .asp?section_id=699&doc_id=162645.

89. *See, e.g.,* Larry Rogers, *What Is a Distributed Denial of Service (DDoS) Attack and What Can I Do About It?* CERT (last updated February 10, 2004), http://www.cert.org/homeusers/ddos.html.

90. *See* Gregg Keizer, *Pro-WikiLeaks Cyber Army Gains Strength*, Computer-World (December 9, 2010), http://www.computerworld.com.

91. Matthew Humphries, *Dutch National Crime Squad Takedown 30 Million PC Botnet Bredolab*, Geek.com (October 25, 2010), http://www.geek.com/

articles/news/dutch-national-crime-squad-takedown-30-million-pc-botnet-bredolab-20101026.

92. Bruce Sterling, *Bredolab Botnet Busted,* Wired (November 11, 2010), http://www.wired.com.

93. *Global Spam E-mail Drops after Hacker Arrests,* BBC News (November 15, 2010), http://www.bbc.co.uk.

94. John Leyden, *RIAA and Anonymous Sites Both Downed by DDoS Assaults,* Register (November 1, 2010), http://www.theregister.co.uk.

95. Dan Goodin, *DDoS Attacks Take Out Asian Nation,* Register (November 3, 2010), http://www.theregister.co.uk.

96. Warwick Ashford, *China-Based DDoS Attack Hits Australian Multinationals,* ComputerWeekly.com (April 15, 2010), http://www.computerweekly.com.

97. Sharon Gaudin, *Twitter Withstands Second DDoS Attack in a Week,* Computer World (August 12, 2009), http://www.computerworld.com

98. Nart Villeneuve, *Koobface: Inside a Crimeware Network,* Infowar Monitor 2 (November 2, 2010), http://www.infowar-monitor.net/koobface.

99. *Iranian Cyber Army Offers Its Botnet for Rental,* InfoSecurity (October 27, 2010), http://www.infosecurity-us.com/view/13516/iranian-cyber-army-offers-its-botnet-for-rental.

100. *Id.*

101. *See, e.g., TwitterNET Builder: New Dangers for Twitter Users,* epagini (May 2010), http://www.epagini.com/2010/05/twitternet-builder-new-dangers-for-twitter-users.

102. Yury Namestnikov, *Information Security Threats in the Second Quarter of 2010,* SecureList (August 23, 2010), http://www.securelist.com/en/analysis/204792133/Information_Security_Threats_in_the_Second_Quarter_of_2010.

103. *Id.*

104. *See id.*

105. *See id.*

106. *See, e.g.,* John Leyden, *Zeus Botnet Raid on UK Bank Accounts under the Spotlight,* Register (August 11, 2010), http://www.theregister.co.uk. *See also Zeus (Trojan Horse),* Wikipedia (last updated February 17, 2012), http://en.wikipedia.org/wiki/Zeus_(trojan_horse).

107. *See, e.g.,* Ellen Messmer, *ZeuS Botnet Still Mutating, Still on the Move,* PC World (March 13, 2010), http://www.pcworld.com.

108. *See Emerging Cyber Threats Report 2011,* Georgia Tech Information Security Center 3 (2010), http://www.gtisc.gatech.edu/pdf/cyberThreatReport 2011.pdf.

109. *Id.*

110. *Id.* at 8.

111. *See* Computer Abuse Amendments Act of 1994 § 290001(b), Pub. L. No. 103-322, 108 Stat. 2097.

112. *See Press Release: "Botherder" Dealt Prison Sentence for Selling and Spreading Malicious Computer Code,* U.S. Department of Justice, Central District of California (May 8, 2006), http://www.cybercrime.gov/anchetaSent.htm. The description of the Ancheta case is taken from this source.

113. *Press Release: Indictment and Arrest for Computer Hacking,* U.S. Department of Justice, Eastern District of California (October 1, 2007).

114. *See Press Release: Computer Hacker Pleads Guilty and Agrees to Two Years in Federal Prison,* U.S. Department of Justice, Eastern District of California (June 10, 2008), http://www.justice.gov/criminal/cybercrimes/kingPlea.pdf.

115. *Id.*

116. *See Press Release: "Bot Roast II" Nets 8 Individuals,* U.S. Department of Justice, Federal Bureau of Investigation (November 29, 2007), http://www.ic3 .gov/media/2007/071129.aspx.

117. *See id.*

118. *See Press Release: Student Charged with Using University Computer Network for Denial of Service Attacks,* U.S. Department of Justice, Northern District of Ohio (May 14, 2010), http://www.justice.gov/criminal/cybercrime/ frostChar.pdf.

119. *See, e.g.,* Barry Leibowitz, *Frost Breached Fox Commentator's Website,* CBS News (November 10, 2010), http://www.cbsnews.com.

120. Angela Moscaritolo, *European Hackers Charged with DDoS Attacks in the U.S.,* SC Magazine (October 7, 2008), http://www.scmagazineus.com.

121. *Id.*

122. *See id.*

123. *See, e.g.,* Kevin Poulsen, *Feds Bust DDoS "Mafia,"* Register (August 27, 2004), http://www.theregister.co.uk.

124. Georgia Code § 16-9-153(a)(1)(C).

125. Ohio Revised Code § 2909.01(F)(3).

126. Ohio Revised Code § 2909.07(6)(b).

127. *See* Model Penal Code § 5.01(1)(c) (1962).

128. South Carolina Code § 16-16-10(k)(3).

129. South Carolina Code § 16-16-20(1)(b).

130. Pennsylvania Consolidated Statutes § 7612(a).

131. Pennsylvania Consolidated Statutes § 7601.

132. *See* 18 Pennsylvania Consolidated Statutes § 7611(a)(1).

133. *See, e.g.*, 18 U.S. Code §§ 1341 and 1343; California Penal Code § 502(c)(1); Colorado Revised Statutes § 18-5.5-102(1)(b); North Carolina General Statutes § 14-454(a)(1).

134. Texas Business and Commerce Code § 324.055(b)–(d).

135. Texas Business and Commerce Code § 324.002(1-a) and (9).

136. Texas Business and Commerce Code § 324.055(f).

Chapter 3. Cybercrimes against Property

1. The account of this hack is taken from *Two Cryptologic Casinos Hacked*, Casinomeister (September 20, 2001), http://www.casinomeister.com/news/september.html.

2. Rollin M. Perkins & Ronald N. Boyce, Criminal Law 292 (3d ed. 1982).

3. *See, e.g.*, Peter J. Henning, *Public Corruption: A Comparative Analysis of International Corruption Conventions and United States Law*, 18 Arizona Journal of International and Comparative Law 793, 856 (2001).

4. *See* Renault UK Limited v. FleetPro Technical Services Limited, Russell Thoms (High Court of Justice Queen's Bench Division) (November 23, 2007), [2007] EWHC 2541. The description of the case in the text is taken from this opinion.

5. *Id.*

6. Alabama Code § 13A-8-2(1).

7. Iowa Code § 701.19.

8. *See, e.g.*, California Penal Code § 484(a).

9. Alabama Code § 18-1A-3(17).

10. Kentucky Revised Statutes § 330.020(9).

11. *See, e.g.*, Wayne R. LaFave, Substantive Criminal Law § 29.4(a) (2008).

12. The account of the Levin case is taken from *How to Catch a Hacker*, USA Today, September 19, 1997, at 12A; and David Gow & Richard Norton-Taylor, *Surfing Superhighwaymen*, Guardian, December 7, 1996, at 28.

13. *See* Michael Newton, The Encyclopedia of High-Tech Crime and Crime Fighting 182 (2004).

14. *See* Gow & Norton-Taylor, *supra* note 12; *The Tale of the Russian Hacker*, Attrition.org (1996), http://attrition.org/~jericho/works/security/pwn-50-15.html.

15. *See* Gow & Norton-Taylor, *supra* note 12.

16. Or. App. 301, 21 P.3d 1128 (Oregon Court of Appeals 2001). The description of the facts in this case is taken entirely from the court's opinion.

17. Or. App. at 303–4, 21 P.3d at 1129–30.

18. Oregon Revised Statutes § 164.015.

19. Or. App. at 311–16, 21 P.3d at 1135–37.

20. Or. App. at 311–16, 21 P.3d at 1135–37.

21. *See, e.g.,* Alabama Code § 13A-8-1(1); Iowa Code § 714.1(1); Washington Code § 9A.56.020.

22. Concise Oxford English Dictionary 385 (Judy Pearsall ed., 10th ed. 2002).

23. William Blackstone, Commentaries on the Laws of England 230–32 (vol. 4 1979).

24. Delaware Code § 857(3). *See also* North Dakota Century Code § 12.1-23-10(2)(3).

25. Pub. L. 104-294, Title I, § 101(a), October 11, 1996, 110 Stat. 3488.

26. U.S. Code § 1839(3).

27. *U.S. v. Aleynikov,* ___ F.Supp.2d ___, 2010 WL 3489383 (S.D.N.Y. 2010). The account of the *Aleynikov* case is taken from this opinion.

28. *Id.*

29. *Id.*

30. *Id.*

31. *Id.* (quoting U.S. v. Santos, 553 U.S. 507 [2008]).

32. *Id.*

33. *Id.*

34. *See* Patricia Hurtado, *Ex-Goldman Programmer Loses Bid to Be Freed Pending Appeal,* Bloomberg (May 3, 2011), http://www.businessweek.com.

35. *See ONCIX Reports to Congress: Foreign Economic and Industrial Espionage,* Office of the National Counterintelligence Executive (accessed February 23, 2012), http://www.ncix.gov/publications/reports/fecie_all/index_fecie .html.

36. *See Wireless Freeloader Charged Because He Never Bought Coffee,* Techweb News (June 22, 2006), 2006 WLNR 10939330.

37. *See, e.g.,* Alabama Code § 13A-8-10(a).

38. American Jurisprudence 2d, Larceny § 66 (2008).

39. *See* Commonwealth v. Rivers, 31 Mass.App.Ct. 669, 671, 583 N.E.2d 867, 869 (Massachusetts Court of Appeals 1991).

40. *See* Model Penal Code § 223.7 (1962).

41. *See* Wayne R. LaFave, Substantive Criminal Law § 19.4 (2008).

42. Tim Ferguson, *Wi-fi Piggybacking Is OK, Say Silicon.com Readers,* Silicon.com (November 19, 2007), http://networks.silicon.com/mobile/0,39024665,39169199,00.htm (quoting e-mail).

43. *Id.*

44. *Id.*

45. *See* Egan Orion, *Wireless Internet Freeloading Might Become a Crime,* Inquirer (March 21, 2008), http://www.theinquirer.net.

46. *See* Model Penal Code § 2.02 (1962).

47. *See Maryland Turns against Wi-Fi Leeching Laws,* Yahoo! Tech (April 16, 2008), http://tech.yahoo.com.

48. *See, e.g.,* Commonwealth v. Thompson, 1989 WL 214494 (Pennsylvania Court of Common Pleas 1989).

49. *See Internet Crime Schemes,* Internet Crime Complaint Center (accessed February 23, 2012), http://www.ic3.gov/crimeschemes.aspx#item-18.

50. *See Willie Sutton,* Federal Bureau of Investigation (accessed February 23, 2012), http://www.fbi.gov/about-us/history/famous-cases/willie-sutton.

51. *See, e.g., The "Nigerian Scam": Costly Compassion,* Federal Trade Commission (July 2003), http://www.ftc.gov/becp/edu/pubs/consumer/alerts/alt117.shtml.

52. *Advance Fee Schemes,* Federal Bureau of Investigation (accessed February 23, 2012), http://www.fbi.gov/scams-safety/fraud.

53. *The Spanish Prisoner: Birth of the 419 Scam,* Security FAQs (accessed February 23, 2012), http://www.security-faqs.com/the-spanish-prisoner-birth-of-the-419-scam.html.

54. *Id.*

55. *Id.*

56. *Id.*

57. *Id.*

58. For examples of such e-mails, see Crimes of Persuasion: Nigerian Scams (accessed February 23, 2012), http://www.crimes-of-persuasion.com/Crimes/Business/nigerian.htm.

59. Jane Corbin, *A Mysterious E-mail,* Daily Mail, January 16, 2010, 2010 WLNR 981281.

60. *Nigeria Scams "Cost UK Billions,"* BBC News (November 20, 2006), http://news.bbc.co.uk.

61. *Former Alcona County Treasurer Charged with Embezzling Public Monies,* Office of the Attorney General (January 17, 2007), http://www.michigan.gov/ag/0,1607,7-164-34739_34811-160250--,00.html.

62. *See* Anna Song, *Woman Out $400K to "Nigerian Scam" Con Artists,* KATU.com (November 13, 2008), http://www.katu.com/news/34292654.html.

63. *See Oregon Woman Loses $400,000 to Nigerian E-Mail Scam,* Fox News (November 17, 2008), http://www.foxnews.com.

64. *Nigeria Scams "Cost UK Billions," supra* note 60.

65. *See, e.g., Reported Dollar Loss from Internet Crime Reaches All Time High,* Internet Crime Complaint Center (April 3, 2008), http://www.ic3.gov/media/2008/080403.aspx.

66. United States v. Godin, 534 F.3d 51 (U.S. Court of Appeals for the First Circuit 2008). The account of the prosecution is taken from this opinion.

67. *Id.*

68. *Id.*

69. *Id.*

70. *Id.*

71. State v. Baron, 2008 WL 2201778 (Wisconsin Court of Appeals). The Wisconsin Supreme Court later upheld Baron's conviction. *See* State v. Baron, 318 Wis.2d 60, 769 N.W.2d 34 (Wisconsin 2009).

72. *See* Wayne R. LaFave, Substantive Criminal Law § 20.4 (2008).

73. *See* Rollin M. Perkins & Ronald N. Boyce, Criminal Law 351 (3d ed. 1982).

74. Alabama Code § 13A-8-13.

75. Model Penal Code § 223.4 (1962).

76. The description of the Tereshchuk case is taken from *Press Release: Wi-Fi Hacker Pleads Guilty to Attempted $17,000,000 Extortion*, United States Department of Justice (2004), http://www.usdoj.gov/criminal/cybercrime/tereshchukPlea.htm; and Robyn Lamb, *Maryland Man Pleads Guilty to Extortion*, Baltimore Daily Record, June 29, 2004.

77. *See, e.g.,* Eric Rich, *Man Accused of Possessing Toxins*, Washington Post, September 30, 2001, at B05.

78. Identity Theft Enforcement and Restitution Act of 2008, Pub. L. 110-326, Title II, §§ 203–8, 122 Stat. 3561 (2008).

79. *See, e.g.,* Rendelman v. State, 175 Md.App. 422, 435–36, 927 A.2d 468, 476 (Maryland Court of Appeals 2007).

80. *See, e.g.,* Dan Mangan, *Guilt in Extort Scheme*, New York Post, May 28, 2003, 2003 WLNR 15019466.

81. The facts are taken from these sources: Brad Hicks, *Sungkook Kim Indicted on Multiple Charges*, Times-Tribune, December 22, 2008, http://www.thetimestribune.com; and Bill Estep, *Indictment: Cumberlands Student Tried to Blackmail Woman with Sex Video*, Lexington Herald-Leader, December 19, 2008, 2008 WLNR 24340196.

82. *See* Wayne R. LaFave, Substantive Criminal Law § 20.4(a) (2008).

83. Kansas Statutes § 21-3428 (emphasis added).

84. Charles Wilson, *Feds: Online "Sextortion" of Teens on the Rise*, MSNBC (August 15, 2010), http://www.msnbc.msn.com.

85. *Id.*

86. Kim Zetter, *Wisconsin Teen Gets 15 Years for Facebook Sex-Extortion Scam*, Wired (February 25, 2010), http://www.wired.com.

87. *Id.*

88. *See* Model Penal Code § 223.4 (1962).

89. The description of the facts in the case are taken from *Cops: Mom Threatened to Post Nude Pics of Daughter's Ex*, CNN (October 9, 2008), http://www.cnn.com.

90. California Penal Code § 451.

91. Colorado Revised Statutes § 18-4-102(1).

92. *See, e.g., Nixon Sues Ameren*, Missouri Attorney General (December 13, 2006), http://ago.mo.gov/newsreleases/2006/121306b.htm.

93. *See, e.g.,* Model Penal Code § 210.1 (1962).

94. *See, e.g.,* Wayne R. LaFave, Substantive Criminal Law § 21.3(h) (2008).

95. *Id.*

96. California Penal Code § 594(a).

97. Metacom, *What Is Hacktivism? 2.0*, The Hacktivist (December 2003), http://www.thehacktivist.com/whatishacktivism.pdf.

98. John Ribeiro, *India Tightens Security on Government Websites after Attack*, PC World (December 15, 2010), http://www.pcworld.com.

99. John Leyden, *Foxconn Website Defaced after iPhone Assembly Plant Suicides*, Register (May 26, 2010), http://www.theregister.co.uk.

100. *See, e.g., Website Defacements (Most Recent) by Country*, NationMaster .com, http://www.nationmaster.com/graph/med_web_def-media-website-defacements.

101. Indictment, U.S. v. Dierking, 2008 WL 6795069 (U.S. District Court for the Southern District of California 2008).

102. U.S. v. Dierking, 2009 WL 648922 (U.S. District Court for the Southern District of California 2009). The description of the facts is taken from this opinion.

103. See Indictment, U.S. v. Dierking, *supra* note 101. Dierking eventually pled guilty. *See* Docket for U.S. v. Dierking, U.S. District Court for the Southern District of California, Case No. 3:08CR03366, entry #55 (07/02/2010).

Chapter 4. Cybercrimes against Persons

1. *See* Susan W. Brenner, *Fantasy Crime: The Role of Criminal Law in Virtual Worlds*, 11 Vanderbilt Journal of Entertainment and Technology Law 1 (2008).

2. *See* Kathleen G. McAnaney, Laura A. Curliss & C. Elizabeth Abeyta-Price, *From Imprudence to Crime: Anti-Stalking Law*, 68 Notre Dame Law Review 819, 863 (1993) (quoting 27 George 2, ch. 15 [1754]).

3. *See, e.g.,* Robert Kurman Kelner, Note, *United States v. Jake Baker: Revisiting Threats and the First Amendment*, 84 Virginia Law Review 287, 311–12 (1998).

4. G. Robert Blakey & Brian J. Murray, *Threats, Free Speech, and the Jurisprudence of the Federal Criminal Law*, 2002 B.Y.U. L. Rev. 829, 1061–62 (2002).

5. United States v. Alkhabaz a/k/a Jake Baker, 104 F.3d 1492 (1997). The description of the facts in the case is taken from this opinion.

6. United States v. Alkhabaz a/k/a Jake Baker, 104 F.3d 1492, 1496 (1997).

7. F.3d 1208 (U.S. Court of Appeals for the Eleventh Circuit 2006).

8. *See, e.g.,* Frank James, *Web Site Sued for Posting Cops' Personal Data*, Chicago Tribune, June 5, 2001. The description of the site and the police reaction to it is taken from this source.

9. *Id.*

10. *Id.*

11. *Id.*

12. Sheehan v. Gregoire, 272 F.Supp.2d 1135 (U.S. District Court—Western District of Washington 2003).

13. Virginia v. Black, 538 U.S. 343, 359 (U.S. Supreme Court 2003).

14. Sheehan v. Gregoire, *supra* note 12.

15. *Id.*

16. Who's a Rat (2007), http://www.whosarat.com.

17. *Id.*

18. *See id.*

19. *See* United States v. Carmichael, 326 F.Supp.2d 1267 (U.S. District Court for the Middle District of Alabama 2004); United States v. Carmichael, 326 F.Supp.2d 1303 (U.S. District Court for the Middle District of Alabama 2004).

20. United States v. Carmichael, 326 F.Supp.2d 1267, *supra* note 19.

21. *Id.*

22. *Id.*

23. *Id.*; United States v. Carmichael, 326 F.Supp.2d 1303, *supra* note 19.

24. For more on this, *see* David L. Snyder, *Nonparty Remote Electronic Access to Plea Agreements in the Second Circuit*, 35 Fordham Urban Law Journal 1263 (2008).

25. Darnell v. State, 72 Tex. Crim. 271, 161 S.W. 971, 971 (Texas Court of Criminal Appeals 1913).

26. *See id. See also* Andrea J. Robinson, Note, *A Remedial Approach to Harassment*, 70 Virginia Law Review 507 (1984).

27. *See* Robinson, *supra* note 26.

28. *See id.*

29. *See* Robert A. Guy Jr., *The Nature and Constitutionality of Stalking Laws*, 46 Vanderbilt Law Review 991, 991–92 (1993).

30. *See* Paul E. Mullen & Michele Pathe, *Stalking*, 29 Crime and Justice 273 (2002).

31. *See* Kimberly Wingteung Seto, *How Should Legislation Deal with Children as the Victims and Perpetrators of Cyberstalking?* 9 Cardozo Women's Law Journal 67 (2002).

32. Guy, *supra* note 29, at 1001.

33. Nick Zimmerman, Comment, *Attempted Stalking: An Attempt-to-Almost-Attempt-to-Act*, 20 Northern Illinois University Law Review 219 (2000).

34. Guy, *supra* note 29, at 1012.

35. *See id.* at 1003–7.

36. *See id.*

37. Naomi Harlin Goodno, *Cyberstalking: A New Crime; Evaluating the Effectiveness of Current State and Federal Laws*, 72 Missouri Law Review 125 (2007).

38. Vernon's Ann. Missouri Stat. § 565.225.

39. Michigan Comp. Laws Ann. § 750.411h(1)(b).

40. *See* Snowden v. State, 677 A.2d 33, 38 (Delaware 1996). *See also* People v. Furey, 2 Misc.3d 1011(A), 784 N.Y.S.2d 922, 2004 WL 869586 *2 (New York City Criminal Court 2004).

41. Florida Stat. Ann. § 784.048(1)(d).

42. *See, e.g.,* Arkansas Code Ann. § 5-71-229(a)(1); Colorado Rev. Stat. § 18-9-111.

43. Massachusetts Gen. Laws Ann. 265 § 43A(a).

44. State v. Cline, 2008 WL 1759091 (Ohio Court of Appeals for the Second District 2008).

45. State v. Parmelee, 108 Wash.App. 702, 32 P.3d 1029 (Court of Appeals of Washington 2001). The facts described in the text come from this opinion.

46. *See* Model Penal Code § 2.06(2)(a) (1962).

47. Davan Maharaj, *Chilling Cyber-Stalking Case Illustrates New Breed of Crime*, Los Angeles Times, January 23, 1999. 1999 WLNR 6626941.

48. For the facts in the case, *see* Corinne Rose, *Wabash Sisters Cyber-stalked*, Indiana's NewsCenter (August 13, 2008), http://www.indianasnewscenter.com.

49. *See* Anonymous, comment, *Weird Cyberstalking Case*, CYB3RCRIM3 (August 14, 2008), http://cyb3rcrim3.blogspot.com/2008/08/weird-cyber-stalking-case.html (post from one of the victims).

50. Lamber Royakkers, *The Dutch Approach to Stalking Laws*, 3 California Criminal Law Review 2, 20 (2000).

51. Rose, *supra* note 48.

52. *Id.*

53. *See* Anonymous, *supra* note 49.

54. *See* Anonymous, *supra* note 49.

55. Mr. X's sister, e-mail message to author, October 7, 2008 (on file with Susan Brenner).

56. Rose, *supra* note 48.

57. Mr. X's sister, *supra* note 55.

58. *See* Anonymous, *supra* note 49.

59. Mr. X's sister, *supra* note 55.

60. *See* Anonymous, *supra* note 49.

61. *See* State v. Baron, 2008 WL 2201778 (Wisconsin Court of Appeals).

62. Wisconsin Stat. § 943.201(2).

63. *See* Susan W. Brenner, *Is There Such a Thing as "Virtual Crime,"* 4 California Criminal Law Review 1 (2001), http://boalt.org/CCLR/v4/v4brenner.htm.

64. *See* Susan Brenner, *Undue Influence in the Criminal Law: A Proposed Analysis of the Criminal Offense of "Causing Suicide,"* 47 Albany Law Review 62 (1982).

65. Model Penal Code § 210.5 (1962).

66. Continuation of Discussion of Model Penal Code, 36 American Law Institute Proceedings 137 (1959).

67. Model Penal Code § 210.5 (1962).

68. The description of the facts in the Megan Meier case is taken from these sources: *Mom: MySpace Hoax Led to Daughter's Suicide,* Fox News (November 16, 2007), http://www.foxnews.com; Steve Pokin, *Pokin Around: A Real Person, a Real Death,* St. Charles Journal, November 10, 2007, http://www.stltoday.com/suburban-journals/stcharles.

69. *See* Model Penal Code §§ 210.1–210.4 (1962).

70. The description of the case is taken from these sources: *Nurse-Hacker Alters Hospital Prescriptions,* Computer Audit Update (February 1, 1994), 1994 WLNR 3804526; *"Hacker" Nurse Risked Boy's Life,* Guardian, December 21, 1993.

71. *Nurse-Hacker, supra* note 70.

72. *Id.*

73. *Id.*

74. *Id.*

75. *See* FX et al., Stealing the Network: How to Own a Continent 53, 66 (2004).

76. *See* Dean Takahashi, *Defcon: Excuse Me While I Turn Off Your Pacemaker,* Venture Beat (August 8, 2008), http://venturebeat.com/2008/08/08/defcon-excuse-me-while-I-turn-off-your-pacemaker.

77. Lauren Cox, *Security Experts: Hackers Could Target Pacemakers,* ABC News (April 1, 2010), http://abcnews.go.com.

78. *See* Roger Highfield, *Hacking Fears over Wireless Pacemakers*, Telegraph, March 14, 2008, http://www.telegraph.co.uk; Chris Soghoian, *Security Researchers to Unveil Pacemaker, Medical Implant Hacks*, CNET News (March 3, 2008), http://news.cnet.com.

Chapter 5. Cyber CSI: The Evidentiary Challenges of Digital Crime Scenes

1. The account of the attack and prosecution is taken from these sources: Alison Purdy, *Hacker Cleared of Causing Biggest US Systems Crash*, Birmingham Post, October 18, 2003, at 5; *Teenager Cleared of US Internet Attack*, Times (London), October 18, 2003, at 7; *Teen Hacker Cleared By Jury*, Sophos (October 17, 2003), http://www.sophos.com/pressoffice/news/articles/2003/10/va_caffrey.html; *Cyber Attack on US Shipping Exploited Known Security Hole*, Computer Weekly (October 13, 2003), http://www.computerweekly.com; Steve Bird, *Lovelorn Hacker Sabotaged Network of U.S. Port*, Times (London), October 7, 2003, at 9.

2. Bird, *supra* note 1.

3. *See* Andy McCue, *"Revenge" Hack Downed US Port Systems*, ZDNet UK (October 7, 2003), http://news.zdnet.co.uk.

4. Purdy, *supra* note 1.

5. John Chapman, *The Nerdy Brit Who Paralysed A U.S. City*, Daily Express (UK), October 7, 2003, at 24, 2003 WLNR 8350946.

6. McCue, *supra* note 3.

7. *Denial of Service Attack Meant for Chatroom User*, Computer Weekly (October 13, 2003), http://www.computerweekly.com.

8. *See, e.g.,* John Leyden, *Caffrey Acquittal a Setback for Cybercrime Prosecutions*, Register (October 17, 2003), http://www.theregister.co.uk.

9. McCue, *supra* note 3.

10. *Id.*

11. *Id.*

12. Neil Barrett, *Scary Whodunit Will Have Sequels*, IT Week (October 27, 2003), 2003 WLNR 4302075.

13. *See* Leyden, *supra* note 8.

14. *Id.* (quoting Neil Barrett).

15. *See* Susan W. Brenner, Brian Carrier & Jef Henninger, *The Trojan Horse Defense in Cybercrime Cases*, 21 Santa Clara Computer and High Technology Law Journal 1, 9 (2004).

16. W. William Hodes, *Seeking the Truth versus Telling the Truth at the Boundaries of the Law: Misdirection, Lying, and "Lying with an Explanation,"* 44 South Texas Law Review 53, 59 note 18 (2002).

17. *See* Brenner, Carrier & Henninger, *supra* note 15, at 7–9.

18. *See id.*

19. *See* Matthew, Gregory & Jeanne Bandy, Justice for Matt (2006), http://www.justice4matt.com.

20. *See, e.g.,* State v. McKinney, 699 N.W.2d 460 (South Dakota 2005).

21. Chapman v. Commonwealth, 56 Va. App. 725, 697 S.E.2d 20 (Virginia App. 2010).

22. *See id.*

23. *Id.*

24. West v. State, 2010 WL 4395452 (Texas App. 2010).

25. *Id.*

26. *Id.*

27. *Id.*

28. *See, e.g.,* State v. Tackett, 2007 WL 4328084 (Ohio Court of Appeals 2007).

29. *See id.*

30. *See, e.g.,* Wilson v. State, 2008 WL 5501146 (Texas Court of Appeals 2009).

31. *See, e.g.,* Micah Joel, *Safe and Insecure,* Salon.com (May 18, 2004), http://www.salon.com.

32. *See* U.S. v. Miller, 527 F.3d 54 (U.S. Court of Appeals for the Third Circuit 2008).

33. John Schwartz, *Acquitted Man Says Virus Put Pornography on Computer,* New York Times, August 11, 2003 (quoting former head of Department of Justice's computer crimes unit).

34. *See, e.g.,* Aluisi v. Elliott Mfg. Co., Inc. Plan, 2009 WL 565544 *6 (Eastern District of California 2009).

35. *State v. Bell,* 145 Ohio Misc.2d 55, 882 N.E.2d 502 (Ohio Court of Common Pleas 2008).

36. *Id.*

37. *Id.*

38. *Id.* (quoting Ohio Rule of Evidence 901[A]).

39. *Id.* (quoting U.S. v. Tin Yat Chin, 371 F.31, 38 (U.S. Court of Appeals for the Second Circuit 2004)).

40. *Id.*

41. U.S. v. Jackson, 488 F. Supp.2d 866 (U.S. District Court for the District of Nebraska 2007).

42. *Id.*

43. *Id.*

44. Corpus Juris Secundum Criminal Law § 1142.

45. U.S. v. Wyss, 2006 WL 1722288 (U.S. District Court for the Southern District of Mississippi 2006).

46. *Id.*

47. *Id.*

48. *Id.*

49. *Id.*

50. *Id.*

51. *Id.*

52. *Id.*

53. State v. Colwell, 715 N.W.2d 768 (Iowa Court of Appeals, 2006).

54. Iowa Code Annotated § 712.7.

55. State v. Colwell, *supra* note 53.

56. *Id.*

57. *Id.*

58. State v. Armstead, 432 So.2d 837 (Louisiana Supreme Court 1983).

59. Thomas v. State, 2008 WL 4629572 (Florida Court of Appeals 2008).

60. *Id.*

61. *Id.*

62. Timberlake Const. Co. v. U.S. Fidelity & Guar. Co., 71 F.3d 335, 341 (U.S. Court of Appeals for the Tenth Circuit 1995).

63. Thomas v. State, *supra* note 59.

64. Florida Statutes § 90.805.

65. Thomas v. State, *supra* note 59.

66. *Id.*

67. State v. Chavez, 225 Ariz. 442, 239 P.3d 761 (Arizona App. 2010).

68. *Id.*

69. *Id.*

70. *Id.*

71. Appellant's Reply Brief, State v. Chavez, 2010 WL 1746591 (Arizona App. 2010).

72. Appellee's Answering Brief, State v. Chavez, 2010 WL 1019033 (Arizona App. 2010).

73. State v. Chavez, *supra* note 67.

74. This discussion is based on the work by Susan W. Brenner and Joseph J. Schwerha IV, *Transnational Evidence-Gathering and Local Prosecution of International Cybercrime*, 20 John Marshall Journal of Computer and Information Law 347 (2002).

75. Franz J. Vancura, *Using Computer Forensics to Enhance the Discovery of Electronically Stored Information*, 7 University of St. Thomas Law Review 727, 728 (2010).

76. Orin S. Kerr, *Searches and Seizures in a Digital World*, 119 Harv. L. Rev. 531, 544 (2005).

77. *See id.* at 540–41.

78. *Id.*

79. *Id.*

80. *See, e.g.,* Talia Buford, *Crooks Now Going Digital*, Providence Journal Bulletin, February 14, 2010, 2010 WLNR 3134592.

81. *See, e.g.,* U.S. v. Rubenstein, 2010 WL 2723186 (Southern District of Florida 2010) (analyst spent four months searching a hard drive).

82. *See, e.g.,* U.S. v. Lantz, 2009 WL 1158818 (Southern District of Ohio 2009).

83. State v. Dingman, 149 Wash. App. 648, 202 P.3d 388 (Washington App. 2009).

84. *See id.*

85. *See id.*

86. *See* Deborah L. Meyer, *Melendez-Diaz v. Massachusetts: What the Expanded Confrontation Clause Ruling Means for Computer Forensics and Electronic Discovery*, 28 Temple Journal of Science, Technology and Environmental Law 243 (2009).

87. *See, e.g.,* Melendez-Diaz v. Massachusetts, 129 S.Ct. 2527 (2009).

88. *See id.*

89. *See id.*

90. *See* Meyer, *supra* note 86.

91. The Sixth Amendment right to confront testing done by other computer processes is already being litigated. *See, e.g.,* David Liebow, *DWI Source Code Motions after Underdahl*, 11 Minnesota Journal of Law, Science and Technology 853 (2010).

Chapter 6. Cybercrime Investigations and Privacy

1. *See* Susan W. Brenner & Leo L. Clarke, *Distributed Security: Preventing Cybercrime*, 23 John Marshall Journal of Computer and Information Law 659, 660–64 (2005).

2. David Sklansky, *The Private Police*, 46 U.C.L.A. Law Review 1165, 1211 (1999).

3. Sean J. Kealy, *The Posse Comitatus Act: Toward a Right to Civil Law Enforcement*, 21 Yale Law and Policy Review 383, 429 note 300 (2003).

4. *See Secret Service History*, United States Secret Service (2010), http://www.secretservice.gov/history.shtml.

5. *See A Brief History of the FBI*, Federal Bureau of Investigation (accessed February 28, 2012) http://www.fbi.gov/about-us/history/brief-history/.

6. *See, e.g.,* Kathleen F. Brickey, *Criminal Mischief: The Federalization of American Criminal Law,* 46 Hastings Law Journal 1135, 1137–46 (1995).

7. Lawrence M. Friedman, Crime and Punishment in American History 209 (1993).

8. *See, e.g.,* American Bar Association, The Federalization of Criminal Law (1998).

9. Brian A. Reaves, *Census of State and Local Law Enforcement Agencies, 2008,* 1–2 U.S. Department of Justice, Bureau of Justice Statistics (July 2011), http://bjs.ojp.usdoj.gov/content/pub/pdf/csllea08.pdf.

10. Brian A. Reaves, *Federal Law Enforcement Officers, 2004,* 1–2, U.S. Department of Justice, Bureau of Justice Statistics (July 2006), http://bjs.ojp.usdoj.gov/content/pub/pdf/fleo04.pdf.

11. *Id.*

12. *See DEA Staffing and Budget,* U.S. Drug Enforcement Administration (accessed February 28, 2012), http://www.usdoj.gov/dea/agency/staffing.htm; *Frequently Asked Questions,* U.S. Secret Service (2010), http://www.secret service.gov/faq.shtml.

13. Daniel C. Richman, *The Changing Boundaries between Federal and Local Law Enforcement,* 2 Criminal Justice 81, 93 (2000).

14. *See id.*

15. *See, e.g.,* William J. Cuddihy, The Fourth Amendment: Origins and Original Meaning 31–75 (PhD diss., Claremont Graduate School, 1990).

16. *See* Nelson B. Lasson, The History and Development of the Fourth Amendment to the United States Constitution 23–25 (1937).

17. *Id.*

18. *Id.*

19. 3 *Blackstone's Commentaries on the Laws of England* 209, Yale Law School Avalon Project (2008), http://avalon.law.yale.edu/18th_century/blackstone_bk3ch12.asp.

20. *See* Patcher v. Sprague, 2 Johns 462, 1807 WL 931 (New York Supreme Court 1807).

21. *See* Lasson, *supra* note 16, at 51–61, 79–82.

22. *See* Maryland v. Buie, 494 U.S. 325, 331 (U.S. Supreme Court 1990).

23. Ex parte Jackson, 96 U.S. 727 (1877).

24. *See* Anisha S. Dasgupta, *Public Finance and the Fortunes of the Early American Lottery,* 24 Quinnipiac Law Review 227 (2006).

25. Ex parte Jackson, 96 U.S. at 728 (1877; emphasis added).

26. *See* Herbert N. Casson, The History of the Telephone 170–98 (1922).

27. *See* Andrew Ayers, *The Police Can Do What? Making Local Governmental*

Entities Pay for Unauthorized Wiretapping, 19 New York Law School Journal of Human Rights 651 (2003).

28. *See Police Espionage in a Democracy*, Outlook 235 (May 31, 1916).

29. *See, e.g.,* Joan Nix & David Gabel, *The Introduction of Automatic Switching into the Bell System*, 30 Journal of Economic Issues 737, 738 (1996).

30. *See* Robert Ellis Smith, Ben Franklin's Web Site: Privacy and Curiosity from Plymouth Rock to the Internet 155–56 (2000).

31. *See* Andrew Sinclair, Prohibition: The Era of Excess 152–70 (1962).

32. The account of Olmstead's career is taken from the work by Samuel Dash, The Intruders 72–76 (2004).

33. Olmstead v. United States, 277 U.S. 438, 455 (U.S. Supreme Court 1928).

34. *See id.* at 473 (Brandeis, J., dissenting).

35. *See* Katz v. United States, 369 F.2d 130 (U.S. Court of Appeals for the Ninth Circuit 1966), reversed 389 U.S. 347 (1967).

36. Katz v. United States, 389 U.S. 347–51 (U.S. Supreme Court 1967).

37. *See id.* (Harlan, J., concurring).

38. Smith v. Maryland, 442 U.S. 735 (1979). The facts are taken from this opinion.

39. United States v. Miller, 425 U.S. 435, 442–43 (U.S. Supreme Court 1976).

40. United States v. Carneiro, 861 F.2d 1171, 1173 (U.S. Court of Appeals for the Ninth Circuit 1988).

41. Omnibus Crime Control and Safe Streets Act of 1968, Senate Report 90-197, 90th Cong., 2d sess. 1968, 1968 U.S.C.C.A.N. 2112, 1968 WL 4956.

42. U.S. Code § 2518(1).

43. *See* Omnibus Crime Control and Safe Streets Act of 1968, *supra* note 41.

44. *See* Electronic Communications Privacy Act of 1986, Pub. L. No. 99-508, 100 Stat. 1848 (codified at 18 U.S. Code §§ 2510–22, 2701–12, 3121–27).

45. Alexander Scolnik, *Protections for Electronic Communications: The Stored Communications Act and the Fourth Amendment*, 78 Fordham Law Review 349, 375 (2009).

46. *See* 18 U.S. Code § 2511(1)(a) (as amended by ECPA).

47. U.S. Code § 2510(12) (as amended by ECPA).

48. *See, e.g.,* Cardinal Health 414, Inc. v. Adams, 582 F.Supp.2d 967, 979 (U.S. District Court for the Middle District of Tennessee 2008).

49. Electronic Communications Privacy Act of 1986, Senate Report No. 541, 99th Cong., 2d sess. 1986 U.S.C.C.A.N. 3555, 1986 WL 31929.

50. U.S. Code § 2703(a).

51. U.S. Code § 2703(b).

52. Scolnik, *supra* note 45, at 377.

53. *See, e.g.,* Final Reply Brief for Defendant-Appellant United States of America, Warshak v. United States, 2007 WL 2085416 (U.S. Court of Appeals for the Sixth Circuit 2007).

54. *See, e.g., Information Technology: Electronic Mail (VII.A.1)*, Purdue University Policies (last updated November 18, 2011), http://www.purdue.edu/policies/information-technology/viia1.html.

55. *See The Case for E-mail Security*, LuxSci FYI (March 13, 2009), http://luxsci.com/blog/the-case-for-email-security.html.

56. Warshak v. United States, 2006 WL 5230332 (U.S. District Court for the Southern District of Ohio 2006), affirmed 490 F.3d 455, opinion vacated 532 F.3d 521 (2008).

57. Warshak v. United States, 490 F.3d 455, rehearing en banc granted, opinion vacated 532 F.3d 521 (Sixth Circuit 2008).

58. Warshak v. United States, 532 F.3d 521 (2008).

59. *See* United States v. Warshak, __ F.3d __, 2010 WL 5071766 (Sixth Circuit 2010).

60. *Id.*

61. *See, e.g.,* State v. Marshall, 123 N.J. 1, 586 A.2d 85 (New Jersey 1991).

62. *See, e.g.,* United States v. Hambrick, 225 F.3d 656, 2000 WL 1062039 (U.S. Court of Appeals for the Fourth Circuit 2000).

63. *See, e.g.,* United States v. Martin, 2008 WL 5095986 (U.S. District Court for the District of Minnesota 2008).

64. United States v. D'Andrea, 497 F.Supp.2d 117 (U.S. District Court for the District of Massachusetts 2007).

65. United States v. Jacobsen, 466 U.S. 109 (U.S. Supreme Court 1984).

66. *See* United States v. R. Enterprises, Etc., 498 U.S. 292 (U.S. Supreme Court 1991).

67. United States v. Forrester, 512 F.3d 500 (U.S. Court of Appeals for the Ninth Circuit 2008).

68. *See Network Basics: Internet Protocol (IP)*, SNMPTools.net (accessed February 29, 2012), http://www.snmptools.net/netbasics/ip.

69. *See What Is Google's IP Address?* Yahoo! Answers (accessed February 29, 2012), http://answers.yahoo.com/question/index?qid=20061120105411AAfToI7.

70. *See What Is an IP Address?* WiseGeek (accessed February 29, 2012), http://www.wisegeek.com/what-is-an-ip-address.htm.

71. United States v. Forrester, *supra* note 67.

72. United States v. Christie, 624 F.3d 558, 573 (2010), *affirmed in part* by United States v. Christie, 2010 WL 3565729 (U.S. Court of Appeals for the Third Circuit 2010).

73. *See, e.g., What You Read Is Your Business*, Secure NNTP (accessed February 29, 2012), http://www.securenntp.com; True Crypt (last updated February 14, 2012), http://www.truecrypt.org.

74. Mary Patricia Jones, *Proposed Rule 12.3: Prosecutorial Discovery and the Defense of Federal Authority*, 72 Virginia Law Review 1299, 1316 note 93 (1986).

75. *See* United States v. Mandujano, 425 U.S. 564 (U.S. Supreme Court 1976).

76. *See* Hiibel v. Sixth Judicial District Court, 542 U.S. 177 (U.S. Supreme Court 2004).

77. *See, e.g.,* Margit Livingston, *Disobedience and Contempt*, 75 Washington Law Review 345 (2000).

78. *See, e.g.,* United States v. Dionisio, 410 U.S. 1 (1973).

79. *See* Hoffman v. United States, 341 U.S. 479 (1951).

80. *See* In re Boucher, 2007 WL 4246473 (U.S. District Court for the District of Vermont 2007).

81. U.S. 391 (U.S. Supreme Court 1976).

82. In re Boucher, 2007 WL 4246473, *supra* note 80.

83. *See* Kastigar v. United States, 406 U.S. 441, 445–48 (1972).

84. United States v. Boucher, 2009 WL 424718 (U.S. District Court for the District of Vermont 2009).

85. *Vermont Child Porn Suspect from Canada Gets 3 Year Prison Sentence*, Guelph Mercury 61 (January 22, 2010).

86. *Id.*

Chapter 7. Transnational Investigation of Cybercrime

1. *See, e.g.,* Susan W. Brenner, *Civilians in Cyberwarfare: Conscripts*, 43 Vanderbilt Journal of Transnational Law 1011 (2010).

2. United States v. Gorshkov, 2001 WL 1024026 *1 (U.S. District Court for the Western District of Washington 2002).

3. *Russian Computer Hacker Convicted by Jury*, U.S. Department of Justice (October 10, 2001), http://www.usdoj.gov/criminal/cybercrime/gorshkov convict.htm.

4. *See* Mike Brunker, *Judge OKs FBI Hack of Russian Computers*, ZDNet (May 31, 2001), http://news.zdnet.com.

5. *See id.*

6. *See* Ariana Eunjung Cha, *A Tempting Offer for Russian Pair*, Washington Post, May 19, 2003, http://www.washingtonpost.com.

7. The account of the company president's negotiations with the Invita hackers is taken primarily from Cha, *supra* note 6.

8. *See id.*

9. Brendan I. Koerner, *From Russia with LØPHT,* Legal Affairs (May–June 2002), http://www.legalaffairs.org/printerfriendly.msp?id=286.

10. *See* Cha, *supra* note 6.

11. *See* Koerner, *supra* note 9.

12. *See id.*

13. United States v. Gorshkov, *supra* note 2.

14. *Russian Hacker Sentenced to Prison,* U.S. Department of Justice (July 25, 2003), http://www.usdoj.gov/usao/nj/press/files/ivo725_r.htm.

15. *See Russian Computer Hacker Sentenced to Three Years in Prison,* U.S. Department of Justice (October 4, 2002), http://www.usdoj.gov/criminal/cybercrime/gorshkovSent.htm.

16. *See* Mike Brunker, *FBI Agent Charged with Hacking,* MSNBC (August 15, 2002), http://www.msnbc.msn.com.

17. *Id.*

18. The account of the attacks is taken from Richard Power, Tangled Web: Tales of Digital Crime from the Shadows of Cyberspace, 66–67 (2000); Jonathan Ungoed-Thomas, *The Schoolboy Spy,* Sunday Times, March 29, 1998, at 1, 1998 WLNR 5838030; and *Security in Cyberspace* (Minority Staff Statement), U.S. Senate, Permanent Subcommittee on Investigations, appendix B (June 5, 1996), http://www.fas.org/irp/congress/1996_hr/s960605b.htm.

19. *Security in Cyberspace, supra* note 18. The account of the investigation is taken from this source.

20. Ungoed-Thomas, *supra* note 18.

21. *Id.*

22. *Id.*

23. *Criminal Resource Manual: 274 Methods,* U.S. Department of Justice (accessed March 6, 2012), http://www.usdoj.gov/usao/eousa/foia_reading_room/usam/title9/crmoo274.htm.

24. Code of Federal Regulations § 92.54.

25. *Criminal Resource Manual: 275 Letters Rogatory,* U.S. Department of Justice (accessed March 6, 2012), http://www.usdoj.gov/usao/eousa/foia_reading_room/usam/title9/crmoo275.htm#275.

26. *See* The Signe, 37 F. Supp. 819, 821 (U.S. District Court for the Eastern District of Louisiana 1941).

27. *See* The Signe, *supra* note 26, 37 F. Supp. at 820.

28. *Criminal Resource Manual: 275, supra* note 25.

29. *See, e.g.,* Nicolai Seitz, *Transborder Search: A New Perspective in Law Enforcement,* 7 Yale Journal of Law and Technology 23 (2004–2005).

30. *Criminal Resource Manual: 276 Treaty Requests,* U.S. Department of Justice (accessed March 6, 2012), http://www.usdoj.gov/usao/eousa/foia_reading_room/usam/title9/crm00276.htm.

31. *See* Peter J. White, *International Judicial Assistance in Antitrust Enforcement: The Shortcomings of Current Practices and Legislation, and the Roles of International Organizations,* 62 Administrative Law Review 263, 264 note 6 (2010).

32. Geoffrey R. Watson, *Offenders Abroad: The Case for Nationality-Based Criminal Jurisdiction,* 17 Yale Journal of International Law 41, 75 (1992).

33. *Criminal Resource Manual: 276,* supra note 30.

34. *Id.*

35. *Id.*

36. Stefan D. Cassella, *Bulk Cash Smuggling and the Globalization of Crime,* 22 Berkeley Journal of International law 98, 99 note 2 (2004).

37. *See, e.g.,* Seitz, *supra* note 29.

38. *See, e.g.,* James J. Varellas, *The Constitutional Political Economy of Free Trade,* 49 Santa Clara Law Review 717, 733 (2009).

39. *Criminal Resource Manual: 277: Executive Agreements and Memoranda of Understanding on Mutual Assistance in Criminal Matters,* U.S. Department of Justice (accessed March 6, 2012), http://www.usdoj.gov/usao/eousa/foia_reading_room/usam/title9/crm00277.htm.

40. Daseul Kim, *"Perfectly Properly Triable" in the United States: Is Extradition a Real and Significant Threat to Foreign Antitrust Offenders?* 28 Northwestern Journal of International Law and Business 583, 599 (2008).

41. *See id.*

42. Elise Keppler, *Preventing Human Rights Abuses by Regulating Arms Brokering,* 19 Berkeley Journal of International Law 381, 402 (2001).

43. *Criminal Resource Manual: 602 Procedures for Requesting Extradition from Abroad,* U.S. Department of Justice (accessed March 19, 12), http://www.usdoj.gov/usao/eousa/foia_reading_room/usam/title9/crm00602.htm.

44. *Criminal Resource Manual: 603 Determination of Extraditability,* U.S. Department of Justice (accessed March 19, 12), http://www.usdoj.gov/usao/eousa/foia_reading_room/usam/title9/crm00603.htm.

45. *Criminal Resource Manual: 603, supra* note 44.

46. *See Criminal Resource Manual: 604–609,* U.S. Department of Justice (accessed March 19, 12), http://www.justice.gov/usao/eousa/foia_reading_room/usam/title9/crm00600.htm.

47. *See, e.g.,* Gabriella Blum, *Bilateralism, Multilateralism, and the Architecture of International Law,* 49 Harvard International Law Journal 323, 260 (2008).

48. *See* Sarah E. Tilstra, *Prosecuting International Terrorists*, 12 Pacific Rim Law and Policy Journal 835, 843–44 (2003).

49. *See* Reese v. United States. 76 U.S. 13, 21–22 (U.S. Supreme Court 1869).

50. *See* United States v. Alvarez-Machain, 504 U.S. 655 (U.S. Supreme Court 1992); Ker v. Illinois, 119 U.S. 436 (U.S. Supreme Court 1886).

51. *See* United States v. Alvarez-Machain, *supra* note 50, at 661–62.

52. *Criminal Resource Manual: 9-15.610 Deportations, Expulsions, or Other Extraordinary Renditions*, U.S. Department of Justice (accessed March 6, 2012), http://www.usdoj.gov/usao/eousa/foia_reading_room/usam/title9/15mcrm .htm#9-15.610.

53. *See About the Organisation for Economic Co-operation and Development (OECD)*, OECD (accessed March 19, 12), http://www.oecd.org/pages/0,3417 ,en_36734052_36734103_1_1_1_1_1,00.html.

54. *See* Marc D. Goodman & Susan W. Brenner, *The Emerging Consensus on Criminal Conduct in Cyberspace*, 2002 UCLA Journal of Law and Technology 3.

55. *See id.*

56. *See Convention on Cybercrime* (ETS No. 185), Council of Europe, November 23, 2001, http://conventions.coe.int/Treaty/en/Treaties/Html/185.htm.

57. *See The United Nations*, Cybercrime Law (accessed March 19, 12), http:// www.cybercrimelaw.net/un.html.

58. See *Overview*, Interpol (accessed March 21, 2012), http://www.interpol .int/About-INTERPOL/Overview.

59. *See Interpol's Four Core Functions*, Interpol (last updated July 7, 2009), https://www.interpol.int/Public/icpo/about.asp.

Chapter 8. Mutating Cyberthreats

1. *See* Susan W. Brenner, Cyberthreats: The Emerging Fault Lines of the Nation-State 13–23 (2009).

2. *See, e.g.,* John J. Goldman, *African Embassy Bomber Gets Life Sentence with No Parole*, Los Angeles Times, June 13, 2001, 2001 WLNR 10560943; and Nunzio Lupo, *America's Moment of Silence as McVeigh Goes Stoically; Somber Nation Looks Within*, Atlanta Journal and Constitution, June 12, 2001, 2001 WLNR 3947198.

3. *See, e.g.,* Matthew Hoisington, *Cyberwarfare and the Use of Force Giving Rise to the Right of Self-Defense*, 32 B.C. Int'l & Comp. L. Rev. 439, 450 (2009).

4. *See, e.g.,* Alan Sipress, *Computer System Under Attack*, Washington Post, October 6, 2006, http://www.washingtonpost.com.

5. *See id.*

6. *See, e.g., Method to Find Stepping Stones by Comparing Network Latency Times from Different Protocol Stack Layers*, National Security Agency (January

15, 2009), http://www.nsa.gov/research/tech_transfer/fact_sheets/stepping _stones.shtml.

7. Mark Landler & John Markoff, *Digital Fears Emerge after Data Siege in Estonia*, New York Times, May 29, 2007, http://www.nytimes.com.

8. *Id.*

9. *See* Steven Lee Myers, *Estonia Computers Blitzed, Possibly by the Russians*, New York Times May 19, 2007, http://www.nytimes.com.

10. *See* Tony Halpin, *Estonia Accuses Russia of "Waging Cyber War,"* Times (London), May 17, 2007, http://www.timesonline.co.uk.

11. *See* Ian Traynor, *Russia Accused of Unleashing Cyberwar to Disable Estonia*, Guardian, May 17, 2007, http://www.guardian.co.uk.

12. *See* Landler & Markoff, *supra* note 7.

13. *See id.*

14. *See generally* Bill Brenner, *Black Hat 2007: Estonian Attacks Were a Cyber Riot, Not Warfare*, SearchSecurity (August 3, 2007), http://searchsecurity .techtarget.com/news/article/0,289142,sid14_gci1266728,00.html.

15. *See, e.g.,* Steven Lee Myers, *Youth Groups Created by Kremlin Serve Putin's Cause*, New York Times, July 8, 2007, http://www.nytimes.com.

16. Noah Shactman, *Kremlin Kids: We Launched the Estonian Cyber War*, Wired (March 11, 2009), http://www.wired.com.

17. *Id.*

18. *See* WikiLeaks, http://www.wikileaks.org.

19. *See WikiLeaks Diplomatic Cable: WikiLeaks FAQ*, Spiegel Online (November 28, 2010), http://www.spiegel.de/international/world/0,1518,731441,00 .html.

20. *See* Mahendra Palsule, *EveryDNS.net Terminates WikiLeaks. org DNS Services; WikiLeaks.ch Back Up in Switzerland*, Skeptic Geek, December 3, 2010, http://www.skepticgeek.com/miscellaneous/ everydns-net-terminates-wikileaks-dns-services.

21. Daniel Shane, *Amazon Web Services Pulls Plug on WikiLeaks Servers*, Information Age (December 2, 2010), http://www.information-age.com; Ashlee Vance, *WikiLeaks Struggles to Stay Online after Attacks*, New York Times, December 3, 2010, http://www.nytimes.com.

22. *See Donations Were Never as Strong as Now*, Spiegel Online (December 13, 2010), 2010 WLNR 24690545.

23. *See Updates on Leak of U.S. Cables*, New York Times, December 7, 2010, 2010 WLNR 24232099.

24. *See* John Hudson, *Why MasterCard, Visa and PayPal Are Wrong to Cut Off WikiLeaks*, Atlantic Wire (December 7, 2010), http://www.theatlanticwire .com.

25. John F. Burns, *Hackers Attack Those Seen as WikiLeaks Enemies*, New York Times, December 8, 2010, http://www.nytimes.com.

26. *See, e.g.,* Mark Phillips, *WikiLeaks Ally Anonymous Launches Cyber War*, CBS News (December 8, 2010), http://www.cbsnews.com.

27. Mark Clayton, *Did WikiLeaks Bring on Cyberwar? Maybe a Cyber Sit-in*, Christian Science Monitor (December 23, 2010), http://www.csmonitor.com.

28. *See Dutch Team High Tech Crime Arrests Second Anonymous Suspect*, vRRitti.com (December 12, 2010), http://vrritti.com.

29. *See Anonymous Hits Dutch National Police and Moneybookers Sites*, Info Security (December 13, 2010), http://www.infosecurity-magazine.com.

30. *See EveryDNS*, Wikipedia (last updated September 15, 2011), http://en.wikipedia.org/wiki/EveryDNS; *DynDNS*, Wikipedia (last updated March 6, 2012), http://en.wikipedia.org/wiki/DynDNS.

31. *See* Kim Zetter, *Claim: WikiLeaks Published Documents Siphoned over File Sharing Software*, Wired (January 20, 2011), http://www.wired.com.

32. *See, e.g.,* Daniella Ashkenazy, The Military in the Service of Society and Democracy: The Challenge of the Dual-Role Military 4–5 (1994).

33. *See, e.g.,* Alan J. Levine, The Strategic Bombing of Germany 1940–1945 27 (1992).

Epilogue

1. Chris Mark, quoted in *FBI Group on Cybercrime: "We're Losing the Battle,"* InterComputer (September 29, 2010), http://www.echeck.org/content.php/?p=511.

2. *See About Infragard*, Federal Bureau of Investigation (accessed March 19, 12), http://www.infragard.net/about.php?mn=1&sm=1-0.

3. *See, e.g.,* Tom Gjelten, *Seeing the Internet as an "Information Weapon,"* NPR (September 23, 2010), http://www.npr.org.

4. *See id.*

5. Quoted in Michael Joseph Gross, *Enter the Cyber-Dragon*, Vanity Fair (September 2011), http://www.vanityfair.com.